A CONNOISSEUR'S
GUIDE TO ANTIQUE
FURNITURE

A CONNOISSEUR'S GUIDE TO ANTIQUE
FURNITURE

RONALD PEARSALL

TIGER BOOKS INTERNATIONAL
LONDON

This edition published in 1997 by
Tiger Books International PLC, Twickenham

This book was designed and produced by
Todtri Productions Limited P.O. Box 572, New York,
NY 10116-0572 FAX: (212) 279-1241

Printed and bound in Singapore

ISBN 1-85501-935-3

CONTENTS

INTRODUCTION

Opposite: Edwardian bureau bookcase with serpentine base, and a curious arrangement of glazing bars. The bureau bookcase is perhaps the supreme achievement of the eighteenth-century cabinetmaker, and this example does not match up to it, high quality as it is. An Edwardian reworking of a Georgian ideal can always be detected by added inlay not strictly necessary for the overall design.

Below: A Victorian chaise longue, remarkably elegant but perhaps betrayed by the dumpy turned legs. It is essentially a daybed, and remained popular well into the Edwardian period, when it became ugly, with a black leatherette covering and spindles at the back. It belongs to the same group as the sofa, which replaced the settee in the nineteenth century. The chaise longue first appeared in England in 1825 but has only been Anglicised in recent years..

urniture is the most important of all antiques. It has everything—style, quality, and usability. There is no substitute for a Georgian tea table, nothing so elegant as an early Victorian chaise longue, nothing as overpowering as a twelve-foot-wide nineteenth-century sideboard. Nor is there a piece of furniture so imbued with history as an old oak chest dating back to the English Civil War or beyond and still buyable at no more than £400 ($640). Sometimes the feet are worn where they have stood for centuries on damp flagstones; sometimes the locks are broken in the search for hidden treasures. They reflect history as nothing else does.

Collecting antique furniture, at whatever level, is a window on the past, even the recent past. The streamlined sideboards with gorgeous walnut veneer of sixty years ago, still not valued and seen in many a junk shop, are as redolent of the age as a classic Buick—and can still be used as they were intended to be.

Furniture was made for use. It did not have built-in obsolescence. Even the French fantasy pieces without a plain surface had a part to play in the everyday life of those who could afford them. Antique furniture fits in with modern life. It is not something stuck behind a glass barrier to be admired at a distance. It is there for use. And it will outlast most of us, to give delight to future generations.

CHAPTER ONE

TO THE AGE OF OAK

Few items of furniture from before the fourteenth century still exist. Much of what was used before that date must be deduced from other sources such as illustrations and carvings. There are exceptions, however. The excavations of Pompeii and Herculaneum, the twin cities buried when Mount Vesuvius erupted, show that ancient Roman furniture was of a sophistication and quality that was not remotely approached for more than a thousand years—marble, bronze, and wooden tables with lion and panther heads as decoration or in the form of supports, couches with elaborate headrests, and cradles. The Romans used cupboards and shelves and much furniture we associate with gracious living. The Greeks evolved the klismos, a seat with plaited thongs on curved legs, considered by some to be the most graceful chair ever invented.

The making of furniture was long governed by the materials and tools available. Ancient civilizations imported much wood; the most valuable was the citron from Africa, so popular that the supply was exhausted. Local supplies were more plentiful in Rome than in Greece; oak, fir, beech, holly, yew, and lime were all used. Bronze, copper, and iron woodworking tools included the adze, the axe, the saw (made on the present-day pattern of teeth protruding right and left alternatively), a kind of hacksaw, the plane (mentioned by Pliny in the first century A.D.), the chisel, and the drill. Since furniture sometimes had turned legs it is likely that the Romans invented the pole lathe. Although Greek, Roman, and Egyptian artefacts are not rare, furniture is not available to collectors. But its existence provides a benchmark for what came later.

Early European Furniture

The abilities of furniture makers in the Dark Ages and the medieval period were far inferior to those evident in Classical times. It is not that the furniture makers did not have skills to do more than provide solid functional objects; it is because furniture occupied no definite role in everyday life.

In the earlier years of European furniture, there seem to have been three main trends—Byzantine in the east, Scandinavian in the north, and Romanesque in central and western Europe, with the faintest of hints of ancient Rome. From the evidence of illuminated manuscripts there were thrones of some grandeur (though their magnificence may have been exaggerated by the artists). European furniture was more advanced than that in Britain. The royal courts on the Continent paid more attention to it, as is evident from elaborate genre paintings of the time, the kind of paintings that are absent in Britain. The most advanced furniture was probably made in Germany, where flat surfaces were veneered with different woods. Northern Europe, including Britain, opted for the Gothic style, as exemplified in church architecture.

Above: Even without the eagle, this gilded mirror would stand apart from the European tradition. The eagle stands on a oval shield, which is painted blue and bordered by thirteen stars representing the original states. The ornamentation is novel, though the structure of the frame, pine covered with gesso (plaster of Paris and size, strung on wires for added strength in the ornament) and then gilded, is traditional.

Opposite: An early American chest on frame, known in the United Kingdom as a chest on stand, from Massachusetts, dating from the last quarter of the eighteenth century, and made from a variety of woods including pine, oak, and possibly maple. It was the custom in America to paint their furniture, and this type of furniture could be painted red with a flower decoration in black.

Above: If this were British, its dating and identification would be difficult, as it does not conform. It is a Massachusetts or Connecticut chest over drawer (known in the United Kingdom as a mule chest) of the period 1680–1710, made of pine with wooden hinges (almost unknown in Britain and Europe), and proof of the American ability to improvise. These chests were frequently painted red, black, or green (though green was often the colour of beds). Chests were multipurpose pieces of furniture, used as seats and tables as well as containers.

Left: Charles II side table from about 1670, of oak with inset panels of contrasting wood, drop handles, and the kind of turning on the sturdy base that his predecessor, Cromwell, approved of. It is backward-looking, and shortly the oak would give way to walnut.

Opposite: An unusual corner cupboard of uncertain date. There are two kinds of corner cupboards: free standing with a base, and hanging. Early hanging corner cupboards were bow fronted, sometimes painted with figurative subjects which were often of Dutch inspiration. Many were custom-made, and as rooms were often not perfect rectangles, these are not symmetrical. Some corner cupboards have no doors—corner fitments rather than cupboards—and many were painted blue or orange inside, often believed to be later and tasteless adornment.

Above: American chest made from six boards, from New England, dated 1680–1710. It represents a style of furniture which had long gone out of fashion in Britain, in particular the device of extending the sides of the chest to form legs. This example has traces of reddish brown stain, suggesting that it was originally painted, and is made of pine.

The wood used in Britain was predominantly oak, though there is no question that any local wood might be used. Oak survives, but most other woods do not. Pine was unquestionably a favourite for the masses; since it is soft, it is easily worked with the most primitive of tools. But pine is the shortest-lived of all woods, and it is doubtful that any furniture used by the common people survives today.

More church furniture than domestic furniture of early times remains extant. In Britain domestic furniture was less important than colourful tapestries and hangings; its main requirement was not to be beautiful or decorative or even to be suited to the purpose for which it was made, but to be portable. As nobles moved from stronghold to stronghold their furniture went with them; some of the furniture doubled as carrying cases. Furniture that stayed where it was known as "dormant" furniture. The "movables" included the most important piece of furniture in the household, the chest, often with intricate locks, made using a technology well ahead of its time. Church chests often had three different locks. Sometimes the chests were hooped and ringed with iron. Food was kept in the ambry or hutch, sometimes with a grille for ventilation. There were also shelved display stands for grandees to show off their treasures. Cupboards were an open structure of shelves on which cups, especially of silver, were stored or displayed. From the late fifteenth century doors were often placed in front of the shelves.

Chests and cupboards do exist from the twelfth century, dogged and uncompromising. The earliest chests were hollowed-out tree trunks, but by the thirteenth century they were made with simple carved geometric decoration on the front, frequently lively and expressive, and a hinged lid. The sides extended below the body of the chest to act as legs. In the fifteenth century thin panels of wood were set in the front of the chest. The fact that they were fitted in only loosely to allow for the shrinkage of wood indicates a certain thoughtfulness. Carved to represent folded

Opposite: Victorian oak hall chair with turned front legs and sabre back legs with a heavily carved grotesque back, though this may have been unintentional. These were always uncomfortable. Their aim seems to have been to deter visitors.

Opposite:Without knowledge of Arabic it is often difficult to decide whether such occasional tables were intended for export or were merely fashionable. The East and the Middle East were sources of inspiration from especially 1870 onwards. Painters were particularly fond of Arabic and similar subjects, and the more wealthy furnished their houses in the Arabic and Persian styles. Novelty tables of the period are described as being of the Quaint style.

Below: Old oak chest of great quality with palmette carving and original lock. Such chests have proved to be the Cinderellas of the antique world and have hardly advanced in value in twenty-five years. The Victorians took plain chests of this period (sixteenth and seventeenth centuries) and carved them, but rarely are their "improvements" convincing, as they lacked the spirit and conviction of the original craftsmen, who worked solely with gouge and chisel.

cloth, these panels were known as linenfold, introduced from Holland. Panels also became a feature of chair backs, not for aesthetic reasons but to keep the oak from cracking. On Continental chests, buttresses were sometimes applied between intricately carved and pierced tracery panels.

Tables were mainly of the trestle type, sometimes twenty-five feet (7.5 m) long, stacked up against the wall when not in use and easily transported when it was time to move again. Small tables with fixed tops were used in the private rooms. In an era when privacy was not in demand, grand beds with hanging curtains and textiles were designed not so much to preserve privacy but to keep out draughts (the ability to make close-fitting doors had not yet arrived). Lesser folk had box beds, and continued to have them until relatively recent times. Truckle beds on wooden wheels, made to push under the main bed, were used by attendants or maids either in the bedroom or an annex.

Important people used chairs; lesser folk had to be content with stools or benches. Chests were true multipurpose pieces since they could used to sit upon as well as to store things. Stools were often three-legged, not for the sake of design but because three-legged stools were more stable on the often uneven floors. Stools are often described as being joint or joynt stools because they were made not by common woodworkers but by a joiner using mortise-and-tenon joints.

Above: A James I court cupboard of the highest quality. Court means 'short', and is not associated with royalty. Cupboard is from 'cup-board', a surface on which to keep cups, etc., but the court cupboard was for the ostentatious display of silver, pewter, and the strange and novel treasures which were being brought into the country. Characteristic of the open court cupboard are the large melon-shaped supports, a device used on table legs. This is power furniture, made to impress. The court cupboard, in a meaner form, was revived in the 1930s for suburban houses; they can still be seen in second-hand furniture warehouses, and, being well made, are due for a revival.

Above: An Elizabeth I oak mule chest, with rich carving, elaborate inlay, a central projecting section, and drawers in the base, all indicating that this was a piece of furniture for the very wealthy. This was at the very pinnacle of sixteenth-century furniture-making.

Left: These are usually referred to as knife boxes, though their purpose must be in doubt. There is all the evidence that this is an eighteenth-century example. This would, as is usually the case, be a country piece; the dovetailing is very much a hit-or-miss effort. The very deficiencies are part of the appeal. And they are incredibly difficult to satisfactorily fake. They have, over the past few years, been much collected, simple and functional as they are.

Renaissance, Tudor, and Stuart Furniture

In Italy carving was initially not so popular, partly because the native woods were softer, and painting was preferred, often executed by well-known artists of the time. As in Britain, the most important piece of furniture was the chest, called in Italy the cassone, often part of a dowry and therefore a status symbol. Traces of Roman influence can be seen in Italian furniture, and around 1500 Italianate styles began to influence the neighbouring countries of the north and beyond, though largely avoiding Britain, which progressed along its own parochial way. The discovery of the ancient world during the Renaissance spread the culture of Italy throughout Europe (and would later help to instigate the Baroque movement in about 1620).

In 1550 Jacques Androuet du Cerceau published patterns for somewhat delicate

Opposite: Victorian, but early Victorian, this is a superior chair with its crimson velvet covering, high-class front legs, (not routinely turned, but executed with some skill), and good quality trefoil cut-outs in the back. The side finials are unfortunate, but this does not detract from a handsome piece. It would probably best be described as a library chair, even though it may never have seen a library in its life. It is Gothic Revival at its cosiest.

Below: A French cradle, of fretted design with spindled sides, of some quality, as the embossed sections imply. British cradles that have survived are generally solid and rugged.

Above An upholstered X-shaped stool of about 1900, indicated by the rectangular stretchers and the almost geometrically accurate curve of the legs. The X-stool never enjoyed the popularity in Britain that it enjoyed on the continent, where they were sometimes of the fold-up variety. The stool was the most important type of seat until the chair became commonly used; in the court of France's Sun King (Louis XIV) even the nobility were obliged to sit on stools. Each stool's quality depended on the status of the one who occupied it.

furniture that were very influential, particularly in France, though probably less so than the pattern books (c. 1580) of Hans de Vredeman de Vries of Holland, who stressed angularity, ponderousness, bulk, and gravity, far more in tune with northern European and Protestant thinking. North German furniture of this period (totally different from that of the south, which was sometimes more Italianate than the Italian) has all these qualities, mostly in oak; walnut and the more subtle woods were preferred by the more Latinate countries.

A strong, almost manic preference for virtuosity arose, particularly in Italy and France. Marquetry and parquetry (inlaying with picture shapes or inlaying with geometric shapes) could be unbelievably complex. In one Italian piece of 1470 more than thirty separate woods have been identified. Furniture was often adorned with staggering wood pictures of lavish scenes, splashed across the front of almost any large piece of furniture irrespective of its purpose. Such finesse was scorned by the British, though much European furniture was imported. This was particularly true of comfortable upholstered ladies' furniture.

The Tudors, who occupied the throne of England between 1485 and 1603, brought internal stability to the country. The upper classes were encouraged to build houses for comfort, not simply as staging posts between potential battles. Many houses now had a great chamber, a long gallery, a dining room, and numerous smaller rooms, all of which needed furnishing and decorating in a style commensu-

rate with an age that saw Britain becoming the prime nation of Europe. Efforts were made to bring Britain into the mainstream of furniture evolution. Henry VIII invited Italian craftsmen to England and there are hazy indications that they did come to work there, though it was certainly not an influx of culture, which was what was needed.

The standard prestige chair was the box chair (also known as the settle chair), with arms, an ornate back, and a box beneath the seat,. The earliest known English example is the Coronation Chair in Westminster Abbey. X-shaped chairs were also used, more portable than the cumbersome box chairs and widely used abroad. From the mid-sixteenth century chests and travelling coffers were fitted out with small drawers in the base. The upper compartment would only open from the top. The chest of drawers gradually emerged from this prototype, though it did not

Above: A nineteenth-century cane-sided rocking cradle of good quality with a medieval-style hood .

become a fully accepted piece of furniture until the seventeenth century.

The massive refectory table was one of the classic pieces of the Tudor period, with low stretchers, bulbous supports, and a carved frieze beneath the top. Correctly called a hall table (the hall was then the main room of a house, not simply a vestibule), it was a general-purpose table, not merely used for dining purposes. Its use faded in the seventeenth century when dining rooms became smaller and intimate eating more fashionable. Panel-back chairs were now used, as well as richly upholstered chairs from the Continent. About 1550 the draw table came into use, with leaves that could extend its length. There was also the "framed" table, in which heavy turned legs were set into a "framing" at the corners. Settles with high sides and backs to keep out draughts were popular. Also used were side tables with undecorated backs, intended to stand against a wall. In addition to stools and benches there was now the back stool, a chair without arms but a half-upholstered back

The most essentially English piece of Elizabethan furniture is the court cupboard. The word "court" in this case has nothing to do with royalty but is French for "short"; the "cup-board" was a board for cups, and by extension a table or sideboard for the display of "cups." At these side tables food was set for preparing, serving, and dressing—thus the origin of the dresser. Court cupboards were large, heavy, ornate sideboards, sometimes with a closed base, and others, more preferable, with an open base. They are usually in two or three tiers, each tier often braced by bulbous melon-shaped supports or heavily carved animal motifs. Court cupboards were predominantly pieces of power furniture, made to impress and mirror the age. Used for display, they had a short existence, though they were revived in the

Above: A country table of sycamore, with four sturdy tapering legs. There is good-quality carving on the frieze beneath the top, which overlaps the frame. Sycamore was not so widely used as other woods, but in high-quality furniture was employed in marquetry and inlay.

Opposite: The variety in Victorian hall chairs was immense; here are are two at the opposite ends of the scale: a bizarre part-ebonised version and a higher-quality chair with inset tile, a broken pediment with urn finial, and well-crafted turned legs. The hall as a term for vestibule or entrance room was first used in 1663.

Left: A miniature oak bureau bookcase of immense charm and eccentricity, dated about 1780. The miniaturisation meant altering proportions, so we have an out-of-scale swan's-neck pediment and a truncated upper section with only two shelves. The quality is high. The three urns are splendidly done.

Opposite: Jacobethan was the name given to Victorian furniture where styles were indiscriminately mixed. Because of the frequent use of lion masks it has been given the name "pussy-cat oak" by antique dealers, and many must be regretting their contempt, as the once plentiful supplies of good-quality Jacobethan oak have dried up (mostly exported, especially to Australia in the 1960s and 1970s), and the crafts-manship involved was of a high standard. Jacobethan was a favourite style of the newly rich, who demand-ed the best.

*Opposite: Most types of furniture originated in the cities, but
two types of furniture were created in the country: the dresser,
and the stick-back chair, of which the Windsor is the best—
in England, often of ash or yew with an elm seat, and in
America, of suitable local woods including maple. This is a
Windsor armchair made in Connecticut about 1800, but
variations were made throughout the eastern seaboard after
they had first been introduced from Britain. Durable and
ageless, the Windsor has never been out of fashion. First mentioned in the United Kingdom in 1724, legs were first
tenoned and wedged into mortice holes bored right through
the seat. After about 1780 the invention of the spoon bit
(without a point) meant that a deep hole could be bored
without coming through the top of the seat.*

1920s and 1930s for the suburban home. The livery cupboard then made its appearance, an enclosed two-tiered cupboard with a perforated door for keeping food, a
replacement for the ambry and hardly differing in form.

There was no shortage of enterprise. Oak was often inset in bold checkered or
flower designs of different woods and materials, some of which were ill matched
and crude compared with the same sort of work carried out on the Continent. Oak
was still the most important wood during the reign of James I, but rather than
emphasising the massive, more skill was developed in elaborate turning and carpentry, with ingenious though ugly inlay, and a reluctant acceptance of the need to keep
up with Europe. Hanging cupboards became popular; as did low, wide chairs and
settees in the form of two chairs side by side.

Items of oak furniture often turn up without a pedigree and it is difficult to place
them in context. References made in inventories are ambiguous. The bible box,
sometimes called a desk box, is supposed to date from the seventeenth century
despite a similar "table desk" appearing in an engraving by Albrecht Dürer
(1471–1528). This uncertainty is even more evident when the furniture is devoid of
decoration or a distinctive style. The bible box was to become an important article
of small American furniture.

By the seventeenth century America was being colonised, and distinctive
American furniture was emerging, often made from local woods such as maple or
hickory. The various colonising nations did not mix but pursued their own individual ways. Function was the main aim, with little ornament, and multipurpose furni-

Right: Known as a Wellington chest, this has seven graduated drawers. It is of mahogany with satinwood inlay and is Edwardian revival in the Georgian style, more restrained than most, with modest banding. The name Wellington chest is a misnomer, as this should be reserved for a similar chest where a hinged full-length flap falls across the drawers to prevent them being opened.

Above: A child's high chair of a particularly American kind, made from the colonial period onwards without much change, though this is most likely eighteenth century. The seat would originally have been of rush or cane. The sturdy no-nonsense front legs have no ornament—not even the simplest turning—and the back is unrelieved except for the most rudimentary of finials on the uprights. It has much in common with the Arts and Crafts Movement of the last half of the nineteenth century, and with Shaker furniture of the United States. It is a minor classic.

Above: A handsome oak dresser, reputedly early nineteenth century, with nice features such as the mouldings round the drawers and cupboards, and a good patina. Why does one feel uneasy about it? Is there an incompatibility between the square-section legs and the exuberant apron (beneath the working surface)? Country furniture makers, who did not deign to call themselves cabinetmakers or adopt city habits, did what they liked, using elements from the furniture they knew. Even so, someone should have smartened up the backboard.

ture was prevalent. It was only in the latter part of the seventeenth century that European fashions caught up with the immigrants—or, indeed, Britain.

Charles I was perhaps the most cultured monarch England had ever had, but despite all his efforts there was still no evidence that there was any will on the part of English furniture makers to improve general design, though there was an increased refinement. Chests of drawers were beginning to assume importance as people wondered how they had managed to do without them for so long, though in these early stages the drawers were concealed behind doors. Even more significant was the popularity of gate-leg tables, a genre that in the following century was to proliferate into a huge variety of customised alterable tables for every imaginable purpose.

Some of the most attractive furniture was made in the provinces: the turned or "thrown" chair in which the legs, stretchers, arms, and back were all turned, often bobbin-turned, giving a very lumpy and often primitive appearance; and the classic Windsor chair, still being made today, with a shaped and comfortable solid wood seat into which the legs and the spindles are dowelled. Stick-back chairs were widely made throughout Britain, many of them bearing the county of their origin. Prior to this date country furniture was not identifiable, though much of what survives from earlier times must have been made a long way from London.

Increased decoration, including inlay of bone and mother-of-pearl, was brought to an abrupt halt with the English Civil War. All ornamentation except simple turning was anathema to the Puritans, but there was a curious fashion for leather half-backs and seats fixed to the wood by prominent brass studs. Whether by accident or design these are among the most attractive pieces of oak furniture.

Opposite: Oak Charles I closed court cupboard, sometimes called a press cupboard (small cupboards at top, larger ones at the bottom). These were never as successful visually as the open court cupboard. The melon-shaped uprights are still present in an abbreviated form. This piece has fine arcaded cupboards in the base.

Left: A very fine quality eighteenth-century oak dresser with turned feet and a convincing lower stage and frieze. Many of the finest dressers originated in Wales and the English counties bordering it, and there are endless subtle variations among the types. Oak and pine were the main woods used; pine dressers are widely faked.

CHAPTER TWO

WALNUT AND LACQUER

In the space of a few years England rejected its cultural isolation and joined Europe. Whether this was an inevitable step is not possible to say, but the move was certainly accelerated by Charles II, who, upon ending his exile abroad and returning to the throne in 1660, brought with him Continental ideas of what furniture should be all about.

Of most importance was the introduction of walnut to replace oak as the favoured wood, though oak continued to be used in quantity, and plain chests were made that were almost indistinguishable from those constructed a hundred years earlier. The main influences came from Holland and France, which often had diverse styles, and the split allegiances sometimes account for certain awkwardness.

The Age of Louis XIV

In the early 1600s furniture design in France was at a low ebb and craftsmen from Holland and Italy were encouraged to settle in France. French furniture makers learned quickly and their products were soon immeasurably better than those of the

Opposite: Incredibly ornate Chinese lacquered cabinet faced by doors, in gilt and black, with vase and flowers painting on the inside of the door. Chinese furniture pursued its own path: It could be austere and functional, or it could be opulent, but great attention was paid to the disposition of the furniture in a room. As in porcelain, the Chinese had techniques more advanced than those in the West, and refinement of taste. They developed the cabriole leg hundreds of years before it arrived in Europe. A unique piece of furniture was the chest or pair of chests with hat cupboards on top; pieces of this kind from about 1600 could be taken at first glance for Arts and Crafts furniture.

Left: French commode (chest of drawers) of modest ambitions—except for the knobs.

Above: Painted furniture was far more common in France than in the United Kingdom, but perhaps not so common as in Italy where softwood was used more often. Even minor pieces, such as this commode, were greatly improved by well-applied designs.

Opposite: Furniture made in the Chinese taste in the late eighteenth century and during the Regency was often constructed of softwood and painted or japanned, the legs and uprights being turned to resemble bamboo, which had suddenly become extraordinarily popular. In 1770, Wedgwood produced cane-coloured pottery, which he named Bamboo ware.

immigrants. The emerging French style produced the cabinet, and, more significantly, the cabinetmaker. By a statute of 1741 ébénistes were obliged to place a distinguishing mark on the furniture they made, immensely useful to future generations and at the time a guarantee of first-rate work. Nothing like this had ever happened in English furniture, even in the great days of the eighteenth century when English furniture was supreme.

The ascent of Charles II to the throne coincided with the arrival of Louis XIV, the Sun King, who determined the route French furniture was to follow. Charles Lebrun (1619–1690) was put in charge of the Gobelins factory in 1667; there, for the glory of the king and of France, everything regarding furniture was made regardless of expense—marquetry, mosaic, joinery, ormolu fittings, mirrors. It was an incentive for great craftsmen to make luxury objects without the need to bother about selling them, as was and always would be the case in England.

Louis XIV furniture is always opulent, but also symmetrical and classical. Taste was controlled. New techniques were developed, such as boulle (sometimes spelled buhl), marquetry of brass and tortoiseshell on an oak backing. The originator of boulle, André-Charles Boulle, also experimented with inlay of pewter, ivory, horn, and a whole range of exotic woods, many of which had only recently been discovered. Ormolu (gilt bronze) was increasingly used; developed from the protective metal corners added to furniture for practical reason, it became an art form in its own right with its own specialist makers.

*Above: Ornate late-nineteenth-century French bed with mir-
rored veneer. This is, to a degree, revivalist, incorporating elements of earlier periods, but not systematically. The workman-
ship is of a high order, but the contrast between pattern
veneer and a plain surface shows a drop in standards of
design. French beds had been noted for their lightness and
delicacy; this is bourgeois furniture.*

*Right: The amazing virtuosity and complexity of this jewel
cabinet defines it as continental, belonging to a group of
astonishing seventeenth-century masterpieces originating
especially in Spain, Italy, and Portugal (Lisbon being the
richest city in the world). It is of walnut with gilt fittings
and had little relation to anything produced in the Britain
of the time; however, many were brought in, especially by the
aristocracy doing the Grand Tour of Europe.*

*Opposite: The truly classical walnut corner cupboard, dating
from about 1720. It is mirror veneered (the pattern on the
one door is echoed by that on the other) and there are details
that mark it out as of supreme quality such as the hinges, the
inlay, and the mouldings, especially on the bottom of the cupboard.*

Above: A French crib made of willow, both intertwined and as spindles. Highly collected, cribs and cradles are often country pieces without elaboration, functional rather than decorative.

Certain types of furniture went out of fashion, and new ones were introduced, such as the armoire, a high or low wardrobe; commodes (chests of drawers); and varieties of desks. Louis XIV was not always forward-looking; at court he was the only person to sit on a chair, even a chair without arms (the chaise). Even duchesses had to be content with stools, which themselves were graded—they had folding stools, the courtiers and minions had more uncomfortable ones.

New Directions for English Furniture

These were the influences that began to affect backward- and inward-looking English furniture. The effect of Dutch furniture was even more important. French design had been fashioned by the will of the king, Dutch design by the demands of perhaps the richest merchant class of Europe—the burghers of Holland. Sober but rich, Dutch furniture featured lavish veneer, and intricate, deep-toned marquetry and parquetry played a significant part, integrated into the design of opulent chests of drawers, not just stuck on as added extras. The Dutch exploited the wood found on their trading routes such as padouk, acacia, and kingwood, and used them in their marquetry and parquetry, often in panel pictures of floral groups.

Opposite: A Tyrolean painted armoire of 1791. These can be massive and are often of the simplest construction, with the makers often relying on the weight of the structure to hold things together. Sometimes an armoire would have a cornice, which would help to bind the piece together. 'Armoire', a word first used in 1571, derives from the earlier 'ambry', a repository for victuals, etc. But it was also used for clothes, and armoires are essentially wardrobes. The painting on this example seems to be original, but many unscrupulous dealers in pine have imported genuine plain armoires and painted them themselves, sanding the paintings down in an attempt to make them look old (which they rarely do).

Left: A late-nineteenth-century American dressing table in a spindly delicate style, with four cabriole legs. The dressing table itself echoes the eighteenth century, but the ornate mirror does not, though it fits well in a very high-class piece, being made of mahogany, rosewood, and other prestige woods (oak was for the mass market). The delicacy is lost with oak; the fragility of the legs is not possible to create. Without mahogany, classic Georgian furniture could not have existed. The brass drawer pulls, batwing type, are too heavy for this dressing table.

Below: Lacquering was a very popular hobby in the 1920s, and many antique pieces were given the treatment, just as valuable cabinets were desecrated to make a home for radios and gramophones (manufacturers such as Victor eventually produced antique-style cabinets). The favourite colour was red; this is black with Japanese genre scenes painted on top of a low-quality table—probably professional and not amateur.

Dutch furniture also influenced that of Sweden and north Germany, especially Prussia, but in England a catastrophe accelerated the process. In 1666 the Great Fire of London destroyed 13,200 houses and 88 churches including old St. Paul's, devastated 396 acres, and caused 200,000 people to flee. The fire lasted four days. Many of the houses were those of the great and the good and when they refurnished their houses they opted for furniture made of the newly fashionable wood, walnut. Around 1670 floral marquetry began to be imported from Holland, and elegant gilded furniture arrived from France.

Notwithstanding the introduction of walnut, there were other factors that propelled English furniture into a new dimension. Some of these were social. Society was becoming more intimate and women were playing an increasingly important role. Dining and the taking of tea were becoming refined rituals and would become even more so in succeeding years. There was a demand for suitable small tables and decorative furniture such as cabinets.

Opposite: A nineteenth-century bookcase, distinctive in that each section (four here) is detachable, making the bookcase as large or small as one wishes, and the glass fronts lift up and pushes back, making open shelves if desired. They are bought for use rather than show as they are the most functional of bookcases.

Above: The Americans had their own names for certain pieces of furniture, and this William and Mary lowboy (1690–1720) from the eastern seaboard as far south as Maryland has as its equivalents in the United Kingdom the side table or dressing table. The X-shaped stretchers give credence to these names in that they make it possible to sit nearer the table. Modern authorities in the United Kingdom have adopted the American terminology for three or four drawer examples. Usually of walnut, they could be made of oak, yew, and fruitwoods. The inverted-cup design of the legs shows a Dutch influence.

Opposite: High Victorianism at its very best: a masterpiece in rosewood, the king of woods, with spiral uprights, fretted work impossible to fault, and small bun knobs perfectly in keeping. A journeyman would have made the knobs larger. The construction echoes that of the whatnot, but it could be described in a number of ways such as a tiered Canterbury (for holding music) or a server, though it would be a foolish hostess who used it as such.

Opposite: This American Hudson Valley kas, a monumental wardrobe up to seven feet in height and eight feet wide, is a type of furniture unknown in the United Kingdom. It was made in all woods, including walnut, pine, and almost any local wood from the late eighteenth century onwards. This example has a drawer beneath the cupboard. Often this is disguised as two separate drawers. The large ball feet are distinctive and functional, meant to bear the heavy weight, and the elaborate cornice has a pronounced overhang. The kas was frequently painted, sometimes with floral scenes.

With the increased use of cosmetics, the dressing table appeared in the bedroom, initially modest but later developing into a piece of furniture often mistaken for a desk. The bookcase, first mentioned by Samuel Pepys in 1666, began to evolve— tall, plain, made of oak with wide glazing bars to minimise the use of glass.

The Dutch East India Company had imported lacquer cabinets and chests from Japan and China since about 1600 and set them on stands. An inventory of the contents of an English noble house in 1614 included a lacquered table. However, there was no great enthusiasm until the close of the century when lacquer became fashionable, with the British among the most enthusiastic.

A flourishing trade in what was known as japanned furniture grew, and in 1688 John Stalker and George Parker wrote A Treatise of Japanning and Varnishing. In response to the pleas of the japanners, the government placed crippling taxes on imported lacquer work. Unlike in the Far East, where lacquer was an art form, japanning was a comparatively easy process for Europeans, who simply applied gesso to a wooden surface and then laid on varnish with a brush. Gesso, a mixture

Right: A round mirror, sometimes known as a Girandole, made of carved and gilded pine, bearing the American eagle, and fitted with two candle holders. The glass is concave or, more often, convex, supposedly useful for hostesses to see her guests at a glance, though one cannot see why, unless she were devious or guilty of something. Made in the late eighteenth and early nineteenth centuries, the fragility of the applied gesso has made them vulnerable, but even in a sad and decrepit state they command high prices. The candle holders and arms have often been the first to go. The convex glass is more likely to have survived than flat glass, due to the technique of manufacturing it.

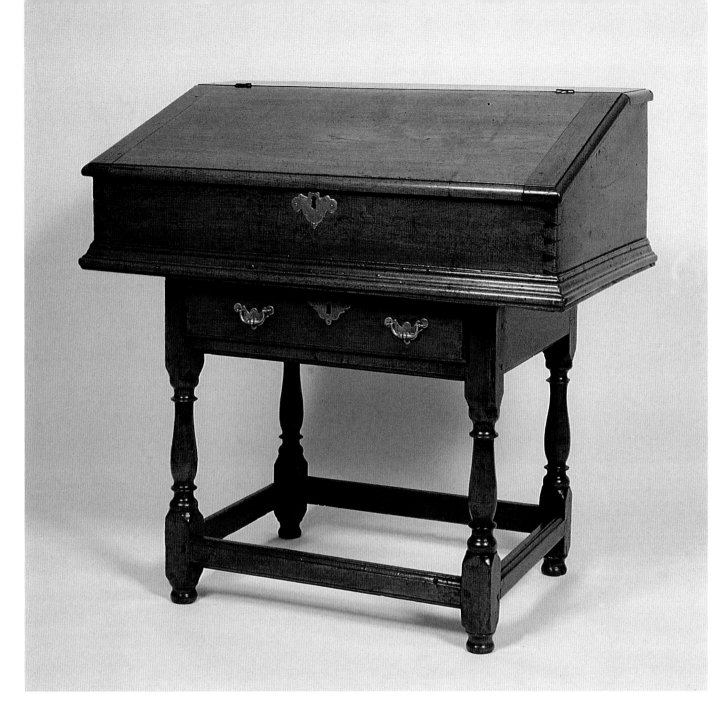

of plaster of paris and size, had been used in furniture decoration from the Middle Ages onward, especially in Italy, where it was used as the base for chest painting. From the end of the seventeenth century, gesso was much used in England for mirror frames and as decoration on chairs and pier tables (designed to be placed against the wall between the windows of grand houses).

The furniture trade in England was greatly helped when the Huguenots immigrated from France to escape religious persecution. Skilled in many of the applied arts, the Huguenots introduced French expertise and enthusiasm. The new discipline of veneering was demanding, as were techniques such as the universal use of dovetailing in "carcase" furniture (chests of drawers and the like). Unlike the mortise-and-tenon joint, which demanded fairly thick wood, dovetailing was ideal for the insides of drawers (linings) in place of nailing. The number of dovetails in a drawer lining increased, and this can often provide a guide to age and quality.

Metal accessories were becoming sophisticated; the earlier attachments to drawers and doors had been wooden knobs, and often there was only a key grasp. Iron handles were an ugly but short-lived interim measure, and brass handles, beginning with the pear-shaped drop, became established until they in their turn gave way to the wooden knob in the nineteenth century.

Above: Totally individual, this American William and Mary desk on stand (or frame) has a robust stand with traditional turning. An unusual feature is that the top either hinges back, or, with additional hinges at front, folds forward to present a writing surface on two pull-out slides. Made in New England and Pennsylvania between about 1700 and 1720, such desks could be in various woods, with oak the most common. Essentially a traditional piece derived from the desk, it was originally a simple box with a canted lid, often referred to erroneously as a Bible box. The drawer beneath the desk is inconveniently placed, as it would have been difficult to use the writing surface without banging the knees.

Opposite: A fine chest of drawers of olive wood with oyster inlay and bun feet, implying a William and Mary date. Oyster wood is walnut, made by slicing branches edgeways. Modest in intentions without extravagance, such chests of drawers represent furniture making at its best.

Below: A modern serving trolley with hinged flaps, superior to most with good quality barley-sugar-twist turning on the uprights, cancelled out by ugly square-section legs. These domestic items appeared in quantity after World War I when domestic servants were few and far between, and ladies had to manage without them. It was a social phenomenon that influenced house and kitchen design to an extent that has never been fully examined.

Standard established furniture was also smartened up. Gate-leg tables had a gap between the leaves, but by making a "rule joint" so that the leaves did not meet at an absolute right angle the gap disappeared. This was important for aesthetic reasons, and the rule joint was subsequently used for high-quality display tables. Throughout Britain and Europe furniture makers aimed toward perfection, not just a quality sufficient to pass muster.

Great quantities of walnut were imported, especially from France, and chests of drawers in veneered walnut were inlaid with holly, sycamore, and boxwood, often in strictly geometric patterns. Oystershell veneer was one of the most popular, slices from the smaller branches of walnut, olive, kingwood, lignum vitae, and other woods laid together in association with light-coloured wood.

The Approach of the Eighteenth Century

As the eighteenth century neared, a great variety of different chairs evolved, lighter and more elegant, and utilising different kinds of feet—hoofed, scrolled, club, and, the most famous, the ball-and-claw, perhaps an echo of Chinese designs. In the 1690s the corner cupboard, full length or hanging, began to make an appearance, and with the fashion for panelled rooms, wardrobes and open cupboards were fitted into the panelling. Comfort was becoming a feature of living, and padded furniture was widely used.

French opulence was reflected, sometimes surpassed, in side tables, sometimes with tops of marble. The lean-to fall-front writing desk, the bureau, developed into the bureau-bookcase. The bureau, like the commode, is a type of furniture whose meanings differ in France and Britain. The bureau plat is a flat writing table with drawers in the frieze; the bureau à cylindre is a roll-top desk. The commode in Britain holds the container of a chamber pot; in France the commode is a chest of

Above: At first glance, this appears to be a corner chair, but the large aprons give a clue. This is a commode. The commode in French was a chest of drawers, in English, a piece of furniture concealing a chamber pot. Stylistically, this is a mishmash, with square legs countered by turned uprights to the rail, and two lyre-shaped splats surrounding a turned centre column. The added ornament is uncertain and purposeless.

drawers. These ambiguities increased as time went by, and have not been resolved with twentieth-century auctioneers' practice of fastening to items of furniture descriptions that relate to something else. A scrutoire may mean almost anything if the will to believe is there.

In 1689 William III of Holland ascended the throne. He encouraged the French Huguenot furniture designer Daniel Marot, who had served the Dutch court, to visit England, and Marot played an important part in further furniture development. Ridding English furniture of some of the ornamental excesses of the age of Charles II, Marot helped impose dignity. William and Mary furniture (1689–1702) was largely transitional, lighter but still distinctly English. One of the new pieces introduced was the card table, illustrating the part activities associated with an increasingly refined society were now playing in the evolution of furniture. Unlike on the Continent, it was a supply-and-demand economy.

The Queen Anne period (1702–14) was one of consolidation, with applied ornament subordinated to good design and fine proportions. Comfort and elegance were pursued, and settees, called love seats, were widely popular. "Cased" furniture such as chests of drawers were increasingly attractive, with finer dovetailing, and bun feet were replaced by bracket feet. Burr-walnut veneer was a popular choice for finish and the fashion for collecting resulted in new types of display cabinet to show off imported Chinese porcelain and silver. The cabriole leg made its appearance. The most characteristic chair, foreshadowing the future, was narrow backed with a curved shape, a central substantial splat, with cabriole legs in front, based on French models, and executed with an elegance that promised well.

*Above: High-quality mid-Victorian walnut swivel-top card table, with characteristic turned
legs and stretcher incorporating bulbous forms, typical of the period. The top has a sensational
grain, highly valued at the time. Although oak enjoyed a renaissance during Victorian times,
walnut was the preferred wood for prestigious showpieces, as this table unquestionably is.*

Early American Furniture

By 1700 English furniture had been accepted as being among the best in the world and was exported throughout Europe, as well to parts of the world where the British had the strongest trading links. Much furniture went to America. By this time American craftsmen were not only copying contemporary English furniture but were developing their own styles. Typical of these was the Carver chair, which was itself a simplified version of the Brewster chair, the most elaborate form of stick furniture made in America, named after an elder of the Massachusetts colony. Inside a robust turned framework was an intricate array of vertical spindles, down the back, down the sides, and between double stretchers, which was itself unusual.

Below: American nineteenth-century dressing box with mirror, of somewhat spare design with routine decoration. This example is of mahogany, but they were made in all woods, including pine covered with leather. The equivalent of the dressing box, made for function when travelling, is the writing box, a far superior genus.

A typical Brewster chair had a total of twenty-six spindles, each one turned in baluster form (a very elongated vase shape). The Carver chair, named after a Massachusetts governor, had spindles just at the back.

They were unique to America, where there was also much effort paid to rocking chairs, never an important feature of European furniture. The early makers often had very little experience of furniture and were learning as they were making, but there was increased awareness of style. Certain items of furniture persisted, such as the chair-table (an armchair with a large back that was hinged forward resting on the arms to form a horizontal surface), whereas in Europe they had enjoyed a half-life on the edge of obscurity.

As in the Middle Ages, chests were essential pieces, and types of chests bore distinctive names such as the Connecticut chest and the Hadley chest. Connecticut chests were mule chests (with drawers at the bottom) whose panels and drawer fronts were carved with tulips and sunflowers; sometimes there is applied half-baluster turning. Hadley chests had fronts engraved with flower motifs, and many came from one of the first firms to be known in American furniture, Belding and Allen, also of Connecticut.

The highboy—a chest of drawers on a stand—was an American product. The lowboy was the name given to both a small dressing table and a low chest of drawers with up to six turned legs, primarily intended for ladies. Walnut is indigenous to America, and was used there long before its introduction to Britain; as a result, colonial walnut furniture was strongly marked with American individualism.

In France the opulent formality of Louis XIV had given way to a lighter more playful furniture (the beginning of the Régence style) and throughout Europe there seems to have been a general relaxation, a feeling that spread to America. Philadelphia was becoming the centre of taste, and the Queen Anne chair proved a stimulus to the new school of fine craftsmen. Furniture was smaller than in England, and straight lines were replaced by curves. The pad foot was preferred, except in New York, where there was a strong Dutch woodworking tradition. The "roundabout" chair, with a curved back and a corner to the front, was an innovation.

Only forty years had passed since the Great Fire of London, but the changes in furniture had been immense, mirroring the great social revolutions that were quietly taking place, as important in their stress on a new quieter and more cultivated society as the Industrial Revolution was to be later in the eighteenth century.

Opposite: The Brewster chair was made of decoratively turned spindles within a substantial framework, and was the most elaborate type of stick furniture made in colonial America in the seventeenth century. It was named after an elder of Massachusetts. Customarily of ash or maple, any wood which could be satisfactorily turned on a lathe was used. This is an incredibly convincing replica made by Wallace Nutting of Massachusetts between about 1920 and 1930.

Left: Less elaborate than the Brewster chair, the Carver chair was named after John Carver, the first governor of Massachusetts Bay Colony, and bears some relationship to English stick chairs, apart from the sturdy framework. An interesting feature in this fine example is that the stretchers are at ground level. The seat is of rush, probably replaced but thankfully not in chintz.

CHAPTER THREE

GEORGIAN FURNITURE

A walnut famine occurred in 1720. Walnut was an indigenous French wood, and the authorities placed an embargo on its export. Supplies from the American colonies were insufficient to meet the demand, so an alternative wood was sought. The look of walnut, however, was incomparable, and when supplies resumed walnut furniture continued to be made until about 1760.

America, possessing sufficient native walnut, initially did not join in the quest, and it kept the Queen Anne style until about 1760. It must be remembered that America had a tiny population; even in 1767 it had hardly more than two and a half million people, and only five cities had a population exceeding 5000—Philadelphia, Boston, New York, Baltimore, and Providence. Only two areas, around Philadelphia and north of Boston, had more than a hundred inhabitants to the square mile. That this country had built and sustained an important furniture interest must be something to marvel upon. English furniture was the main influence throughout the eighteenth century, though it was the nonmahogany Windsor chair that proved to

Opposite: The highboy is often called in Britain a chest on stand, but rarely in Britain is the top so ornately made, with swan's-neck broken pediment and small urn-and-flame finials. The arrangement of drawers is also unusual. Widely made from New England to Virginia between about 1755 and 1775, often in mahogany but also in cherry, walnut, and maple, these are of comparable quality to the work of the great London cabinet-makers. This highboy has cabriole legs with ball-and-claw feet.

Above: Walnut cabinet on stand of about 1690, with a replacement stand. This is entirely in period. It is not surprising that the stand has been replaced, as stands frequently collapsed under the weight of the cabinets or chests.

Left: Made throughout the eastern United States between about 1790 and 1820, this type of furniture is unmistakably American, and known as a server, the server itself being the upper section of three small drawers. Both this and the base have an overhanging top. The turned leg was rehabilitated after the supremacy of the tapering square leg. The server is entirely devoid of ornament, even modest stringing.

Opposite: Shaker washstand from the Shaker communities in New England—of an astonishing simplicity, considering the period (1820–1850). The design was based on a standard washstand of the Federal period. Characteristic of Shaker furniture is the fine finishing and construction, gently sloping sides and backs, and fine dovetailing. The washstand fits flush to the floor, again an unusual feature.

be the most significant, imitated and developed into a particularly American form, especially when painted black and green, which was never done in Britain.

In the 1760s in Manchester, England, Ann Lee founded a Quaker splinter group, known as the Shakers from their habit of shaking and dancing when worshipping. Shunned in England, a small band went to America in 1774, settling near Albany. Shakers believed in celibacy, sexual equality, and common ownership, and their furniture—perhaps the most distinctive of all American furniture—is simple and functional, with uncluttered lines. It has a quality not found in Britain until the best of the Arts and Crafts movement in the late nineteenth century. Maple and pine were the woods most often used, and it was not unusual for the furniture to be painted. Beds were always painted green.

The Lure of Mahogany

Walnut's supremely successful alternative was mahogany, a wood that had been known for many years but that for some reason had not been taken up. The earliest variety of mahogany, mainly from San Domingo and Jamaica, was "Spanish" mahogany—close-grained, dark, and heavy. Later Cuba and Honduras supplied their mahogany, lighter in colour but with a spectacular grain, known as "figure."

Mahogany possesses something distinctive and even magical. It is immensely strong; does not warp, mark, or crack; can be brought up to a magnificent sheen by polishing; and resists the inroads of woodworm, a factor it shares with oak but not with walnut. Because of its strength it does not need stretchers or other members to support it, and legs could thus be made almost pencil-thin without danger of the superstructure collapsing. Since walnut lacked this strength, the ubiquitous chests on stands often feature bases weighed down by heavy tops. (This was so common that the replacements were known as Hackney Road bases from the area in London

Below: Utterly unknown as a type of furniture in Britain, this is a double-door dry sink of the nineteenth century with the surface completely covered with shallow engraving. These were made in all woods, but most often of pine and the less prestigious woods, as they were domestic pieces without high status. There were two doors in the base, and occasionally additional drawers. The well was zinc-, tin- or enamel-lined. For its period, the bracket feet are out of step with generally accepted furniture design. The widespread existence of such furniture is a reminder that in the United States of the nineteenth century, constant running water could not be taken for granted.

where they were made.) Mahogany furniture was not restricted to London; pattern books were widely distributed.

Oak continued to be used in country furniture. If there was contact with the capital elements of mahogany styling might be evident, often not successful. There was no substitute for what might be termed the king of woods, and even ill-equipped provincial woodworkers tried their hand at it

Workers in wood adored mahogany. Although the eighteenth century was dominated by four major stylists who exerted a previously unheard-of influence, much of the credit for furniture that has no equal in its power, elegance, and unforced beauty must be laid at the door of unknown woodworkers. Since furniture makers went out of business if they failed to please the buyer, deference must also be paid to the taste of the men and women who bought the furniture.

The Four Major British Stylists

Architect William Kent (1685–1748) journeyed to Rome in 1710 and returned to promote classical styles, in his case known as Palladian. He died before mahogany was completely established as the only suitable wood for the new age. His work is

Above: Traditional country pine drop-leaf table, widely used throughout the United States during the first half of the nineteenth century. It was without pretention, though pine was sometimes stained or painted.

Opposite: American country-made server of between 1810 and 1840, painted to imitate the veneer and inlay of city versions. This adds to the value to American collectors. The painting is often meticulous with serious efforts to render satinwood, as in the medallions in the front of the piece. American country-made furniture is distinct from British country-made furniture in that the furniture makers were often hundreds of miles from the nearest large town, often working in isolation and not needing to compete with colleagues nearby, whereas in Britain there always was a nod towards London. Otherwise, more up-to-date competitors would take the trade.

powerful and massive, often displaying a brooding, overpowering quality. His interest was in the rich people and only in the rich—country-house and court furniture on the grand scale.

Like Kent, Robert Adam (1728–1792) went to Rome, studying there for four years and returning in 1758. He was an architect, interior decorator, and designer not only of furniture but also of metalwork, carpets, chimneypieces, and almost anything else that can be placed under the heading of applied arts. In partnership with his brother James he created the Adam style, which swept England in the 1760s and quickly spread to France and the United States, as well as further afield in Europe, where it was realised that Britain was eclipsing France in style. This was especially true of nations such as Sweden, where the prettiness and frivolity of some eighteenth-century French furniture was out of character with their own British-style reserve.

Above: The military chest was first used in the Napoleonic wars, and ideally there should have been no external projections such as handles. The corners were protected with brass (the original purpose of ormolu before it was used purely decoratively). Besides mahogany, padouk, camphor, and cedar woods were used. This specimen is damaged, lacking brass protection plates, and has external carrying handles rather than inset ones. Military chests were sometimes made with a secretaire (writing box) feature.

Opposite: Washstand with circular cutout for a bowl, made in the United States in the early nineteenth century in all woods, with or without a drawer above the short legs.

Adam did not restrict himself to one style, and was not averse to picking up hints from contemporary French furniture, which he adapted to his own needs. His wall furniture such as mirrors featured intricate tracery composed of composition on wire. He also designed pier tables, carved and gilded wood sconces known as girandoles, urns, torchères (candlestands), tripods, French-style commodes, and console tables fixed to a wall, often with marble tops and supported by one or two ornate and massive supports, sometimes in the shape of a griffin or animal.

Adam is believed to have invented the sideboard, which in early days had urns set at either end. He occasionally designed Gothic furniture, but the majority of his work incorporates classical motifs such as husks, scrolls, palmettes, anthemions (friezes of flowers and other plants), and paterae (bell flowers, shells, honeysuckle, and small circular or oval ornaments containing representations of acanthus leaves). The classic Adam fireplace was an ideal setting for paterae.

Thomas Chippendale (1718?–1779) is known for his designs rather than for the actual furniture he produced (no piece of furniture has ever been assigned to Chippendale, and no expert has been rash enough to do so). Yet the Chippendale style embraced influences from all over the world, and his Gentleman and Cabinet-Maker's Directory of 1754 is perhaps the most important book of designs ever published. Makers, sellers, and buyers of furniture were provided with a book of patterns. He ventured into every known style, including that of Adam, and his directory features fretwork, lacquerwork, pagoda, and other Chinese shapes, and he twisted and transformed French designs so that they appeared distinctly English.

Of all the designers, Chippendale had the most influence in America, where cabi-

Opposite: Monumental Regency plant stand in giltwood made for the Royal Horticultural Society in 1810, and demonstrating the strength and power of the best Regency furniture after the classic mahogany age had begun to lose its edge. Although the Napoleonic Wars had financially drained Britain (and they were still not over) there was a vibrance about the time, a consciousness that a new age was dawning. There are echoes in this piece of the powerful marble-topped console tables of 1725 onwards.

Below: It is easy to shout "Masterpiece!" when something extra special appears, but in the case of this marble-topped console table of about 1780, it is justified. Made in amboyna wood with gilt, and the lower stage surrounded by an immaculate gallery with tiny hoops, it is made even more memorable by the Wedgwood blue-and-white jasper plaque.

netmaking was reaching great heights, as exemplified by Duncan Phyfe (1768–1854), the greatest American cabinetmaker, who employed a hundred men in his New York workhouse. He based much of his work on Sheraton pattern books, but he lived into the Victorian age and was obliged to make what he called "butcher pieces." Some say that other American cabinetmakers were his equal, but he is one of the few American cabinetmakers to stand out as an individual.

As with Chippendale, no piece of furniture can be ascribed directly to George Hepplewhite (died 1786), whose chief influence comes from a pattern book, The Cabinet-maker and Upholsterer's Guide, published after his death. Hepplewhite furniture—directed at the common people, in this case the affluent middle class-es—was simple, rational, and refined, lightly but strongly built, using a good deal of satinwood. Said to have invented the stylish Pembroke table, Hepplewhite also produced bow- and serpentine-fronted chests of drawers, as well as oval, heart-shaped, and shield-back chairs of great beauty. He introduced the Prince of Wales feathers on the shield-backs of his chairs. Hepplewhite is never obtrusive, and he avoids the occasional excesses of Chippendale

Thomas Sheraton (1751-1806) set up as a drawing master in London and supplied designs to cabinet makers. It is improbable that he ever owned a workshop or was actually involved in the manufacture of any article of furniture. The Cabinet-Maker and Upholsterer's Drawing Book (1791-94) contained 113 plates and a list of 600 makers throughout the United Kingdom. His invention was fluent, he favoured square-backed chaires, and also advocated plain chairs made of beech and plane, japanned black or in colour, or sometimes gilded. He introduced to the wider public such curios as the lady's screen desk, which served as both a fire screen and an impracti-cal fall-front desk. His ladies' cabinets were intricate and elaborate—far too inge-

Above: New York Chippendale cabriole-legged arm-chair dated 1760–70, displaying the ample proportions of true classic eighteenth-century chairs. It has spooned arms, a characteristic of New York furniture, and a "knuckled" character to the ball-and-claw feet.

Left: American Chippendale-style cabriole-legged card table with a fifth leg to support a swing-out leaf. It dates from about 1760 to 1770, is of mahogany, and has a shell motif on the frieze. Made in Philadelphia, it is cabinetmaking of which Chippendale himself would have been proud. It has robust ball-and-claw feet. The three great furniture centres of mid-eighteenth-century America were Philadelphia, Newport, and New York.

nious for many a cabinet maker. He demonstrates the *possibilities* of furniture. Sheraton died in poverty, deranged.

Hepplewhite's designs have a unity, and many display a delicate feminine quality. At his best in informal pieces, he had a penchant for simple, severe outlines, and flat painted or inlaid decoration. He clearly had a love of wood, and his stringing and veneers in geometric patterns often stress the wood's grain. He evolved new French-style motifs such as the lattice and the lozenge, and had a fondness for strong perpendicular lines in his chair backs.

Left: In the United Kingdom, this would be termed a bureau bookcase, in the United States, a secretary. In Britain the secretaire (not secretary) is reserved for bureaux with a straight, not sloping, fall front to the writing section. This piece has a superb broken pediment and the typical three-urn motifs. The hidden writing section has twelve to seventeen pigeonholes and drawers. The upper section has up to seventeen pigeonholes, together with the shelving and two candle slides. The secretaries of United States Chippendale style 1755–80 were made in all the major furniture-producing cities.

Above: American serpentine-front sideboard in mahogany with satinwood inlay dating 1790–1815, rather heavier than the English Hepplewhite equivalents, with more pronounced handles, while the serpentine front contains bow-front elements. It has characteristic tapering legs. The wine cupboards at the side do not bear the large handles.

Opposite: William and Mary walnut chest on stand with X-stretcher and legs, showing Dutch influence. With five tiers of graduated drawers in the corniced chest, this chest on stand would have led a precarious life, and although reasonably sturdy, the legs would not have supported it for any length of time.

Right: The Pembroke table was one of the large family of drop-leaf tables that proliferated in the late eighteenth and early nineteenth century. This example is of harewood and satinwood, with truncated spade feet and a drawer beneath the top. The date would be about 1785.

Above: American serpentine-front chest of drawers of about 1785 to 1805, somewhat later than the equivalent in the United Kingdom. Made in mahogany, maple and cherry, sometimes with bird's-eye maple or satinwood veneer. The apron is restrained as is the piece itself. Soberness brings its own problems, and during the earlier part of the nineteenth century, as in Britain, such chests of drawers were made less and less, possibly because they were expensive to produce, traditional cabinetmaking was on the decline, and there was an urge for change.

Opposite: A doleful Victorian octagonal occasional table, with machine-made tripod legs. The turned pedestal is decorated with meaningless ornament.

Chairs and Tables

Many of the classic pieces of eighteenth-century furniture are not mentioned in any of the handbooks and directories, though it is possible that guidelines were laid down to enable furniture makers to create their own particular pieces using the designers' criteria. Basically there are only a limited number of types of furniture, but no end to the variations played upon them. Names of furniture are often imposed simply for classification purposes; a breakfast table can be almost anything. The butterfly table is an American drop-leaf with a single drawer; the name comes from the butterfly supports that flip out to hold the leaves horizontal.

Characteristically, many eighteenth-century chairs, especially those designed by Chippendale, have very large seats. Despite often intricate tracery they have a bold look. Proportions did count—the Victorians took over the Chippendale chair, but they made the seats much smaller; although the decoration is scaled down the chairs look distinctly ill at ease. Comparison of an early Georgian open armchair with a French fauteils à la reine of the same period (also an open armchair) reveals

Above: A high-quality Regency rosewood folding card table, with platform feet and a pedestal with lotus motif, a popular decorative device. These also served as occasional or side tables.

Opposite: American Chippendale-style corner chair of New York, origin of about 1760 to 1770. Note the ball-and-claw feet, deep apron, and solid satisfactory splats. The corner chair was more popular in America than the United Kingdom, where it was never in the mainstream.

that the French example has a pinched look compared with the confident bravura of the Georgian chair. It sometimes seems that the French gilded everything in sight; in English furniture, gilding was used with decorum. Gilding went well with the more classical designs.

Reading chairs, an eighteenth-century design, were armless leather chairs with a hinged adjustable book rest on top; reader sat astride the chair. Some chairs had a box to hold pencils that swung out from the side. Dining tables were produced in all sizes, supported by small tripods, or by three tripods for long tables of fourteen feet or more. Leaves were retracted or extended by ingenious means. Other long tables might be supported by as many as seventeen tapering legs.

All-purpose tables proliferated; there were drop-leaf tables, tilt-top tables, sofa tables, Pembroke tables, and envelope tables (in which extended leaves were pushed up to cover the top). The sofa table often had drawers on both sides so that the lady of the house could move it to the sofa and write or draw. Writing tables are a catch-all category, and only if they have a leather top can they definitely be assigned as such. Demi-lune tables were semicircular, frequently of satinwood with marquetry inlay. Small tripods were often known as kettle stands, though they are just as likely to have been used as display tables. The same is true of urn tables, meant to hold a tea urn.

The drum table—variously known as a capstan table or rent table—is round,

Above: Double pedestal Georgian mahogany dining table. The pedestal was the best answer to the basic problem of dining tables: The legs get in the way of diners. Many methods were used to solve this predicament. Very long tables could have as many as four pedestal supports.

Left: Superb late-eighteenth-century chair in the Sheraton style. It is likely that Sheraton himself never made a single piece of furniture but his designs had a great influence. They were characterised by lightness, innovation, and perfect proportions.

Opposite: Rosewood marble-topped occasional table of superb quality from about 1815. Marble had been little used in Britain as compared with France, except for console tables and grand house furniture. The technique of using marble in intricate patterns had been brought to a pitch of perfection by the Italians. Marble was imported from Italy at £4 a ton.

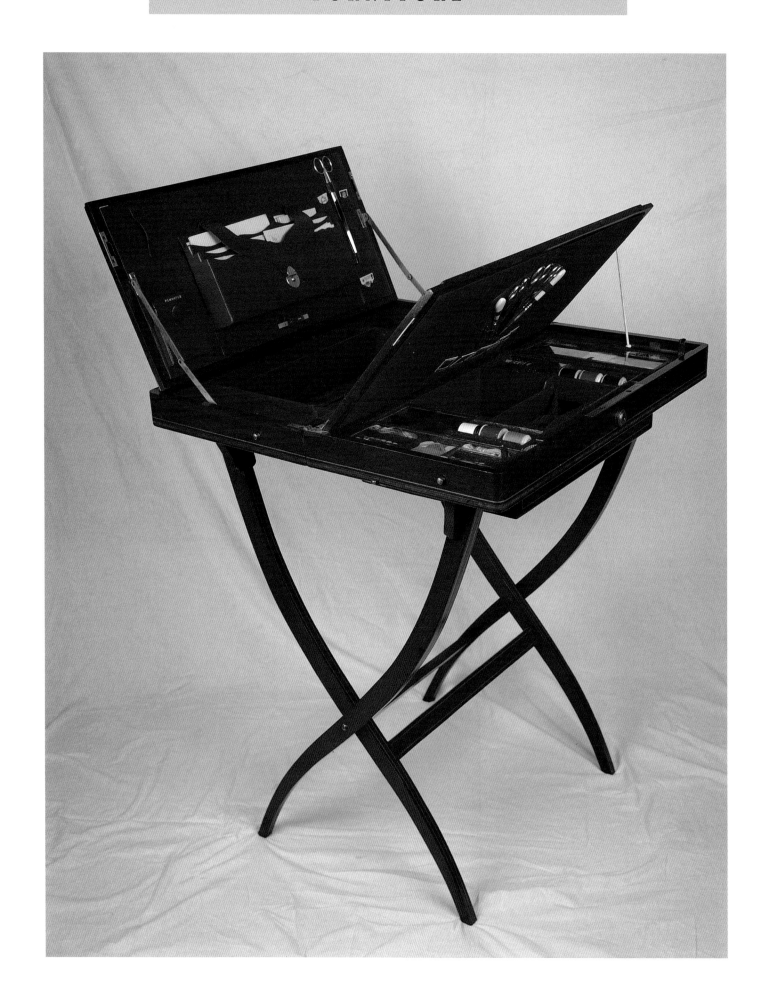

with curved drawers beneath the top (a marvel of cabinetmaking), usually on a tripod base. Introduced from France, kidney tables have a kidney-shaped top, not especially common. Pedestal tables with a tripod or platform base were produced in enormous quantities. The swing-leg table, often mistaken for a gate-leg, is a drop leaf with four legs, two of which swing across to support the leaf. Work tables, introduced at the end of the century, were small, low, blocklike tables with compartments (and sometimes a suspended bag) for wool, silks, bobbins, thread, and other supplies. Dressing tables were often of the kneehole desk type, sometimes with mirrors; what are today described as Georgian dressing tables are more often than not converted sideboards, as evidenced by the two outer cupboards intended to hold wine in coolers.

The most spectacular of all tables is the Carlton House table, really a desk, curved around the sides, with a low superstructure and two or three tiers of drawers. Though described four years earlier, it was given the name in 1796, probably after the residence of the Prince Regent (later King George IV). Much reproduced, it is one of the most desirable pieces on the antique circuit.

D r e s s e r s ,   C h e s t s ,   a n d   B u r e a u s

Legs of Neoclassical furniture were tapered, often ending with spade feet, though chests of drawers had outward-curving feet and an apron beneath the frame. Dressers, which were long low tables with substantial drawers, were replaced by sideboards, usually with eight tapered spade-feet legs; some had a raised brass rail at

Opposite: Edwardian combined needlework and writing desk of the compendium type, much liked in the Victorian age, in mahogany with satinwood stringing. Edwardian furniture is still mistaken for Georgian furniture, and sometimes vice versa. The fittings might lead one to believe that this piece is even later, in what might be called Edwardian revival style.

Below: Massive early-nineteenth-century rosewood drum table with drawers round the rim. These are sometimes called rent tables as there is a tradition that tenants or workers were paid from them. They are also known as capstan tables. The three-sided support is known as a monopodium.

Above:Walnut chest of drawers of classic design with inlay, dating from about 1710.

the back. Serving tables were dressers in all but name (dressers were for dressing food), and these too had brass rails, seemingly for decorative purposes, though they might have held cloths and napkins for handling hot dishes. Washstands were often three-legged corner-fitting, with a stage halfway down containing drawers, or spindly tripods with a rim to hold a bowl.

More chests of drawers have survived than might be imagined, many with bow and serpentine fronts, usually modestly decorated and relying on the wood figure in the veneer. Handles evolved from the teardrop, through an open semicircular type, through an escutcheon shape, to the classic swan-neck design. This is not necessarily a help in dating, since many chests of drawers were survivors—almost impossible to destroy and always useful, they were refitted with Victorian wooden knobs, now replaced by suitably aged reproduction period handles.

English chests of drawers were no match for opulence of the French equivalents, where ormolu runs wild and bow, serpentine, and bombé (bulging out) shapes are often combined in one awe-inspiring piece. The reason is perhaps social; English chests of drawers were bedroom pieces, seen only by owners, servants, and transient lovers. In France, by contrast, the grand hostesses of the day often held court

in their bedrooms, and their commodes were therefore showpieces.

Chests on stands, tallboys, and presses (wardrobes) were inclined to be severe, the modest veneer set off by gleaming brass handles. They could be topped by broken-arch pediments with a finial in the centre, or graceful curved "bonnet-top" pediments, though this was more common in American furniture. Cabinets in Britain were classical in form, sometimes half glazed, often with quartered veneer (in which veneers from the same section of wood are arranged to give a symmetrical mirror-image effect). European cabinets could be supreme showpieces, often incorporating pietra dura (semiprecious stones and marble) and endless grotesquerie, a housemaid's nightmare to keep clean. Lacquer was still used for cabinets. In France lacquering had been brought to a high art, closely approaching that of Japan (Chinese lacquering was never of Japanese quality). Side cabinets were often made in pairs and used between windows in place of pier tables.

Bureaus, plain on the outside, often had the most intricate interiors, with miniature pillars, pigeonholes, and exquisitely fashioned drawers. They sometimes had pull-out slides to increase the writing surface. It was fashionable to include a secret drawer, sometimes operated on the press-button principle, but often difficult to

locate without taking the furniture apart.

Minor drawing-room furniture included torchères, or candlestands, either in the form of a tripod-leg column or a small tripod table with a low gallery; ornate squat cylindrical tubs called jardinières for holding flowers and plants; cellarets to hold plates and cutlery; and tiered dumbwaiters with splayed tripod legs, each tier a round table through which a central column ran.

Library Furniture

Both Sheraton and Hepplewhite produced designs for roll-top desks. There are two main types. The most common has slats of wood glued to linen or canvas; the other, which uses a hollow semicylindre, was the more prestigious because the cylindre required great skill to produce. They are functional pieces that have never been improved upon. Other library furniture includes architect's tables with collapsible slides, and library steps that double as chairs. Sheraton was desperate to show how mechanical furniture could be used for tasks no one has ever wanted to do, such as inordinately complex tables known as the harlequin Pembroke table, with banks of pigeonholes rising and falling by the turn of a key. The table was termed 'halequin', wrote Sheraton, 'for no other reason but because in exhibitions of that sort, there is generally a great deal of machinary introduced in the scewnery'. Much of his work exists as drawings only.

Every gentleman had his library, whether he dipped into his books or not, and the bookcase demonstrated his taste. Those with a real library kept their books either on open shelves occupying an entire wall or room, or on glazed shelves. As glass became less expensive (sparked by the opening of a glass factory in Vauxhall in 1660), middle-class book lovers could afford bookcases. Mirror glass was still expensive, however, so overmantel mirrors made with lively mahogany framing often featured glass made in three parts. In a period of restraint, mirrors were often lavish and gilded, with applied gesso decoration; the influence of French Rococo styles of the 1730s was much in evidence here

Library furniture was often built on castors for ease of movement. Early castors were wood, followed by leather, but in the eighteenth century the preference was for brass. As was the case with much bedroom furniture, library furniture was generally restrained in tone.

Opposite: Although dating from about 1790 to 1820, this American chest on frame is akin to English furniture of a much earlier date, except for the turned legs. Mahogany was used far less in the United States in the eighteenth century than in Britain, where it was almost a crime not to use it (except by country makers), and maple, cherry, walnut, or birch were often employed. The chest on frame or stand was never a satisfactory design; it made the top drawers difficult to reach and the stand was always in danger of collapse, especially when there were many graduated drawers, as here.

CHAPTER FOUR

EXCESS AND REVIVALISM

I n 1807 Thomas Hope's Household Furniture and Interior Decoration sketched out the path ahead. The Neoclassical revival had run out of steam, accelerated by the French Revolution and the Napoleonic Wars, which had induced a state of uncertainty and distrust.

The Regency Period

Regency furniture and its near equivalent in France, Consulat and Empire furniture (the titles refer to the status of Napoleon at the time), broke cleanly with the lightness, elegance, and friendliness of the preceding age. It favoured straight lines; low, unbroken surfaces; and exotic woods such as zebrawood, amboyna, and, most important, rosewood, with its dark dramatic colouring and figuring. Instead of using satinwood as a foil, metal was used, often solid on the feet and applied ornament; metal stringing replaced wood. Typical of Regency furniture were low bookcases with brass trellis frontages often backed by silk curtains; chiffoniers—low dis-

Opposite: The Davenport desk is said to have been named after a Captain Davenport, who ordered one from the great makers Gillow, the only truly important furniture maker outside London. The early ones were simple, but they became increasingly complicated, with secret drawers and pop-up sections. This walnut piano-type is among the best, with S-curve uprights and a delicate brass gallery.

Below: A Regency rosewood two-pedestal library table. The claw feet were a common feature in both wood and metal. The library table was a masculine version of the sofa table without the flaps at the short ends.

play cabinets—with brass galleries; and heavy round tripod tables with massive brass claw feet. The favoured leg for chairs was the sabre leg, which curved outward in a gentle arc.

In Britain and France classical motifs were applied rigorously. One of the key influences came from Egypt, which had been rediscovered by Napoleon, who was fascinated by the evidence of ancient cultures. Winged sphinxes, lotus leaves, and other Egyptian motifs were used extensively in the new stern, masculine furniture, short on subtlety and charm, but powerful. Grecian chairs were fashionable, based on the classical klismos. The Trafalgar chair with naval motifs commemorating Nelson's sea victory was a short-lived novelty

In Germany, Austria, and, to some degree, Sweden, Biedermeier furniture appeared. Biedermeier—a fictional character epitomising the German bourgeoisie—was solid, homely, and full of commonsense, and this was true of Biedermeier furniture, with simplicity and clean lines, and so stripped of ornament that it looks surprisingly modern. The accent was on light-coloured woods such as maple, cherry, and apple, little used in France and Britain. Almost all furniture was below eye level.

As the wars became history, furniture returned to the gentler nature of eighteenth-century styles, with elegant cheval mirrors (full-length swivelling mirrors on a stand), nests of tables, and novelties such as tea caddies in the shape of sarcophagi, directly inspired by Egypt. The Sutherland table, with two large flaps and a narrow top, might appear a typical eighteenth-century design but it dates only from about 1850.

Opposite: Regency mahogany architect's table with tapering round legs, shaped cup casters, and confident carving on the upper part of the legs. Architects' tables are a general name for several specialised forms—others are artists' tables (less robust) and writing tables. They are part of the fascination for multi-purpose furniture (such as library steps that fold down into a chair), which was intensely promoted by Sheraton.

Left: By the middle of the eighteenth century, the night table had become sophisticated in design and was included in the repertoire of the leading furniture makers, disguised as a small chest of drawers with false drawers, or in a more distinct tray-top form, as here. Later, the night table was called a pot holder—later still, a commode—as it was made to hold a chamber pot. The most desirable pot holder is in the form of three steps, often elaborately inlaid.

Below: German Biedermeier cradle of the period 1820–1840, and, but for the formalised decoration at the cradle head and foot, it could be taken for Arts and Crafts furniture of at least fifty years later, especially because of details such as the angular side slats and the extraordinary block feet.

Much was made of the Davenport kneehole desk, particularly since it was ideal for such gadgetry as secret drawers and pop-up inkwells. Neat and compact, the Davenport customarily had a brass gallery, a slightly sloping leather-covered top, and a superstructure of drawers. Though the drawers ran down each side, those on the left were false—appearance was becoming more important than reality.

A variety of couches went under innumerable names—chaise longue, récamier, confidante, veilleuse, and lit de repos. The English had one name, daybed, though the chaise longue was Anglicized and was a standard piece of furniture for eighty years or more.

Mahogany was still used. The Regency largely bypassed country furniture where there was no access to expensive brass fittings. Usually country furniture had London antecedents, but the Welsh dresser sprang up ready formed, the standard long-table dresser with a superstructure of shelves, sometimes in oak, often in pine. Except as a base for veneered furniture, pine was a cheap and disposable wood never featured in pattern books, and only since World War II has it attracted any attention, partly due to promotion by life-style-oriented interior decorators who realised that women needed a change from the all-singing, all-dancing functional kitchen.

The Regency came and went. In France mahogany became fashionable, sixty years after Britain. The Empire style meant monumentality and discomfort; everything was sacrificed to appearance. Drawer handles and key plates were omitted because they distracted from the visual appeal. Chairs were rigid and uncomfortable. Ormolu, previously just part of the ensemble, now positively boomed. The boat-shaped bed was one of the few worthwhile developments of this era. It was compact, useful, and beautiful. The French bourgeoisie and those who wanted to be up to date were heartily glad when the Empire period drifted into anonymity and French furniture began to recover from the excesses of Napoleonic dreams.

Opposite: George III-style dresser with open shelves, which should merit a careful examination. Easy to make up, and easy to sell, especially if the surface lifts slightly, as here.

Below: The earliest forms of settee were extended versions of armchairs, or two-, three- or four-fold repeats of the single chair without divisions, as in Chippendale designs. Unupholstered, they are a specialist taste, and not particularly comfortable. In About 1770, the fully upholstered settee appeared, the daybed and chaise longue following later. Most elegant were the early Victorian cabriole legs; this example has the classic serpentine twist, but is spoiled by its curious and inappropriate legs.

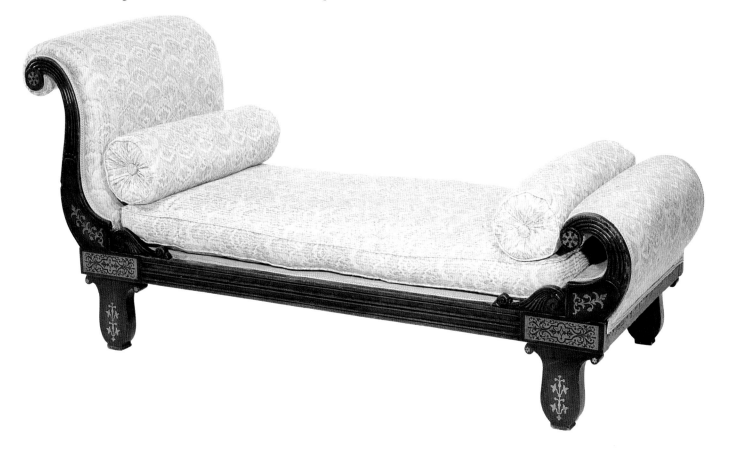

The Victorian Era

Opposite: A High Victorian walnut chiffonier of the very highest quality, demonstrating what could be done when virtuosity and exuberance stopped just short of vulgarity. The great advantage of such furniture is that it is never faked; no-one can make it today.

Below: One of the most common afflictions of the Victorian man was gout, and stools were specially made for this disability. Women of a certain means were fond of lolling; they were also fond of Berlin woolwork, immensely popular between about 1830 and 1860. A respectable hobby and easy, it consisted of applying embroidery to designs copied onto canvas from paper patterns imported from Berlin. The only difficulty presented was counting the squares. Five of these stools have Berlin woolwork, one has velvet, and one has the kind of camouflage used on ships at war. Stools were often made just to show off woolwork, as in the three examples in the foreground. The double stool at the back with pad feet is the only one of quality.

In 1833 J. C. Loudon's Encyclopaedia of Cottage, Farm and Villa Architecture and Furniture predicted that the new styles would be Grecian, Gothic, Elizabethan, and Louis XIV. The idea that they would be used in cottages was wishful thinking, but the styles were certainly used, often together.

By this time, almost all types of furniture had been evolved. The Victorians were obliged to resort to making furniture that looked like something else, or using new material, such as papier mâché ("pulped paper"). Cast-iron furniture appeared. Suitable for hall stands, beds, chairs, and tables, cast iron was best suited to garden furniture. Beds were later to be of brass; many firms made these and nothing else. They were prestige items for the poor. Derbyshire marble had been used for novelties in the eighteenth century, but from the 1840s it was used for table inlay in a debased form of the traditional and expensive Italian process, with slate often substituted for marble. Other furniture was made of coal, deer antlers, and composition imitating wood including gutta-percha (India rubber). Most fell by the wayside.

All types of furniture were developed in the tastes of the times. Sometimes it seems that designers were not employed and the furniture was made on the spur of the moment. It is more likely that designers were confused by the lack of purpose that animated many of the applied arts. There was no easy distinction between

Right: If the Victorians created one genre they could be proud of and call their own, it was the balloon-back chair, which came in many variations and was popular for many decades, either plain or ornate, as in this rosewood example, with its oval velvet splat, the Rococo carving, and the cabriole legs with motifs above the knees.

Gothic and Classical as there was in architecture. As in many eras, there was good taste and bad taste. Chippendale-style furniture was still being made, and much Victorian furniture has stood the test of time.

Machinery became widely used. "Carved" decoration was pressed into wood using red-hot iron templates, wood was stamped with ornament, and carving machines could accomplish undercutting so that ornamentation could be carried out in the round. Most of these processes needed hand-finishing. But there were carvers aplenty—it was truly an art form, and there were staggering display pieces, often made for exhibitions such as the Great Exhibition of 1851. The Chevy Chase sideboard exhibited in 1865, the Robinson Crusoe sideboard, and furniture with Shakespearean themes staggered the groundlings. There was great wealth about, and rich industrialists could afford to buy these overwhelming pieces.

For a long time these gargantuan objects were incorrectly believed to epitomise everyday taste. The great majority of the people were poor, often desperately so, and made do either with what furniture was available within the family, or with rejects. These included fine eighteenth-century pieces that were passed from generation to generation, contemptuously rejected by the wealthy who considered them old-fashioned, and that still occasionally appear in working-class homes.

The most honest piece of furniture was the balloon-back chair, in which the splat is replaced by an ovoid shape. The balloons varied, sometimes appearing in a squashed-in form, but they are samples of good taste. There is style too in the heavy tripod tables, with bases in solid rosewood and the top intricately set with marquetry. Large oval tables are known as loo tables, probably a name given by the antique trade.

Partners' desks (huge flat-topped writing tables with drawers at the side), Davenports, dressing tables in the French style, gadget-filled wardrobes, upholstered furniture of great comfort (helped by the invention of the spiral spring), button-backed chaise longues of great elegance with cabriole legs and serpentine backs, the gentleman's Chesterfield (a double-ended button-backed couch), armless easy chairs with cameo backs made for women wearing crinolines and wide-spreading dresses, ingenious work and games tables, ottomans, charming three-seater sofas arranged in a circle around a central core—there was no end to the furniture that flowed from the factories and workshops to the middle-class householder, who often kept all the furniture in one room. An entire wall might be filled by a Gothic-style bookcase. Surfaces were entirely covered with nicknacks and framed photographs, the clutter kept clean by armies of servants. Palms in great containers

Below: A fine French card table of about 1870, with lavish decoration of great elegance on the frieze and legs. Although this was a standard form of leg in Britain, the tendency was to misjudge the proportions. Were the legs on this table six inches shorter the effect would be entirely different.

Above Massive Victorian library table with heavy reeded legs and four drawers on the long sides. When large Victorian furniture was scorned, it was broken up for the wood. Today, it is very scarce.

Above: Incredibly elegant satinwood breakfront bookcase of about 1880, showing the influence of the Aesthetic movement in the marquetry panels depicting classical scenes. The arrangement and narrowness of the glazing bars is proof of high quality.

Opposite, top: Made in about 1874 to 1882, the Wooton desk (by W.S. Wooton of Indianapolis) is one of the crowning glories of Victorianism, whether in the United States, the United Kingdom, or Europe. It is an office in itself and was only made to special order, so that no two are alike. Even in its day, it was tremendously expensive as only the best woods were used. In the righthand section alone there are up to seventy pigeonholes. The width of the central section can be up to four feet.

vied with pianos for floor space.

Pianos were important pieces of furniture, ranging from the £20 "cottage" piano to grand pianos set upon their side, the "giraffe" piano. Toward the end of the century they were inlaid and veneered with a good deal of fretted work and were often fitted out with candlesticks extending from the front board. The superior Bechstein pianos of Germany were usually ebonised. Harps were popular instruments too, as much for their aesthetic appeal as for their playability. Grand and upright pianos replaced the eighteenth-century square piano, which after World War II were converted into dressing tables.

There were periodic outbursts against muddle. In 1830 a Viennese craftsmen used steam to bend beechwood into a circular shape, creating spare, functional furniture much used in hotels, clubs, and restaurants of the time. Purists such as Pugin wanted a return to pure Gothic. John Ruskin, reformer and art critic, fulminated against vulgarity and the modern world and went slowly mad. William Morris, who hated the industrial age and wanted to return to the handmade era, bade the world not to have anything in their homes that was not useful and beautiful. His Sussex chair of about 1865—made of ebonised beechwood with a straight back and rush seat—was a reformist's ideal but not possible to mass produce. It may still not be possible to make a rush seat mechanically.

Opposite: French vitrines, or display cabinets, of about 1910, with painted pastoral scenes on the bases in the style of Watteau and Fragonard. The French interest in eighteenth-century revivalism was not as intense as that in Britain. There is something of the quality of French Art Nouveau furniture in the proportions, especially the stubby feet.

Below: The name bergere is often given to caned furniture, though its original meaning was a chair upholstered at the sides, usually with a loose cushion. This caned two-seater settee is French, stylistically mixed up, and destined to be expensive to the owner when the cane begins to fray—as it inevitably does.

Above: During the second half of the nineteenth century, style followed style with bewildering speed, often overlapping, and America was no exception. The so-called Rococo revival period (1840–1870) used the latest furniture-making machinery to remarkable effect, making intricate fretwork in a matter of minutes instead of several hours. The top of this centre table is marble, the wood walnut, and the cabriole legs are pierced— hazardous, considering the weight they had to bear.

But what they wanted was already in existence, often in the provinces, produced by journeymen who had never been to London and never seen a book of designs, and who stuck to the old ways. The pine dresser, the Windsor-type chairs (in over a hundred distinct types), which could not be assembled except by hand, the plain tables, and the settles—these were the staple furniture of the farm. Urban and rural dwellers were still evenly matched in terms of population.

European equivalents to High Victorianism, Neo-Gothic in inspiration, were given names such as the Troubadour style or the Cathedral style in France. As in Britain, designers ransacked the past for ideas, particularly the furniture of Louis XV and Louis XVI. Pattern books explored the potential of Chinese, Assyrian, Egyptian, and Persian motifs, especially if they could be applied using machinery. Craftsmen were governed by the law of supply and demand. The monarchs of the Second Empire did little to encourage sobriety and taste, as their own taste was retrogressive, even though Paris was the cultural centre of Europe. Russia revived earlier French furniture, but with a magnificence and a taste sadly lacking in France. The conservative nations—Austria, Sweden, Spain, and Holland—largely avoided the descent into thoughtless eclecticism, though Germany had its share of aimless revivals. Italian furniture, known as "Dantesque," was always looking back at past glories.

A m e r i c a n   S t y l e s

The War of Independence had delayed the Neoclassical movement, and so it lingered longer in the United States than elsewhere. It was a powerful influence, epitomised by the architecture of the White House. The Hitchcock chair, based on

Sheraton designs, was made by the thousands, often sent by mail order throughout the country.

Regency and Empire styles arrived late, but if the European designs were heavy and monumental, American furniture emphasised these qualities still more. Even during the 1850s Regency and Empire influences persisted, mingling with echoes of earlier American furniture and the middle-class urge for the new, the status symbols, the exhibition-style pieces. The industrial middle classes throughout the Western world shared the same basic tastes and appetites. Power furniture had once been the prerogative of royalty and the aristocracy; now it belonged to the rich.

The characteristic piece of American furniture is the unique Wooton desk, which sums up an ethos. Patented in 1874 and used well into the 1890s, the desk has a vertical pull-down writing flap on the front. The front swings away to reveal banks of pigeonholes and drawers fixed to the doors; beneath and above it are more drawers and divisions. Altogether there are well over a hundred different compartments. The wood is ornately carved walnut with satinwood inlay; marquetry using ebony and various other woods appears on the fall-front. The idea seems to have been that if you want to do anything, do it in style. With the Wooton desk, too long looked upon as an oddity, this idea triumphantly succeeds. There is nothing quite like it in European furniture, just as there is nothing like Shaker furniture at the other extreme.

For all who wanted to see, the future beckoned. It may be that those who cried out for furniture reform did not look around them, but saw only the stereotypes, as a succeeding generation did until long after World War II. The nineteenth century was the age of mix-and-match. A century later it is very much the same.

Above: Victorian coat stand with oval mirror. Coat stands, often with facilities for umbrellas and a draining trough at the bottom, could range from the bearable to the ghastly, often being made of unlikely materials. Perhaps they served as conversation pieces; perhaps they awed commoners who should have gone to the tradesman's entrance. This one is so convoluted as to be scarcely credible.

Left: The rocking chair was far more popular in America than in Britain and Europe. This example with iron springs and twenty-seven spindles in the back topped by rosette-patterned hemispheres is made of maple, and dates from about 1880.

CHAPTER FIVE

ART FURNITURE AND BEYOND

One of the most significant features of the last half of the nineteenth century was the international exhibition. Held throughout Europe and the United States, many of them were larger than the Great Exhibition of 1851. In 1862 entries from Japan excited furniture makers, and completely new influences were brought to bear: Art Furniture had arrived. It was a great age of furniture, and because of its startling novelty it was difficult for it to be corrupted by the get-rich-quick furniture makers.

The stylish, sophisticated, sometimes capricious, Anglo-Japanese style of furniture designer E. W. Godwin (1833–1866) appealed to aesthetes such as Oscar Wilde, for whom Godwin decorated his house in Tithe Street, London. Godwin combined his interest in Japanese design with a reverence for eighteenth-century furniture, which he found complementary. His favourite material was ebonised wood, and his designs were made for mechanical reproduction. Godwin embraced simplicity, subtlety, and lightness; he had no interest in revivalism or in handmade parochialism. His sideboard now in the Victoria and Albert Museum would not have looked out of place in the 1920s.

Opposite: The last flourish of high Victorianism was the monumental cabinet in several woods. In this American piece, walnut, maple, and ash, among others, are only partly discernible under a welter of painting, satinwood inlay, gilding, and porcelain plaques.

Left: Rosewood table of about 1880 in the Aesthetic style by Edward William Godwin (1833–86), called "the greatest aesthete of them all" by Oscar Wilde. A pioneer of Anglo-Japanese furniture from 1862, Godwin was an architect as well as a designer, and he aimed at effects "by the mere grouping of solid and void and by more or less broken outline". His furniture was regarded as quaint; it became known as the "Quaint Style". Unfair, as it was bold and innovative, and the spiders'-web stretchers on this table are brilliantly conceived.

There was a downside to the enthusiasm. About 1880 the Japanese craze resulted in oddities of spindly furniture with a multitude of legs, known as the "Quaint" style. Lacquer was applied to the most inappropriate objects (the same thing happened in the 1920s). But the 1862 exhibition also showed that a number of furniture makers, such as William Burges and Norman Shaw, were turning away from revivalist excesses with massive, uncompromising, thoroughly Victorian furniture, fantastic yet compelling. For those who have yet to discover Burges, one of the great names of Victorian furniture, a visit to Wales's Cardiff Castle and nearby Castle Coch is a must. The furniture, decoration, and overall presentation of Castle Coch is the masterpiece of High Victorianism.

The Arts and Crafts and Art Nouveau Movements

It is in the nature of things that progressives form themselves into groups. The first was the Century Guild, whose work foreshadows Art Nouveau. Architect A. H. Mackmurdo instituted the guild in 1882, and in 1884 he started a magazine, The Hobby Horse, to put forward his views. His own furniture in the William Morris style is not particularly important but he was a vital talent, an inspiration to others.

Other guilds and associations followed in quick succession—St. George's Art Society in 1883; the Art Workers' Guild in 1884; C. R. Ashbee's Guild and School of Handicraft in 1888; and also in 1888, the Arts and Crafts Exhibition Society, which gave a new description to the English language—"arty-crafty." Probably no other period in English cultural life saw so much buzz and enthusiasm and so much

Above: Art Deco sideboard of maple with contrasting grey maple veneer, imaginatively designed by Jules Bouy, one of the many European furniture designers who went to the United States after World War I. The surface is finished in green lacquer with ebonisation on the plinth and at the top of the drawer units. The back is plywood; this was not for economy, but was an expected component of even the best furniture.

Opposite: Mistakenly called by some a nursing chair, this is a mid-Victorian prie dieu with Berlin woolwork upholstery. It has a high back and was intended for prayer, the user kneeling on the seat with arms resting on the back of the chair.

unbridled talent, talent such as that of W. R. Lethaby (1857–1931), Professor of Design at the Royal College of Art from 1900, who favoured unpolished oak, and Ernest Gimson, who set up a workshop near Cirencester in the Cotswolds, far away from the metropolis where he produced furniture of the utmost taste and simplicity, partly in the Morris style but without the Morris propaganda.

In Europe C. F. A. Voysey was the most influential British furniture designer. Rush-seated chairs with heart-shaped holes in their high backs, cabinets with elaborate external hinges, unpolished oak, all contributed to an intensely individual style. Furniture firms such as Liberty's, J. S. Henry, and William Birch of High Wycombe took advantage of English design, which was far in advance of anything being done in Europe, though Arts and Crafts furniture had its talented practitioners in America. Voysey influenced the Scotsman Charles Rennie Mackintosh (1868–1928), the most modern of all architects and designers, whose furniture is still ahead of its time a century later.

Other devices appeared, often from apparently nowhere. Uprights (which could extend well above the body of the piece and serve no useful purpose), and feet were provided with squat triangular caps; stretchers on tables and chairs were often at ground level; and although carving was unfashionable inlay was used, often of pewter, sometimes in the form of panels. Mottoes, usually of a wholesome and life-

Above: Art nouveau shaving stand incorporating bentwood stained to resemble mahogany; only a few woods can be shaped under steam to become bentwood. This was imported to America from Austria-Hungary between 1900 and 1905.

Left: Child's wicker rocking chair with cane seat, made throughout the United States in the last quarter of the nineteenth century. These are rarely found in reasonable condition as the wicker "unravels".

Opposite: American Art Deco china cabinet made for the department store B. Altman & Co. of New York City, in conscious emulation of high-quality French Art Deco, but with cheaper materials.

Above: This may be described as an Art Nouveau washstand, is certainly in period, but the addition of curved wooden ornament and ornamental tiles does not make this washstand adventurous. A committed designer would not have used conventional turned legs; these were turned out by furniture factories by the hundredweight.

Opposite: It is often assumed that there was a click when the nineteenth century became the twentieth, but there was not, and the period 1870–1914 has to be looked on as a time when all the possible styles were jostling for position. The result was often an intermingling, as in this sideboard, with the Arts and Crafts use of light wood, selected spaces for decoration with the rest left plain, and Art Nouveau handles. In essence it is cosy suburban furniture without pretension.

Above: This credenza, or side cabinet, marks the change from clutter to simplicity with a wonderful counterpoint of light and ebonised woods and the positioning of decorative features such as the roundels in the door. Much of this work is anonymous, but credit must be paid to innovative writers such as Eastlake (whose own furniture was not up to much), who made this type of furniture acceptable and contemporary.

Opposite: An Aesthetic-style cabinet ebonised with mother-of-pearl inlay for the flowers on the twin doors, and two fine tiles. It is not of the highest quality; there is too much meaningless scratch carving and the spindles on the top do not convince. It would date from about 1870, but could be a little later as the style was fashionable and fitted in with current decor and furnishings. The Art Nouveau pewter complements the dark-coloured wood.

enhancing nature, were featured not only on walls and above mantelpieces but on furniture itself. In the mid-Victorian period oak furniture was often antiqued or "fumed," stained nearly black by placing it in ammonia-filled chambers; now oak was stained green.

Basic, cheap furniture suddenly boasted random Art Nouveau features, such as leaf and lily motifs, carved in low relief or inlaid, and the bold hinges originally intended as part of the design were increasingly added extras. At its most commercial level, Art Nouveau is seen in the decoration on tiles on the splash-backs of marble-topped washstands, far more interesting to collectors than the washstand itself.

The period brought forth its own unique piece of furniture—the cosy corner, a comfortable, cushioned right-angled settle made for the corners of rooms. Bookshelves pierced with heart-shaped holes were made in abundance, sometimes small for the pocket-sized volumes of the Everyman library, then published for the first time. A suite consisting of a washstand, toilet table, chest of drawers, towel rack, and chair cost between £3 and £4. If this seems absurdly cheap it must be remembered that this was more than a working person's weekly wage. The ideal that even the most mundane furniture should be affordable to those at the bottom of the social scale was still not realised, and would not be realised until after World War II and the consumer boom of the 1950s. It was an article of faith that the poor

did not have new furniture—or new anything else, for that matter.

America had its own Arts and Crafts movement from the 1870s, and its later flowering is epitomised in furniture by the architect Frank Lloyd Wright (1867–1959), who developed his furniture along with his architectural and indoor decoration work. Wright's furniture—even more pared down than that of his English contemporaries—demonstrated emphasis on verticals, a liking for angularity, and the use of long narrow slats. His "Prairie House" made great use of stained wood. He wrote that "the most satisfactory apartments are those in which most or all of the furniture is built in as part of the original scheme. The whole must always be considered as an integral unit." Many European designers thought the same, though sometimes with ominous effects.

Elbert Hubbard (1856–1915) was a rich industrialist who founded a community of craftsmen, the Roycrofters, at East Aurora, New York. His early work was simple in the William Morris style: oak benches, tables, and stools known as Mission Furniture. His later influences were European, especially those of the Viennese avant-garde, and he brought in brilliant craftsmen such as Dard Hunter, Karl Kipp, and Frederick Kranz.

Whereas English Art Nouveau was often angular, crisp, and geometric, French Art Nouveau was sinuous, curved, and extravagant, almost harking back to Louis XIV both in taste and expense. It has been called slithery with the look of seaweed, but malevolently creepy is as good a description. Hector Guimard (1867–1942) was one of the key designers; Art Nouveau was even known as the style Guimard or style bouche de Métro (Guimard designed the Métro stations and their marvel-

Previous page, left: Made in America from 1930 onwards, this combination clothespress, or wardrobe, and chest of drawers is Art Deco brought into the home, made in mahogany and bleached maple with some ebonisation, and, as it was made for mass production, it reflects well on public taste. Art Deco persisted longer in the United States than in Europe because of World War II; the austerity years in Britain, which lasted until about 1955, killed off adventure in favour of simplified uniformity.

Previous page, right: Late-Victorian sideboard, with a typical distinguishing feature: the large mirror. Tasteful, with surprisingly plain square legs, it has Aesthetic-style elements without being of that style.

Left: A chain-store drop-leaf table of oak, with bobbin turning on the legs, the fourth leg swinging out from a slot in the stretcher to support the leaf, and a carved top.

Opposite: It is always a delight to see objects in a setting, though there in a curious schizophrenic clash among the sturdy leather-covered armchair, the glitzy chrome, the non-Art-Deco wind-up gramophone with a brass horn, and the unbearably cute print on the wall, not to mention the floor covering, whatever that is made of.

Opposite A high-quality Edwardian Georgian-revival display cabinet, rather too free with the ornament, and with an ugly stretcher between the tapering square-section legs.

Below: The brass bed was a Victorian innovation to promote hygiene, and there were many variations on the basic model. Most used brass tubing rather than solid brass; rectangular uprights, as here, were more uncommon. The centre of the industry was Birmingham, and so great was the demand that many factories were devoted to the production of brass beds and nothing else.

lous lettering). Despite the manner in which he viewed wood as a substitute for plasticine, the furniture he designed for his own house was forward looking, with L-shaped and asymmetrical desks. French Art Nouveau was totally uncommercial, and when it was debased and mass-marketed it was a disaster. Nor was there an antidote; France had never had a century of Georges.

Many of the innovative designers loved the restraint and elegance of eighteenth-century furniture. As the reaction against Art Nouveau set in, classical mahogany furniture enjoyed a sudden and overwhelming revival. At the important St. Louis Exhibition of 1904 virtually all the English furniture was Georgian revival. Long scorned, only recently reevaluated, mahogany with satinwood inlay furniture of the opening years of the twentieth century is often superb. The proportions may not be

quite the same as in the eighteenth century and the inlay is more elaborate and on an increased scale, but there is an elegance and user-friendliness that mirrors the age before the lights went out all over Europe.

Above: Art Deco-style walnut armchair with cane back and sides, impossible to date accurately as there is a clash between the curved classic Deco arms and the ungainly feet.

The Early Twentieth Century

World War I ended European culture and brought a shift of allegiances. Germany, which before the war had trailed along in the wake of English enterprise, emerged as the most forward-looking, with its fitness-for-function message. The Bauhaus, the most influential design school of the twentieth century, was started in 1919 by Walter Gropius (1883–1969). His manifesto was "to co-ordinate all creative effort, to achieve in a new architecture the unification of all training in art and design. The ultimate, if distant, goal of the Bauhaus is the collective work of art—the Building—in which no barriers exist between the structural and decorative arts." Its workshops were "really laboratories in which practical designs for present-day goods were conscientiously worked out as models for mass production."

A Brave New World, indeed, that fortunately did not succeed. Bauhaus furniture

Opposite: An American dressing table ('dresser' in the United States) of pine, of a type painted or grained and intended for a mass market, though with a good deal of elaboration. These were usually made in sets, with accompanying bed, wardrobe, chest of drawers, and sometimes washstand—or any permutation of these. The use of a fixed mirror was a determining point in dressing-table design; it ended the widespread use of the portable toilet mirror.

is bare, impersonal, often uncomfortable, modernist sculpture, not unlike modern office furniture. (The tubular-steel chair may be laid at its door, for better or worse.) Yet the influence of Gropius was worldwide. In England, Herbert Read was a key acolyte who rather resented comfort. "An easy chair of pleasing lines has been evolved, but only slowly and painfully, leaving in its traces some of the ugliest and most shapeless forms ever devised by man."

Fortunately not everyone saw eye to eye with Gropius. Designers and manufacturers all over Europe—especially Sweden—took what they wanted and watered down the austerity. In doing so they produced some delightful products such as the geometric radio set, the "Plan" steel chair by Serge Chermayeff (one of the greatest twentieth-century designers), and electric hanging lamps of a type largely unaltered. The Aga cooker designed by Gustaf Dalén in the 1920s (the best are 1930s models) is fitness for function at its very best.

Left: Dressing table in mahogany and maple, made in America from about 1930 onwards, and notable for its large frameless mirror. Each pedestal has two drawers, which cut across the exterior pattern.

Opposite: Art Deco wardrobe with block feet. These can still be found at absurdly low prices in secondhand furniture warehouses as they are so well constructed that they have been in constant use for more than fifty years. Customarily, the spectacular veneer is glued to plywood, which, except in damp conditions, is very durable.

Art Deco Furniture

In 1925 the Exposition Internationale des Arts Décoratifs Modernes was held in Paris. Art Deco had arrived—bubbly, full of adventure, fizzy, jazzy, rather like the Bauhaus on LSD, throwing overboard everything that savoured of the past yet open to the influence of Art Nouveau and Arts and Crafts, as well as of Aztec, Mayan, Egyptian, and ethnic styles; Russian ballet; Cubism; Russian abstract art; and almost anything else if it was glitzy enough.

Art Deco furniture utilized exotic and unusual materials. Wood was covered with parchment, and chrome and glass were omniscient. Aluminum was discovered as a furniture-making component, and bent plywood proliferated, not because of its cheapness but because of its utility. Streamlining was in vogue. If a sofa automatically ejected its occupants to the floor, so be it; if a glass-topped table was dysfunctional and would crack if stared at too long, that was par for the course. True exhibition-standard Art Deco furniture was handmade, expensive, and intended for rich clientele.

Commercial Art Deco furniture was seen by the masses in cinema foyers, hotels, restaurants—and in the department stores. And they liked it. Wood was cheap, and wafer-thin walnut and flame mahogany veneers on five-ply plywood gave the impression of great luxury. Uncut moquette upholstery in geometric patterns was used on three-piece suites in the most modest of homes. Art Deco combined with fitness for function set styles for electrical equipment, radios, and the new labour-saving devices. But more than anything, the movies gave a credibility to modernistic furniture, even if it was traditional furniture vamped up.

In America the impact was immense. The skyscraper was the incarnation of Art Deco; Packards and Chryslers were Art Deco on wheels. Designers discovered how to combine visual appeal with comfort in furniture and everything else, helped by clever advertising. There was something shameful about being out of date.

The Modern Age

Americans were among the first to realise the potential of plastic. In 1940 the Museum of Modern Art in New York ran a competition for "Organic Design in Home Furnishings." First prize was for a one-piece chair. Moulded plastic and fibreglass led to the influential "womb chair."

Furniture was being seen anew. A chair was no longer a seat, a back, and legs; a table was not necessarily a piece of flat wood with legs. Fitness for purpose was revived in World War II in Britain with Utility furniture—cheap but decent wood, no frills, no ornament. Postwar furniture carried on this trend with G-plan and Habitat. Vying with brightly coloured plastic, smoothly finished furniture has no dust traps, and scooped-out fingerholes often replace knobs and handles. It is all very neat and uncomplicated. Though handmade furniture is still being made (as is art pottery), the comfort of most modern upholstered furniture would have staggered the inventor of the spiral spring. But it is difficult to know who in the future would want to collect all these admirable objects. Hence the appeal of antique furniture, whose like will never be seen again.

Opposite: Quintessential American cottage furniture represented by this commode—elaborately painted, though others were grained to present the pine as a prestige wood. Although they were made in the last quarter of the nineteenth century, they were cherished well into the twentieth, particularly if the painting had been done by someone in the family. Many no doubt regret the passing of such homely, friendly pieces of furniture.

GLOSSARY OF FURNITURE TERMS

Acanthus A stylised leaf decoration.

Amorini Cupids or cherubs.

Anthemion Honeysuckle design.

Apron A decorative piece under the front of a piece of furniture.

Arabesque Figures, fruit, flowers, and other decorative devices in groups or combinations, often used in parquetry.

Arcading A sequence of ornamental arches.

Astragal A type of moulding on the bars of bookcases.

Bail A hinged drawer pull, usually pear-shaped.

Ball-and-claw A type of foot on cabriole-legged furniture.

Baluster A vase-shaped decorative design. A half baluster (a baluster cut in half vertically) was fixed to chests and the like.

Banding A plain or ornate border around doors, panels, drawers, tables, and other items. Straight banding runs with the grain, cross banding against the grain. Feather banding and herringbone banding is in the form of chevrons.

Barley-sugar twist Spiral turning.

Beading A moulding—plain, semicircular, or in the form of a string of beads—placed around drawers and the like. Alternate round and oblong beads are known as "bead and reel."

Bevel A sloping cut in wood or glass.

Blind fret A fretted design on a solid background.

Bobbin turning Turning in the shape of bobbins, akin to squashed spiral turning.

Bombé "Blown out" furniture, especially chests and chests of drawers swollen out at the front.

Boulle work Inlay using brass and tortoiseshell.

Bow front A gentle curve on the front of furniture.

Bracket foot A shaped projecting foot, replacing the bun foot.

Breakfront A bookcase in which the central section juts out.

Broken pediment A formal pediment in which the middle section is omitted but symmetry retained.

Bulb The bulging shape in furniture uprights between tiers.

Bun foot A foot shaped like a flattened orb.

Cabochon A raised oval with a rim, most often used on chairs.

Cabriole leg A sinuous leg curving outward at the top, and tapering in a smooth arc to the foot.

Cameo back A chair back consisting of an open oval.

Carcase The basic structure of "case" furniture (chests and so on) before the application of veneer.

Cartouche A shield or circular shape surrounded by a scroll. Originally meant to imitate a sheet of paper with the ends curled over.

Chamfer A bevelled edge on right-angled furniture surfaces.

Channel moulding Grooved decoration.

Chip-carving Early surface decoration on oak using a gouge and chisel.

Cleat A piece of wood added to give strength.

Cockbeading Simple bead moulding on drawer fronts.

Column turning Turning to give the effect of a column.

Cornice The top of a piece of furniture.

Cresting rail The top rail of a chair.

Cup-and-cover Bulbous decoration used on old oak.

Diaper Diamond shapes adorned with dots or other interior motifs.

Dished corner A tabletop with a depression in the corner, used on card tables for chips or money.

Distressing The practise of superficially damaging new furniture to make it appear old.

Dovetail A jointing method using interlacing V shapes.

Dowel A wooden peg holding parts together.

Ear Unseen reinforcement on vulnerable furniture parts, especially on chairs.

Egg-and-dart Moulding of alternative oval and V shapes.

Escutcheon A shield shape for crests or monograms, or a plate pierced with a keyhole.

Fall front Hinged writing surface of a desk that folds down from the body.

Fielded panel A bevel-edged panel.

Figure The pattern in wood.

Fillet Narrow strip of wood.

Finial Termination topping a piece of furniture, in the shape of a spike or other form.

Fluting Grooving, usually on furniture legs.

Fly-leg A normally hidden table leg that swings to support a table leaf.

Frieze A thin, horizontal decorated section under a the front of a tabletop or other object.

Gadrooning Moulding using concave and/or convex shapes.

Gallery A low plain or ornamental railing at the top of a piece of furniture, usually of brass or wood.

Gesso A composition used for mirror frames or as a suitable surface to paint on, based on plaster of Paris.

Guilloche A pattern of interlinked circles.

Hoop back A chair back where the uprights merge with the top rail to form a hoop.

Husk Cornhusk or bluebell design, used in sequence or in combination with other classical motifs.

Inlay Contrasting material inserted flush in⁰⁰

Key pattern Repetitive key shapes, first used in ancient Greece.

Ladder back A chair back with several horizontal rails, sometimes slightly curved.
Latticework Fretwork.
Linenfold Early carving imitating the folds of cloth.
Linings The sides and backs of drawer interiors.
Lion mask Applied carving in the form of the face of a lion.
Loper Pull-out supports for a fall front of a desk or other piece of furniture.
Lozenge Diamond-shaped motif, sometimes with interior decoration.
Lunette Half moon or fan shape, much used in inlay.

Marquetry Contrasting veneers applied to a surface to form a picture or decoration.
Marriage A made-up piece of furniture using components from other related furniture.
Medallion An applied device, usually circular or oval.
Mitre joint Two surfaces fitting together at right angles.
Monopodium A single support for a heavy object such as a console table.
Mortise and tenon The most important joint in carpentry in which the tongue (tenon) slots into a rectangular hole (mortise).
Moulding A shaped narrow strip of wood for decoration or to hide the edges of joints.

Ogee A design in the form of a stretched S.
Ormolu Gilded bronze used for furniture decoration.
Ovolo Moulding with quarter-circle sections.

Pad foot A flattish, rounded foot.
Parquetry Geometric marquetry.
Patera An oval or round frame depicting a flower.
Patina The surface of antiques after wear, polishing, rubbing, and the changes in texture due to age.
Paw foot A foot in the form of an animal claw or paw.
Pediment The prominent horizontally oriented top of a bookcase or similar piece of furniture.
Pie crust A form of edging for tables and other objects in shallow-scallop form.
Pilaster A flat-sided column.
Plinth A square or rectangular base.

Quartering Four pieces of veneer of identical figuration placed to make a mirror image.

Ram's head A popular decorative device.

Rebate A groove cut to receive an edge or section.

Reeding The opposite of fluting—the surface of a leg or the like built up instead of grooved.

Roundel A circular ornament.

Rule joint A joint allowing the leaf of a table to close without leaving a gap.

Runner A strip of wood to help the smooth opening and closing of a drawer.

Sabre leg A Regency feature, a leg of square tapering section curving gently outward from the seat.

Saltire An X shape, formed by stretchers of tables and chairs.

Scroll Curved or spiral decoration.

Serpentine Elongated S shape for the front of chests and the like.

Shell A favourite decorative motif.

Shoe-piece A strengthening piece of wood at the base of the central splat of a chair back.

Skirt The apron of a chair.

Spiral twist Barley-sugar turning.

Splat The central upright in the back of a chair.

Spoon back A type of chair in which the back gently turns and folds over.

Stile An upright in framing or panelling.

Strapwork Carved ornamentation imitating straps of leather.

Stretcher Strengthening strut between chair or table legs.

Striation The filament-like grain of some woods.

Stringing Narrow straight inlay of wood or metal.

Sunburst A design of radiating lines from a central core.

Swag A hanging assembly of husks, flowers,or the like.

Swan neck A gentle rolling curve, a term applied to handles and to types of pediments.

Terminal The end of the arm of a chair.

Turning Shaping lengths of wood using a lathe.

Veneer A thin sheet of decorative wood glued to a carcase of inferior wood such as pine.

Volute A spiral scroll.

Wainscot Timber used for panelling.

INDEX

Page numbers in **boldface** indicate photo captions.

127

PICTURE CREDITS

Esto
8, 9, 11 (top & bottom), 12, 27, 28 (left), 41 (left),
43, 44, 45, 47, 50, 52, 53, 54, 55, 56, 57 (left), 58,
59, 60, 61, 62, 66 (top & bottom), 67, 68 (top), 70, 73, 77 (top & bottom),
79, 80, 84, 89, 94 (top), 98 (top), 99 (left & right), 100, 103, 104,
105 (left & right), 110, 116, 119, 120

MC Picture Library
6, 7, 10, 13, 15, 18, 19, 20, 21, 22, 23, 24, 26, 29, 31,
32, 33, 34, 35, 36 (top), 39, 40, 48, 49, 51, 63, 71, 72, 76,
77, 83, 86, 87 (bottom), 88, 90, 91, 97, 98, 102, 106, 107,
109, 111, 112, 113, 114, 115, 116, 117 (left & right), 118

Ronald Pearsall
11 (bottom), 14, 16, 17 (top), 25, 28 (right), 30, 36 (bottom),
37, 38, 41 (right), 42, 46, 57 (right), 64, 65, 68 (bottom), 69,
74, 75 (top & bottom), 78, 82, 85, 95, 87 (top), 92, 93, 94 (bottom),
95, 96, 101, 108

The Wright Family Collection
17 (bottom)

European Art
in the 14th Century

Text by
Karel Stejskal

Photographs by
Karel Neubert

European Art
in the 14th Century

Translated by Till Gottheinerová
Graphic design by Aleš Krejča
© 1978 Artia, Prague
Text © Karel Stejskal

English version first published 1978
by Octopus Books Limited
59 Grosvenor Street, London W 1
ISBN 0 7064 0935 3
Printed in Czechoslovakia
2/99/63-51-01

Photographs

Karel Neubert: 2—8, 12—23, 25, 27,
32, 35, 36, 39—41, 45, 49—52, 55, 56,
58—65, 68—71, 73, 74, 76, 78—95,
98—100, 103—115, 117—125,
127—130, 132, 134—139, 141—171,
172—180, 182, 186, 187, 192
Archives of the Institute for Theory
and History of Art, Prague: 9 (P. Paul),
26 (J. Krása), 57 (F. Krejča), 116 (J.
Hampl), 131
Archives of the Knihtisk Printing
Office (earlier Štenc), Prague: 11, 24,
31, 66
Archives of the Prague Castle, Prague:
140 (A. Paul)
Bibliothek der Frauenkirche, Nurem-
berg: 190
Bibliothèque historique de la ville de
Paris, Paris: 77
Bibliothèque Nationale, Paris: 75, 188
Bildarchiv Preussischer Kulturbesitz,
Berlin: 42
Chorherrenstift, Vorau: 30
Christ Church, Oxford: 37
Kunsthistorisches Museum, Vienna:
67
Museum of Fine Arts, Boston: 28
Muzeum śląskie, Wrocław: 29
National Museum, Prague: 10, 43, 44,
46, 48, 97 (J. Bláha)
Österreichische Nationalbibliothek,
Vienna: 53, 54
M. Pierpont Morgan Library, New
York: 38
Rheinisches Bildarchiv, Kölner Stadt-
museum, Cologne: 189
State Institute for Care of Monuments
and Preservation of Nature, Prague: 1,
47, 96, 101, 102, 126
Universitätsbibliothek Erlangen, Nu-
remberg: 133
Vereinigung der Freunde der Staatli-
chen Kunsthalle, Karlsruhe E. V.: 33

(Frontispiece)
The Holy Rood chapel at
Karlstein castle in its original
light. Before 1367.

/1/
Charles IV on a pen drawing in
the Jihlava manuscript of the
Zbraslav Chronicle. Jihlava,
District and City Archives.
C. 1393.

Contents

The reign of Charles IV was a period when the ekonomic and cultural differences between individual parts of Europe became, to some extent, levelled out. At the time when England and France were weakened by the Hundred Years' War and Italy was politically split up, Central Europe lived at peace for several decades and enjoyed relative economic prosperity. This was largely the result of the beneficial policies of Charles IV, who in 1346 was crowned King of the Holy Roman Empire in Bonn. Soon after, he ascended the royal throne of Bohemia vacated by the tragic death of his father John of Luxemburg at the battle of Crécy. By that time the thirty-year-old Charles was already considered one of the most experienced statesmen in Europe. He had been educated in Prague and at the Court of Paris. In his youth he travelled in Luxemburg, Italy, Lithuania, Austria, Hungary and Croatia. Apart from his Czech mother tongue he had a mastery of Latin, French, German and Italian. He maintained diplomatic relations with numerous courts in the western Christian world as well as with the 'Czar of the Serbs and Greeks', Stephen Dushan and with John V Palaeologus, the Byzantine Emperor. Charles gave expression to his European-wide plans as monarch by having himself crowned King of Lombardy in Milan in the year 1355 and that same year also Roman Emperor in Rome. Later, in 1365, he accepted the crown of the Kingdom of Arles in the town of Arles on the Rhône.   :
: Charles IV used his immense political power in the first place for revolutionary measures in European economic life, in which he was far ahead of his time. He has rightly been called 'the first merchant on the imperial throne'. He tirelessly endeavoured to extend and provide safe conduct along the trade routes that led from Venice to Gdansk, Riga and Novgorod and from the towns of Flanders in the direction of Kiev and Constantinople. He even saw to the development of the Vltava—Elbe waterways linking Prague with Hamburg and with other Hanseatic towns. The Emperor's interest in the development of overland trade led him to build up towns like Nuremberg, Wrocław, Tangermünde and others. At the same time he was interested in the spread of education: six European universities owe their charters of foundation to Emperor Charles IV.   :

: Charles was greatly interested in the fine arts which he put to deliberate use in support of his power as monarch. He founded his first castle and the town of Monte Carlo near Lucca when he was sixteen years old. He strengthened his position by establishing new castles, such as Wenzelsburg near Lauf not far from Nuremberg and Beheimstein near the town of Pegnitz. In some of his foundations he intentionally followed up the traditions of his imperial predecessor St. Charlemagne. For instance, in 1355 he laid the foundation stone of a new choir of Aachen cathedral, to whose ancient treasure he donated valuable goldsmiths' works.   :
: Charles made his greatest contribution to artistic development in the Kingdom of Bohemia, whose frontiers he extended by what became known as the Lesser Lands of the Czech Crown. He chose Prague as his residential city and thanks to him it became the third largest town, after Rome and Constantinople. At the present time when Prague as a city is beginning to spread far beyond the horizon of the overcrowded Vltava basin, one appreciates the true greatness of Charles's project for the New Town. Prague developed inside the New Town walls right up to the Industrial Revolution. To this day the New Town serves as a great and busy historical core thanks to the perfection of the town planning, the spaciousness of its squares and streets and the effective layout of the main architectonic features.   :
: The advancement of the Czech Lands and Prague in particular was to be visibly expressed by monumental symbols of art that were to make an impact upon the public. The new buildings, their sculptural and pictorial decorations, often carried out in techniques and materials that were new to the Czech Lands at that time, the magnificently illuminated books and the precious objects of gold exhibited to the crowds of pilgrims once a year were meant to rouse admiration. They were an explicit expression of the aims of Charles's reign and convincingly showed that he was the heir of the local Přemyslide dynasty and the ·legitimate Emperor of the Holy Roman Empire.   :
: Both the Emperor and his circle of counsellors paid systematic attention to works of art. They devoted much thought to these and often changed their form in the course of the work. They gathered ideas on their journeys through Germany, France and Italy, where

Introduction

they encountered the older traditions in art: the ruins of antique Rome and the imperial monuments of the early and culminating Middle Ages. Court masters were selected from among foreign as well as local artists. These masters have fittingly been called the artistic avantgarde of Europe of the time. The age of Charles brought a far-reaching expansion in general education. So solid a basis was laid for cultural values that all subsequent periods have turned back to it and derived benefit from it. The first to uphold this tradition was Wenceslas IV, who tried to follow up the works of art of Charles IV's era that were being fashioned insofar as the growing European crisis of late feudalism made this possible. :*

: The six hundredth anniversary of the death of Charles IV gives art historians a stimulus to try and sum up the results of widespread analytical work carried out over the last few years and to present it to the broader public. The author of the following chapters is a scholar of long standing and has published numerous studies on the subjects touched upon. He is well qualified to guide the reader through the entire field and acquaint him with the latest facts, even if we are left with many hypotheses in view of heavy losses and gaps in sources. We are introduced to highly topical questions of contemporary research in the history of art; attention is drawn not only to newly discovered works but also to artifacts that thanks to new methods of interpretation are now ascribed to the period of Charles IV. The author incorporates traditional forms of study tracing Charles on the Czech and on the European scene in the dual role as King of Bohemia and Emperor of Rome. He clearly understands the decisive role of childhood and youth in the formation of Charles's personality: he shows what he derived from the wealth of French and Italian culture and how ingeniously he managed to make use of the local traditions. By providing inspiration and acting as bountiful donor and cultural strategist of European significance he contributed to the creation of a rich syncretic Court art. Thanks to his own interests in collecting he added to it a specific feature of historicism, which we have become fully aware of only in recent years. :*

: The book evokes the entire cultural context and the significance of the environment with its humanist respect for the arts. The physical and mental character

of Charles IV himself is presented here in a non-traditional manner, reconstructed on the basis of a combination of all available direct and indirect literary evidence, works of art and the results of two independent anthropological analyses of the Emperor's bodily remains. :*

: The attraction and value of the ARTIA volume on Charles IV lies in the exceptional wealth of pictorial material which it has been possible to put together in this book. The pictures evoke the setting that Emperor Charles created and the places where pivotal events in the course of his life occurred. The entire range of works of Court art is presented here in detail. Certain works of art, scattered later in art collections abroad, are published for the first time ever; others are presented in more perfect form than ever laid before the readers. :*

Josef Krása

/2/
The battlefield at Crécy in northern France, where King John of Luxemburg fell on 26 August 1346.

Chapter I

The Luxemburgs
and Europe

The measure of a monarch's importance is the impact which he makes upon the course of history and the results of endeavours which he initiated and executed. In the case of Emperor Charles IV, who was born in Prague on 14 May 1316 and died there on 29 November 1378, the activity which he pursued in the most varied spheres of contemporary life is remarkable. The extent of his ventures is indicated by the towns he visited; they included Brussels, Paris, Zurich, Rome, Königsberg (now Kaliningrad), Krakow, Budapest, Dalmatian Senj . . . :
: Charles's Europeanism can be traced to his family origins. His father John came from Luxemburg on the western borders of the Empire, where for centuries German and French elements had intermixed. His mother, Elizabeth, was the last Queen of the Bohemian Přemyslide dynasty. The Slavonic origin of that dynasty had been strengthened by relations to other ruling Slavonic dynasties (e. g. the Russian), but, at the same time, through frequent intermarriage their blood contained German, Hungarian and Greek elements. At an early age Charles had command of Latin, Czech, German, French and Italian. He became so conversant with the traditions, culture and style of life of many countries that he could move about in them like a native. :
: His noble origin, outstanding abilities and education predetermined him to continue the work begun by his grandfather Henry VII, who in 1308, when he was still a little known Count of Luxemburg, a feoffee of the French crown, had been elected King of Rome at Frankfurt-on-Main. It was to be expected that, like his predecessors, Henry would use his election merely to extend the territorial base of his power. And, indeed, he sent his fourteen-year-old son John to Bohemia, where the orphaned princess Elizabeth had been offered to him in a marriage which would bring with it the Kingdom of Bohemia and Moravia as well as a claim to the Polish crown. :
: At the same time the new king set off for Rome at the head of his army. The inspiration for that campaign must have come from his brother Balduin who, in his archiepiscopal town of Trier — once the residence of St. Constantine the Great and a centre of the cult of that first Christian Emperor — had begun to devise plans to elevate the House of Luxemburg. :
: Henry had supporters among the Italian patriots, who were dreaming of a renewal of the Roman Empire. Dante Alighieri dedicated to him his De Monarchia (which was later denounced by the Church) and in the thirtieth chapter of his Paradise prepared a crown for him. The first theoretician of constitutional monarchy, Marsilius of Padua, accompanied Henry VII on his campaign. After sharp clashes with the Guelphs he accomplished his aim of being crowned Emperor in the Lateran basilica in Rome in the year 1312. His phenomenal rise found self-confident expression in the conviction that 'the law of God lays down that every creature be subject to the Roman Emperor' to whom 'the whole world belongs'. Like Balduin in Trier, he felt himself in Rome to be the owner of the monuments of his imperial ancestors, among them the Flavian amphitheatre, the famous Colosseum, which he presented as a gift 'to the Senate and people of Rome'. Before long, he found himself at odds with the Pope, became embroiled in the turbulent Italian situation, and died of malaria near Siena in 1313. :
: Emperor Henry's tragic end once again proved that the imperial crown could be held only by the ruler of a larger empire. Henry's son, King John of Bohemia, for a time managed to extend dynastic power to the Tyrol and Carinthia. With the help of his son Charles he made a bold but unsuccessful attempt to establish Luxemburg rule in northern and central Italy. For some years after his death the most easternly domain of the Luxemburgs was Polish Mazovia on the Lithuanian-Russian border. John achieved more permanent success at territorial expansion closer to the Kingdom of Bohemia. He extended its frontiers to the west by including the Eger (Cheb) region and to the north by gaining control over a large part of Silesia. He met an untimely but gallant death when fighting on the side of the French against the English at the battle of Crécy in 1346. Together with Balduin of Trier John managed to persuade the majority of Imperial Electors to elect Charles King of Rome at a meeting held in Rhens on the Rhine in the year 1346. That same year Charles was crowned King of Rome in Bonn and the following year King of Bohemia in Prague. :
: In the years 1354—55 Charles undertook his first journey to Rome as monarch, where the great poet Francesco Petrarch was lauding him as a ruler bearing comparison with the great emperors of the past. In Milan Charles accepted the crown of Lombardy, and then, in St. Peter's in Rome, he was anointed and crowned as Emperor of the entire lands on Earth. During this, as on later visits to Rome, (1368—69) he used his imperial rights to levy taxes in Italy. He was the first Emperor after Frederick Barbarossa to have himself crowned in Arles in

/3/
Rhens, a town on a peninsula in the Rhine, where on 11 July 1346 Charles was elected King of Rome. In 1376 he founded a 'Royal Throne' here on an hectagonal ground-plan.

/4/
Pisa baptistry and cathedral, in which Emperor Henry VII of Luxemburg is buried. In 1355 Charles suppressed an anti-imperial uprising in Pisa.

southern France in 1365, asserting thereby his imperial claim to the Kingdom of Arles.

: The fact that Charles had become the generally acknowledged head of the Holy Roman Empire enabled him to raise the kingdom he had inherited to a higher status and to incorporate the Lands of the Bohemian Crown in it. He added the Upper Palatinate to its western frontiers, to the north the remaining part of Silesia and the two Lusatias, and finally in 1373 the extensive lands of Brandenburg. In this way a large, multi-national state came into being in central Europe, a pattern for subsequent similar formations under the Jagiellon and the Hapsburg dynasties. The Lands of the Czech Crown, however, formed a separate territory, unconnected with the old core of dynastic power, Luxemburg, to which, under the rule of the Emperor's step-brother, Duke Wenceslas, the rich duchy of Brabant was added. For that reason Charles aimed at building a kind of corridor out of the numerous feoffs and estates which he had acquired by marriage or purchase in Germany. This corridor was to link up his two domains. As his successor he appointed his eldest son Wenceslas IV, who as a two-year-old child in 1363 had been crowned King of Bohemia and in the year 1376 was made King of Rome. The Emperor came very near to winning the Polish Crown for his younger son Sigismund, who, however, was to become King of Hungary, Dalmatia and Croatia.   :

: The rise of the Luxemburgs was the more remarkable for not involving bloodshed. The reason for this lay in the fact that death removed the most dangerous of opponents, Emperor Ludwig IV of Bavaria, as early as 1347. From then on Charles was able to adhere to the principle mentioned in a letter to Petrarch, namely, that in politics as in medicine 'everything else should be tried before iron is resorted to'. He achieved his aims by deliberate, cold-blooded diplomatic activity, circumspect marriage policy and by money. In contrast to his extravagant father, who would at times resort to blackmailing his subjects, the Emperor was aware that the yield from his country depended on its prosperity. For that reason he tried to raise this by introducing various measures in the economic sphere, in international trade and in town planning, in which he was far ahead of his time. This applied equally to the organization of the efficient imperial chancellery, in which the entire extensive administration of his lands was centralized.   :

: Views on Charles IV tend to be highly controversial. This is due not so much to the complexity of his character as to the contradictory nature of the later Middle Ages, when the germs of a new era were beginning to sprout, often in an old guise; for example the stress on the divine origin of the Empire served as a means of overcoming the medieval feudal fragmentation. There is, however, one sphere where all those who pass judgment are in agreement: they acknowledge Charles's great appreciation of culture. This Emperor left his mark upon the history of education by founding universities in Prague, Arezzo, Pavia, Lucca, Orange and Geneva, and by granting royal charters to other universities. Himself a writer, he encouraged the development of literature and he attracted outstanding scholars and creative artists into his service.   :

: The Emperor's attitude to culture found its most striking expression in the sphere of the fine arts. From the year 1333 to his death he laid the foundations of important buildings of secular and church architecture and acquired by purchase or commission works of art of every kind. For him art was a matter of deliberate 'cultural policy' and a means of spreading the ideas of imperialism. The sovereign's endeavours in this sphere were supported by his educated and art-loving counsellors, who, as patrons of the arts, likewise gave employment to the court artists. The taste of these men was shaped through permanent contact with the most progressive European art of the time.   :

: It is the aim of this book to indicate what influences existed in this sphere, and to outline the development of art under Charles IV, giving a brief survey of the work of the leading artists and assessing the strength of their influence upon work undertaken elsewhere.   :

/5/
Sedlec near Kutná Hora, former
Cistercian church. The end of the
choir and the ambulatory
chapels. 1290—1320.

Chapter II

The causes of the success of the Emperor Charles IV can be ascribed to the fact that by contrast to his father he fully understood that dynastic power would spread only if based upon the strength and might of the Czech state. Bohemia and Moravia formed a relatively large connected territorial unit without any foreign enclaves. The agrarian and urban revolutions and the discovery of precious metals led to profound economic and social changes in the thirteenth century, during which the local population increased when German colonists came to settle. The economic advance of the country enabled King Přemysl Otakar II (1253—78) to carry out a foreign policy which brought Austria, Styria, Carinthia, Carniola and Pordenone to the Kingdom of Bohemia. He was also sovereign of Cividale and Aquileia and afforded protection to Verona and Treviso. He was the first Czech monarch to reach out for the imperial crown. Přemysl Otakar II defended his empire successfully against Bela IV of Hungary, but he succumbed in the war against Rudolph of Hapsburg and lost his life on the battlefield. His son Wenceslas II (1271—1305) renewed royal power in the Czech Lands. Wenceslas's coronation as King of Poland at Gnesen (Gniezno) in 1300 presents a direct precedent for Luxemburg rule over Mazovia and Silesia.   :

: The Luxemburgs took over the Kingdom of Bohemia as it had been established during the reign of these two kings. The land had a comparatively dense network of chartered towns and castles.   :

: In the thirteenth century monasteries flourished in the Czech Lands. In the reign of Přemysl II the Early Gothic trend of Burgundian-Cistercian architecture prevailed, which in clear spatial disposition and massive solidity of walls corresponded to the local Romanesque tradition. Hence this style was used not only for Cistercian buildings but also by the other orders and for town churches and castles. :

: Mention must be made of an important masonic lodge, which built the castle at Písek for King Přemysl II and Zvíkov castle, which has survived in a fairly complete state. Its wings on a ground-plan of an irregular pentagon open on to an arcaded courtyard, in which the heavy granite pillars provide a rhythm. The building is based on a type of disposition that spread from the Mediterranean via the

The Heritage of the Přemyslides

Tyrol to the Frankish region (e. g. the imperial castle at Nuremberg dating from the late twelfth century). In the chapel of the ostentatious castle palace where the walls are broken up by broad windows, the robust courtyard arcades are replaced by somewhat lighter shapes of compound piers, and out of these rise the ribs of the two compartments of sexpartite vaulting.   :

: The builder of the chapel was clearly influenced by classical French Gothic architecture as interpreted through the Rhineland. A masonic lodge that was summoned from Saxony to build the royal Bezděz castle from 1274—8 solved similar problems in a different manner. The elongated layout of the castle is adapted to the sloping ground, on which the castle buildings are fitted in a masterly manner to form a picturesque configuration. The chapel is fortified by a single storey outer gallery so that this part is enveloped in two layers of walling with unequal sized windows. As in the case of Zvíkov chapel the solid wall under the heavy window cornice is lightened by means of blind arcades of the sedilia; the rhythmical design of the articulation is here of a more advanced type.   :

: At this time the development of architecture in Bohemia and Moravia was entering a new phase. While on the older buildings—built to the Burgundian-Cistercian principles — the new elements of classical French Gothic often lacked organic application, after the year 1280 the new style began to appear in pure form. The church of St. Saviour can serve as an example; this is the final part added to the St. Francis monastery in Prague, with a building history lasting over half a century. It was the first Minorite convent in central Europe and perhaps north of the Alps. The convent was founded by an aunt of King Přemysl II, the Blessed Agnes, who kept up a correspondence with St. Clara. With its complex layout the Agnes convent shows a certain relation to the Cistercian nunnery of her cousin St. Hedwig in Silesian Třebnice. The most remarkable part is the choir of the church of St. Saviour, in which large windows with highly intricate traceries, derived from patterns in Champagne, were set among slim compound piers.   :

: A work of outstanding quality is the chapter hall in the Cistercian monastery at Vyšší Brod on the estate of the mighty southern Bohemian family of the Rožmberks. The compound pier in the centre of the square room supports vaulting of an unusual pattern applied so that the consoles might avoid the rose window. This ingenious design foresaw the complex vaulting systems of double-nave churches in the fourteenth century.   :

: The Czech Lands contributed to the development of central European architecture through the Cistercian church at Sedlec built in the years 1290—1320. It has a nave, double aisles and a treble transept. Funds for the erection of this church came from the profits of the silver mines at nearby Kutná Hora. In planning the layout of the Sedlec church the builder availed himself of the ground-plan of Cologne cathedral, but he boldly doubled the number of chapels along the gallery of the main choir. This led to an innovation which was to prove important for development: the alternation of cross and tripartite compartments in the gallery. In regard to style this builder was influenced by the rapidly developing architecture of Swabia. The Cistercian ideal of simplicity did not permit the full development of a system of buttresses even in this mighty building, which is more than 30 m high. But this does not in any way detract from its monumentality.   :

: In Bohemia and Moravia not a single church has survived in which the Gothic portal with monumental sculptural decorations has been further developed. The only existing example is at Předklášteří near Tišnov, where it was built before the middle of the thirteenth century. The antique statues of that portal, derived from Saxony, show certain residues of the Romanesque, and these were not overcome even in the figure of the kneeling King Přemysl II on the badly damaged tympanum of the portal to the palace chapel at Zvíkov. Far more advanced in style is the head of a man on the figural console in the sacristy of that same chapel. The stress on the physiognomical features reflects west European naturalism as do the crowned heads on the entrance portal to the church of St. Saviour in the St. Francis monastery in Prague. Other stonemasons' work of the period shows complexity of style and uneven quality. The somewhat roughly hewn tympanum of St. Bartholomew's church at Kolín holds the scene of the Annunciation, composed into a broken arch and lined with crude plant ornaments. The almost baroque pathos is due to Byzantine patterns used by the painters. On the other hand, the leaves on the outstanding portal to the monastery church at Hradiště nad Jizerou, those in the crypt of St. Stephen's church at Kouřim and elsewhere can easily compete with their French patterns in regard to precision of observation and finesse of work. Fragments of tombstones in the (now pulled down) Benedictine monastery at

/6/
*Zvíkov, castle on the confluence of
the rivers Vltava and Otava,
founded before 1230. Arcaded
gallery in the courtyard. Charles
stayed at the castle in 1352.*

Ostrov often are outstanding; they show figures in shallow relief or engraved and stylized in the spirit of the post-classical Gothic style. It is difficult to pass judgment on the development of sculpture as certain works of greater importance are lost, among them the stone monument with figures set up in Prague in 1257 in memory of Wenceslas I and the stone tombstone with a plastic figure of Wenceslas II in the Cistercian monastery at Zbraslav.

: It can, however, be assumed that certain wooden sculptures reflect older works done in stone which have not survived. This is true of the larger than life-size Madonna from the cloisters of the commandery of the Order of St. John at Strakonice castle, the origin of which dates back to the beginning of the fourteenth century. The broad base of the statue narrows towards the head, to which the eyes of the spectator are drawn by a line of folds of the high-belted garment. The expressly monumental conception and the great simplification of the securely felt form recalls work in stone. The starting point of this important work must have been French sculpture of the thirteenth century. From there derives the Virgin with the open cloak as well as the Byzantine motif of the Child touching the Mother's chin.

: Under the last Přemyslides the other branches of the arts similarly abandoned Romanesque. In the royal chapel at Plasy monastery, finished before 1265, elongated figures of saints and donors in thick draperies are composed into painted architecture. Their unusually precise geometrical construction makes it possible to assign this decoratively effective work to an architect of the Burgundian-Cistercian masonic lodge. The picture of the Madonna Enthroned and a pathetic scene of the Crucifixion on the eastern pillars of the dean's church at Písek with exalted heads and draperies made up of dense folds, bear a striking similarity to the miniatures in English Early Gothic manuscripts (the Evesham Psalter and others).

: A precious globe of the stars was probably commissioned by King Přemysl II; it was later purchased together with other astronomical devices and manuscripts of the Czech kings by Nicholas Cusanius and is kept to this day in the library of his hospital at Bernkastel-Cues in Germany. The wood-

/7/
The Madonna of Strakonice.
Prague, National Gallery. Wood.
Early 14th century.

en core of the globe is covered with canvas and a layer of chalk, into which the drawings are engraved. Originally it served as a pattern for painting but with constant use the drawings were rubbed off. The painter tried to get close to his pattern, which must have been either a now lost work of classical antiquity or a good copy of it. This would explain the stress on the anatomy of the figures, most of them in the nude, their classical profiles, natural movements and the illusive depiction of hair and beards. Andromeda's draperies show fine, dense pinfolds, common in sculpture and painting of the Early Gothic 'classical style'. A similar interest in the anatomy of the naked body but with less pliant draperies which often form wedges of some size, can be found on the rich figural decorations carried out in niello technique on a gilded silver cross which is part of the cathedral treasure at Regensburg. Its inscription is proof that it was made for Přemysl II. The style of the niello corresponds to that of works made in western Europe, particularly English painting of the third quarter of the thirteenth century. The chronicles reveal that the man who commissioned the cross, called the 'King of Iron and Gold' in view of his power and wealth, possessed many precious works in gold. His high artistic demands are evidenced on dual-sided Seals of Majesty with reliefs of the monarch sitting upon a throne and riding a horse. Despite its miniature scale it leaves a monumental impression so that its relation to Paris cathedral sculpture is in no way surprising.   :

: In the Prague Minorite convent of St. Francis a workshop was active at that time, in which the second part of the Franciscan Bible was illuminated and later, around 1290, also the two-volume Osek Lectionary. One of the bible illuminators, Frater Godefridus, depicted himself on it. It is remarkable how these monks had mastered the Byzantine style represented in the Padua Epistolary, the miniatures of which were made in 1259 by the Venetian disciples of local Greek masters. The Franciscans' liking for valuable codices of that type is further shown in five antiphonaries belonging to their monastery at Zadar. In the rich subject-matter and beautiful colouring of the miniatures, in the initials and drolleries of the Prague Franciscans, a good deal of the

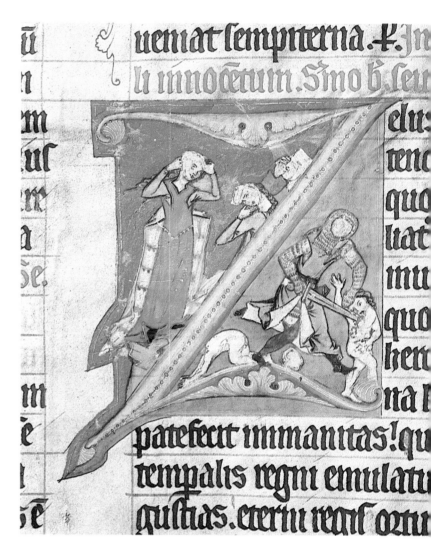

/8/
The Murder of the Innocents.
Lectionary of Arnold of Meissen
called of Osek. Winter part.
Prague, State Library of the
Czech Socialist Republic. C. 1290.

tradition of Mediterranean Hellenism continued. At the same time, however, a number of Gothic architectonic elements and figural types appeared, which reveal a knowledge of Anglo-French book painting of the third quarter of the thirteenth century. Some miniatures are not far removed from the niello of the Regensburg cross of Přemysl II.　:

: Unfortunately Wenceslas II's castle chapel has not survived. The chronicler reports it to have been 'magnificent far beyond the princedoms of his time'. An engraved drawing on part of a tombstone in the St. Francis convent in Prague gives an idea of the level of painting at his court. The tombstone once covered the tomb of the Queen Mother Kunigunde of Hungary († 1285). Its mature style can be explained by the fact that it was made in the masonic lodge of French orientation engaged in building St. Saviour's church. There is a relationship between this tombstone and another in St. Francis convent made for Guta, Wenceslas II's daughter († 1294 or 1297). The engraved tombstone to Wenceslas's sister, the Abbess Kunigunde († 1321) can be ascribed to the same master. With these and other quality tombstones the style of post-classical Gothic penetrated into Bohemia. On the elegant court figures of the Master of Guta's tombstone the draperies fall in effective curves, losing their organic connection with the body and giving an impression of almost playful eurhythmics; but they are based on a rational geometrical scheme of construction.　:

: When in 1292 the Cistercian abbots were returning to Bohemia from the general chapter at Cîteaux, they purchased in Paris 'many volumes of books' for the two hundred talents of silver which King Wenceslas II had given them for that specific purpose. Some of these Paris manuscripts have survived in the Czech Lands to this day (e. g. the illuminated collection of Aristotle's works in Zbraslav monastery). They served the local illuminators as patterns, though some of them learned their craft in Paris itself. This is true of the first illuminator of the Life of St. Francis in the Nostitz Library. This manuscript might be considered Parisian, but for the fact that it contains Czech names and the description of miracles that took place in Prague. The works of the second manuscript painter, who was trained in Bologna, are closer to painting and differ from the delicately drawn little pictures of the first artist in their sparse use of flat colours.　:

: Wenceslas II took a personal interest in culture. He composed German poems in the style of the minnesingers and liked to lead learned theological discussions. He even attempted to set up a university in Prague. It is typical of the man that he attracted priests and monks to his court not only from the west but 'some from Russia, some from Greece, others from Prussia and quite a few from remote regions in Hungary and overseas . . .' and '. . . often

21

they would recite mass before him in the Greek and the Slavonic tongue'. These Orthodox clergy probably added to the treasures of Byzantine art brought to Prague castle by King Vladislav II. Among Wenceslas II's court artists there is mention of a goldsmith John of Greece. Byzantine influences on early fourteenth century painting can be detected, e. g. on the picture of the Descent from the Cross on one of the pillars of the dean's church at Písek. The painter of that picture, who was acquainted with post-classical Gothic, interpreted a compositional scheme used in the preceding century in the work of a Greek artist working at Montegaldo castle near Vicenza. :

: The Abbess Kunigunde prolonged the tradition of Přemyslide art. Her convent of St. George at Prague castle gave shelter to her niece Elizabeth, Charles IV's mother, during the turbulent period 1306—1310. These two Přemyslide women are depicted by the side of the throne of the Holy Trinity

on a miniature which Kunigunde had inserted into the Strahov Plenary together with embossed golden reliefs. The but average miniature is connected with nine liturgical codices, which, from 1315 onwards, were ornamented by painters working for Kunigunde's sister-in-law, the widowed Queen Elizabeth Rycheza. Two of the painters are even known by name: Oldřich and Pešek. :

: The famous Passional of the Abbess Kunigunde is of far higher quality. Into this manuscript Canon Beneš, the librarian of St. George's, copied, in the years 1313 and 1320—1, the compositions of the Prague Dominican monk Kolda of Koldice, who had come under the influence of the heretical mystic Johann Eckart, together with other spiritually elating precepts. To these Beneš added his own rhymes and magnificent illustrations. He thus creat ed a work that is a parable of Kunigunde's eventful life and, at the same time, he expressed in symbols a cosmology founded upon neo-Platonic and Augustinian metaphysics of light. The monumental conception of the carefully drawn architecture and the richly draped figures placed ingeniously in a complex geometrical pattern show that Beneš must have known the work of the Master of Guta's tombstone and some of the local mural painting. The northern French character of his lettering at the same time shows that the artist had broadened his education in the west, probably in Paris. It was there that the epoch-making Breviary of Philippe le Bel arose within close range of the cathedral sculpture. At that time, too, English, Flemish and other illustrators were busy at work in Paris. While the artistic effect of the illustrations in the first part of the Passional rests in the virtuosity of its drawings, in the second, made later, more emphasis was placed on physical volume and values in painting. This part differs from west European manuscripts by its pathos of expression, achieved by the painter's choice of types, compositional principles and an approach of Byzantine origin. :

: The preceding outline gives a highly condensed picture of development, for many works have been omitted for the sake of clarity. It does show, however, that Bohemia and Moravia, which had been lagging behind as artistic centres, had largely made up lost ground by the time Charles was born. Through

/11/
St. John the Evangelist. Plenary from St. George's convent. Prague, church of Our Lady at Strahov. Gilded silver. Embossed relief. C. 1307.

the work of three generations of artists of various nationalities the country had accumulated considerable numbers of works of art. Foreign influences continued to be adopted but the local setting militated against one-sided dependence. Relations extended no longer merely to the neighbouring countries of Germany, as had been the case previously, but far to the west and south. Individual works contained a variety of stimuli. There was a characteristic interpenetration of Gothic and Byzantine elements on the Kolín tympanum and on paintings. The specific local conditions and the distinctive aspect of work led some of the builders and artists to resort to highly original solutions.   :

: Charles's attitude to the traditions of the Kingdom of Bohemia found expression also in the sphere of the arts. When after ten continuous years abroad he returned to Bohemia in October 1333, his first steps led to his mother's grave in the monastery church at Zbraslav. There was also to be found the tomb of his grandfather Wenceslas II, who founded the church in 1297. Immediately after his return Charles initiated the renovation of the Přemyslide palace at Prague castle, which had been devastated by fire in 1304. He retrieved from bail a number of Přemyslide castles in Bohemia and Moravia and began to repair some of them. In 1334 an illustrated astronomical almanac was finished for him, and today is deposited in the hospital library of Nicholas Cusanius. Wenceslas II had the first part of this copied in 1301. From it can be deduced that the collection of astronomical devices and the manuscripts of the Czech kings, which the famous German cardinal later acquired, must have passed through Charles's hands. The same is true of the funeral insignia discovered in 1976 in the tomb of Přemysl II in Prague cathedral. These insignia, the royal crown, orb and sceptre, the latter being the oldest of its kind to have survived, were made at the expense of Queen Kunigunde of Hungary or Wenceslas II. Charles had a rim with an inscription added to the crown and a further inscription on a small slab of lead, which was laid into the royal tomb. He must have been fully aware of the material, memorial and undoubtedly artistic value of the works from the Přemyslide epoch.   :

/12/
Canon Beneš: Mystical Embrace. Passional of Abbess Kunigunde, 2nd part. State Library of the Czech Socialist Republic. 1320—21.

/13/
Paris, cathedral of Notre-Dame.
Founded 1163.

Chapter III

The Czech Prince
as Scholar in Paris
and as Venetian Condottiere

In April 1323 King John of Luxemburg had his seven-year-old son taken from Bohemia to the royal court in Paris, to his aunt Jane, who was married to the King of France Charles IV, called le Bel. The young Bohemian prince was engaged to Blanche of Valois, the sister of the future French King Philippe VI. A further marriage bound King John more closely to Paris, where he received as a gift from King Philippe an official residence, Palais Nesle. It could be reached from Prague in a mere ten days.   :

: In the new setting John's son disclaimed his Christian name Wenceslas and adopted that of his French uncle, Charles, as he himself relates in 'Vita Caroli', the first medieval biography written by a monarch. He recalls that his uncle had taken a great liking to him and, though he himself could not write, ordered the chaplain to teach Charles his letters. At that time the boy also acquired a passing knowledge of Latin, a prerequisite for his later studies at the university of Paris (probably from 1328). The Paris university had been a magnet for foreign scholars from the thirteenth century, and among them were some from Bohemia. The reports of Charles's university studies are given by the chronicler Beneš Krabice and there is no reason to doubt them. Later Charles proved his sympathies for medieval scholars many times over: he issued foundation documents for numerous universities, granted privileges to them and actively participated in writing the Lexicon of Master Barholomew of Chlumec. He showed theological and juristical knowledge in parts of his own literary work and was deeply interested in astronomy. His nephew, the Dauphin and later King of France Charles V, showed similar leanings. He is shown in the gown of a university master on the many miniatures and reliquary scenes at Karlstein castle. Charles's one-time relation to the university would explain the ostentatious homage which numerous representatives of all its faculties paid to him when he visited Charles V in the Louvre on 9 January 1378. The young Charles was undoubtedly introduced on the university campus by one of its outstanding members, court preacher Master Pierre Roger de Rosiers, the abbot of the ancient Benedictine monastery at Fécamp. He kept up contact with Charles even

26

when he was Cardinal of Avignon and later Pope Clement VI. And it was Master Roger who drew his attention to the teaching of St. Augustine, whose cosmological and aesthetic views, especially the neo-Platonic metaphysics of light, left a mark on his artistic work.

: Charles was greatly impressed by the magnificent art of Paris, as can be deduced from the fact that the new palace at Prague castle was built, in 1333, to the pattern of the residence of the kings of France. The oratory of the Palais de la Cité, the Sainte-Chapelle, must have made a deep impression on Charles who attended divine service there as a member of the royal family. This ingenious building in classical Gothic style, founded by King Louis le Saint, was consecrated in 1248. It was designed as a vast lit-up tabernacle for the most precious relic of the Kingdom of France, Christ's Crown of Thorns. For that reason stained glass windows occupied the entire wall on the first floor. They were conceived as 'divine writing casting the light of the true Sun, i.e. God, into the Church, i.e. the hearts of the believers'. Sainte-Chapelle became the pattern for the court chapel of All Saints at Prague castle, which Peter Parler built in the years 1370—8. There can be little doubt that the Czech prince also visited the abbey church of Saint-Denis, which enjoyed great respect as the centre of the cult of the national patron saint and the burial ground of the kings of France. The reconstruction of that church under the Abbot Suger in the years 1132—44 marks the onset of the history of Gothic. Saint-Denis probably had been at the back of the mind of Wenceslas II when he founded the Cistercian church at Zbraslav as a royal burial place. This trend continued under Charles with the Parler tombs of the Přemyslide dynasty in Prague cathedral, as these show a certain relationship to the tombs of the French ruling dynasty at Saint-Denis. And even the Golden Gate of Prague cathedral with the mosaic of the Last Judgment has one of its precedents in the golden mosaic on the tympanum over the left side portal to Suger's church.

: In Paris Charles came to realize that art can be a pillar of royal might. At the same time, he received the first incentives for his passion of collecting objects and books. Immediately on arrival his uncle gave him a Book of Hours, which served the boy as a reader. One can form an idea of the book, now lost, from the psalter belonging to Charles's sister Bonne of Luxemburg, the wife of the Duke of Normandy and later King of France, Jean II le Bon. The psalter was decorated with paintings done in masterly manner by Jean Pucelle, whose Paris workshop kept a monopoly over several decades on commissions from highly placed persons. It can be assumed that Charles's wife Blanche of Valois had a similar manuscript in her dowry.

: The outstanding position that the Czech prince enjoyed at the court of France gave him access not only to precious manuscripts but also to other valuable objects. Paris had a multitude of antique and Byzantine cameos with carved reliefs; the best-known of these was the Grande Camée de Sainte-Chapelle with the Apotheosis of Germanicus. It is attributed to Dioscorides, a famous carver at the time of Augustus and Tiberius. It probably came to the Chapelle under St. Louis, who perhaps had it given to him by the Emperor Balduin II of Constantinople. In 1334 it became for a time the property of Charles's one-time teacher Clement VI, who collected such antiquities. A row of cameos adorned the reliquary tomb of St. Charlemagne at Saint-Denis. A follow-up of this was the valuable tomb which Charles ordered to be built for St. Wenceslas in Prague cathedral. Abbot Suger had enriched his church treasure with an antique vase, on which he had mounted a golden eagle's head and wings and a chalice of sardonyx with a golden stem and ornamental work. This last object seems to have anticipated the onyx chalice in a gilded silver mount, which Charles presented to the St. Vitus's treasure in 1350. The core of his later immense collections of antiquities of all kinds, precious minerals and many other items, must have come with him from Paris. But he could not fully devote himself to his university studies nor to his liking for books and his collections. Other duties were imposed upon him, outstandingly the need for a military education.

: This was a must for the future monarch, as shown in March 1331, when his father suddenly summoned him to Italy. During his stay at Trento in September 1330 King John had managed to extend his rule over sixteen important Italian towns and their surroundings. By creating Luxemburg enclaves in this way he found himself facing numerous opponents.

: Charles set out from Luxemburg with his escort to help his father, crossing the mountains at Brieg. For the first time in his life he stood on an Alpine pass, though later in life he was to cross the Alps on many occasions. At sixteen, he won his first battle near the fortress of San Felice in the Modena district. 'Then we came to Lucca in Tuscany', he wrote in his autobiography, 'and prepared war against Florence; and we built a beautiful castle with a little walled town on the top of a hill, which is ten miles from Lucca... and gave it the name of Monte Carlo'. It was perhaps the influence of Italian individualism that made Charles give his first castle his own name, later borne by many other castles that he established. Lucca, which he mentions in his autobiography, is famous for its gold brocades. From here came at least six pieces of valuable materials found in the royal tombs in St. Vitus's cathedral. In the rich and profligate environment of the town the Czech prince forgot the faithfulness he had promised his distant wife Blanche. This resulted in a warning dream he had at Tarenzo on the way to Parma: it stirred him so much that in 1355 he founded an Augustinian monastery there.   :

: These events marked the beginning of Charles's attitude towards Italy, to which he moved his residence a total of six times and where altogether he spent more than five years. Soon after his first arrival in Bohemia he fell into disgrace with his father so that he was forced to escape to the Tyrol where his younger brother John Henry was living. Since King John forbad money to be sent to him, 'he was forced', as the well-informed chronicler Peter of Žitava (Zittau) relates, 'to accept pay from the Venetians and other Lombardian towns and out of that provide for himself and his retinue all the essentials of life'. As an aristocratic condottiere he took up the services of the League which the Venetians had formed with some of their neighbours against the mighty tyrant of Verona, Mastino II della Scala. It was at this time, when Charles had to act entirely on his own, that he was given a number of stimuli for his later foundations and art commissions.   :

: In April of the year 1337 Charles went down the Danube as far as Buda and from there undertook a journey across Hungary, Croatia and Dalmatia to Senj on the Adriatic coast. There he became acquainted with the Slavonic liturgy current in the Orthodox East. In the Church of Rome the Slavonic liturgy was permitted by the Lyons rescript of Pope Innocent IV in 1248, but only for the dioceses of Split, Senj and Aquileia. Later Charles named his chaplain and counsellor, the Dominican priest John Protiva of Dlouhá Ves, Bishop of Senj, and his stepbrother Nicholas of Luxemburg was appointed Patriarch of Aquileia. Charles clearly realized a relationship between Church Slavonic as a liturgical tongue and the national language used not only in the Kingdom of Bohemia but in extensive areas through which he had traversed in the course of his Lithuanian expedition and during his two visits to Hungary.   :

: It was probably in Senj that he became acquainted with some of the future members of the one hundred strong monastery of the Slavonic Brethren, which he founded in Prague ten years later. Most of

/15/
*The upper floor of
Sainte-Chapelle reserved for the
royal family. Interior.*

/16/
Monte Carlo. Castle founded by
Charles in 1333 to protect Lucca
from the Florentine armies.

the monks of that monastery came from the Benedictine Slavonic abbey on a beautiful island near
Zadar in Dalmatia.   :
: During his journey Charles travelled via Parenzo
in Istria (Poreč today), using a vessel belonging to
Count Bartholomew Frankopan of Krk. The Parenzo early Christian basilica from the sixth century is
often given as the source of inspiration for the incrustation on the walls of the Holy Rood chapel at
Karlstein castle with its polished semi-precious
stones. After several adventurous episodes, e. g. escape from captivity by pirates at Grad, he was finally able to carry out in June 1337 a speedy operation
outside Venice with a small troop of Bohemian and
Tyrolean cavalry. He used a stratagem to conquer
Primiero castle, the town of Belluno and lastly,
aided by strong enforcements entrusted to his command by the Venetians, the town of Feltre. He received the lifetime rank of captain in both these
towns. Then he marched his troops to Venice where
he was welcomed with great honour by the Doge
Francesco Dandolo and the wealthy patricians.   :
: In Venice his hosts must certainly have taken him
to the church of their patron saint, the basilica of St.
Mark, built on the pattern of the Justinian church
of the Apostles at Constantinople. In the cupolas of
the narthex Charles saw the 13th century Old Testament scenes in mosaics, made on the pattern of
miniatures in a Greeco-Egyptian manuscript, which
even at that time was some eight hundred years old.
He will have realized that Venice is full of mosaics

incomparably richer than those he had seen in the
abbey church of Saint-Denis. Suger's mosaics remained a mere curio in the west, which were never
continued since the ancient technique of mosaic-
making had fallen into oblivion. In Venice, however, the art still flourished and in the years
1370—1 the Emperor Charles commissioned the
local mosaic-makers to carry out the decorations of
the Golden Gate to Prague cathedral.   :
: The aesthetic impression on entering St. Mark's is
based on that special contrast aroused by the shining
gilded tessera of the mosaics and the dull patina of the
four bronze horses by the Greek sculptor Lysippus (4th century B.C.), brought from Constantinople as loot and set up on the balcony of the
church. Is it mere chance that a similar combination of materials can be found in Prague, where the
bronze equestrian statue of St. George stands close
to the mosaic on the Golden Gate?   :
: In the interior of St. Mark's basilica Charles saw

/17/
*San Felice near Modena. The
fortress at the foot of which the
16 year old Charles won his first
victory on 26 November 1332.*

the Byzantine iconostasis, which was not removed until the second half of the fourteenth century. He might also have seen an iconostasis in the cathedral on Torcello island nearby. The connection of those iconostases with the set of pictures by Theodoric in the Holy Rood chapel at Karlstein castle, which also cover a whole wall, is all the more striking since the gilded lids with the constellations on the vaulting of the Karlstein chapel were made of thin-walled Venetian glass. At the time of Charles's stay in Venice the town was affected by a wave of Palaeologus neo-Hellenism from Constantinople. No family was without its Byzantine icon which protected the home. Paolo Veneziano was painting his panel pictures with their severe expressions and solemn colour schemes, which before long were to find a strong reflection in Czech panel painting. :

: In his autobiography Charles recorded that he concluded several agreements and treaties with his hosts but does not disclose their content. There can be little doubt that he might have kept both towns he had conquered. He was, at that time, no longer a landless person at the mercy of his brother's support or pay. He later extended his possessions in northern Italy and used both sword and diplomacy to strengthen his hold over them in expeditions in 1340, 1347 and 1354. But another fact is far more revealing: he had the entire revenue of his first Roman expedition transferred by Tuscan bankers to his account in the Fondaco dei Tedeschi in Venice in August 1355. In agreement with the doges, whose interests were represented on the Imperial Council by Marino Faliero, their probable relative, he aimed at extending and protecting the overland

/18/
Tarenzo in northern Italy, where Charles had a frightening dream in 1332. In 1355 he founded an Augustinian monastery here.

/19/
Tyrol castle on the river Adige where Charles stayed with his brother John Henry in 1337. In 1347 he vainly tried to conquer this strong fortress defended by the 'Ugly Duchess' Margaret Maultasch.

/20/
Venice, balcony of St. Mark's basilica. The bronze statues of the horses by the Greek sculptor Lysippus (4th cent. B. C.) were brought from the Constantinople hippodrome in 1204.

routes from the harbour at Venice via Prague to northern and north-eastern Europe. In this manner Charles developed the ancient economic and cultural ties between the Czech lands and the 'Ruler of the Adriatic'. This led in the early thirteenth century to numerous places in Prague and elsewhere being given the name of Venice — not in the Italian form but in a Czech version, related to the Slovene name 'Benetke'. In this trade luxury articles of the applied arts came from Venice to Bohemia, some of which added to the St. Vitus's treasure under Charles.   :

: The childhood which Charles spent in Paris and his adolescence in the sunny south are important for the understanding of the later development of art at his court. Special circumstances provided the future Emperor with a broad understanding and exquisite taste in matters of the arts by the time he reached the age of twenty-one. It was, without exaggeration, European in breadth. The same can be said of his courtiers. His future prime counsellor, Archbishop Ernest of Pardubice, spent the whole of the fourteen years which we have just traced in the life of the young Charles at his studies in Bologna and Padua. In Italy he financed many a poor cleric from Bohemia and even provided them with books. He was at home in Italy so that during his first expedition Charles could without fear entrust him with the command of his reserves. It is not surprising therefore that the paintings made for Ernest are Italian in character.   :

: Other Bohemian prelates had close knowledge of Avignon in southern France, where after 1309 the papal court had its residence. John IV of Dražice, the Bishop of Prague, spent eleven years there. It was from Avignon that in 1333 he summoned William, the builder of the now damaged bridge across the Elbe at Roudnice, and other stone-masons. The bishop brought many books back from Avignon as did the later imperial diplomat, the Dean of Vyšehrad, William of Lestkov. Charles personally visited Avignon in the years 1323, 1339, 1344, 1346 and 1365. In the year 1344 he made the acquaintance of Matthias of Arras, the first builder of Prague cathedral, there. Charles witnessed the steady growth of the papal residence and saw it becoming more and more ostentatious. Under Pope John XXII there

/21/
Venice. Byzantine basilica of St.
Mark from the 11th century.
Mosaic in the cupola of the
narthex made in the 13th century
from the 5th century
Greeco-Egyptian patterns.

had been a mighty fortress of the southern type with plain square towers rising on a cliff above the bridge that spanned the Rhône. The new palace of Pope Clement VI and Innocent VI was redesigned by Jean de Loubies to provide greater comfort and style in its interior. Its most beautiful part was the main audience hall in the shape of a spacious double nave. In the forties of the fourteenth century Avignon became an important centre of painting. Apart from local artists, Simone Martini of Siena, a naturalized Frenchman, was working there side by side with the solemn Matteo Giovanetti and other Italians.

The similarity between Avignon painting and the work of some of the imperial masters can perhaps be explained by the fact that the works were analogically but independently derived from two traditions in painting, the French and the Italian. But before the court art in Bohemia reached results commensurable with the work of the leading art centres in the west and south, it had to undergo a long and complex process of development.

/22/
The Papal palace at Avignon (14th cent.) with the bridge across the Rhône (12th cent.). Charles and his courtiers paid frequent visits to the palace.

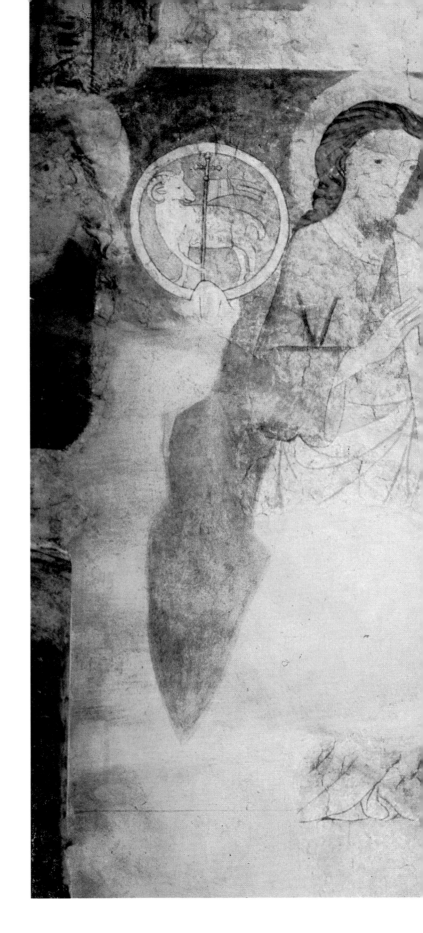

/23/
Strakonice castle, formerly the commandery of the Order of St. John. The figures of John the Baptist and the Apostles above the choir loft. Mural paintings from before 1330.

Chapter IV

Art in Bohemia at the Beginning of the Reign of Charles IV

The conflict which gradually intensified between King John and the young Charles left its marks in the sphere of the arts. Its onset dates from an event reported to have happened in 1336 when the king had five hundred talents of silver coined from melted-down statues of apostles, which his son had been preparing as adornment for the tomb of St. Wenceslas in St. Vitus's cathedral. In the eyes of the historians John's greatest vice, extravagance, was joined by another—his lack of appreciation of culture. No work that might have shed light on this accusation has survived. We do not know, for instance, what goldsmith John of Greece produced for King John, after he had been granted in 1318 a feudal rent to make up for a debt left by Wenceslas II and given three hundred talents of silver.   :

: Another later tombstone to Wenceslas II at Zbraslav monastery, made by metal-caster John of Brabant after 1310, has also been destroyed. This craftsman must have been summoned by King John from the country of his mother Margaret. The same fate met the tombstone to Queen Elizabeth, which the king had erected for his wife in the same monastery in the years 1330—33. The manuscript of the History of Troy has also disappeared. This was the book from which the king liked to be read to at his castle of Durboy in Luxemburg, furnished—if we are to believe the poet Guillaume de Machaut—with a magnificence that was almost oriental. Nothing has survived of buildings 'in the French style' built by John at Prague castle and in the Old Town of Prague in 1335, nor of the Carthusian monastery, which he founded in Prague in 1341 and to which he presented books, vestments and jewels. St. James's church, which King John had commissioned in the Old Town of Prague in 1318 underwent considerable changes during the baroque period.   ·

: The works of art made on the initiative of the king's wife, Elizabeth Přemyslide, suffered the same fate: they included numerous masterpieces in gold and embroidered work (the latter often carried out by herself), nine chapels and altars which she set up in Zbraslav monastery in 1329 as well as breviaries valued in her last will, the following year, at the unusually high sum of sixteen threescores of groschen. These losses are probably responsible for the mistaken impression that art at the court of Charles IV grew up on entirely unprepared ground.   :

: The only authentic works of art attributed to King John until recently were small works of craftsmanship, mainly coins. In 1325 the Florentine mint coined the first Czech ducats, which came to be known as florins. What is interesting is the Italian-type parvus with the king's portrait in three-quarter profile and the half-groschen with his bust, which he ordered to be coined in his Italian signoria in 1331—33. Artistically the most valuable work, how-

/24 a, b/
The Majestic and Rider's Seal of the Czech King John of Luxemburg. Prague, State Archives. Wax. 1310—19.

a

c

d

/24 c, d/
A gold coin known as a florin with the picture of John the Baptist and a lily. Work of Florentine minters invited to Bohemia by King John of Luxemburg. 1325.

b

ever, is the two-sided Seal of Majesty dating from the years 1310—19. The relief of the monarch on the throne and the rider in armour on that seal show such purity of form and finesse of execution that they rank among the finest medieval works of its kind.   :

: Some years ago several small and larger stone fragments were found in the wall of the originally Gothic house At the Bell on the Old Town Square in Prague. This house had later been re-built in baroque style, but the fragments undoubtedly belonged to the rich sculptural decorations that were made at the time of King John. Recent reconstruction work has made it clear that these fragments are remnants of statues of two figures seated on a throne and two standing shield-bearers, and that they must have been located on the niches between the windows of the façade of the three-storey house. Another fragment, a horse's haunch, suggests that there must have been a relief of a man on horseback on the tympanum over the portal. If the figures on the throne truly represented King John and his wife Elizabeth Přemyslide, it would be possible to date their origin to the end of the period 1310—30. Such dating fits into the style of the fragments of works made by the Frankish-Flemish sculptor Jean Pepin de Huy and his followers. These fragments are closely linked with the beautiful tombstone to Henry IV Probus in the Holy Rood church in Wrocław, as has been found recently. Several later strata of mural decorations connected with the work of one of Charles's court painters prove that the royal family indeed owned the house At the Bell.   :

: Similarly representative in character is the monumental tympanum placed at a subsequent date over

the portal to the cemetery of the church of Our Lady of the Snows in Prague. Its upper strip bears a carved relief of the Trinity, the lower strip showing the Coronation of the Virgin. The relation of Father to Son, the central theological problem of the Trinity, has its secular parallel in the figures of the donors kneeling at each side of the lower strip. The first represents King John, the second Charles as Margrave of Moravia, his belt bearing the initial K. The tympanum must have been made in the period close to 11 June 1341, when King John, by then completely blind, designated Charles as his successor at a meeting of the Bohemian Estates. The sculptural decorations were intended to express Charles's complete reconciliation with his father, who had often treated his son harshly but who was preparing him for his future dominant position in European politics. Unfortunately, not a single head has survived on the tympanum so that it is impossible to judge its importance for the development of portraiture. The manner in which the draperies are laid out in tiny parallel folds reveals that the sculptor had learned his craft in the Rottweil masonic lodge in Swabia, i.e. in an area from which, about ten years later, the greatest German stone-mason of his time, Peter Parler, was to come to Prague.   :

: The meagre remains of stone-masons' work are numerically far smaller than wood carvings. The Madonna of Michle in the Prague National Gallery from the period around 1340, is a masterpiece made in a workshop in Brno, as is the Madonna of Strakonice, based on French sculpture (the Madonna of Saint-Aignan in Notre-Dame in Paris). This knowledge had come to Brno through work done in the Strasbourg-Freiburg circle. Any comparison of the Madonna of Michle with that of Strakonice shows that the former is a more progressive work in the sense of post-classical Gothic development leading towards abstraction and formalist stress on the calligraphic line. Nonetheless, it does appear that this general trend in development was balanced by the influence of Bohemian painting of the type of the Vyšší Brod cycle, which shows Italian influences. An even closer relationship to painting can be found in the slightly later Crucifixion, which originally came from the Carmelite nunnery in Prague and belongs now to the Prague National Gallery. It

/26/
Tympanum with reliefs of the
Holy Trinity, the Coronation of
the Virgin and figures of King
John and the Margrave Charles.
Prague, originally the portal of
the church of Our Lady of the
Snows, now in the National
Gallery in Prague. Sandstone.
Before 1346.

shows far greater physical volume. It should be taken into account that the sculptor might have been affected by influences radiating from the circle of Giovanni Pisano. The high quality of the Crucifixion (which is regarded as an artistic expression of early Humanism) and its most likely origin at Hradčany, make it possible to believe that it is the work of one of Charles's court artists.   :

: In the years 1301—34 a very interesting astronomical almanac came into being at Prague castle. The origin of its two full-page finely drawn pen sketches showing the planets can be traced to the years 1310—20. The nude figures of Helios, Venus and Selene are a free version of antique iconography, while the figures of Saturn, Jupiter and Mars, depicted as representatives of various professions, derive from the pre-antique tradition of Babylon as interpreted in medieval Europe by the Arabs. The manuscript was finished at a time when King John had temporarily appointed Charles as Regent of Bohemia and Moravia. It was to him that the astronomers turned with a satirical comment on the year 1334: 'The Regent thunders above us with his constant presence and severely reprimands the people for their sins, but his wife (Blanche of Valois) in her glistening sheen has not shown herself on any occasion'. The 'thundering Regent' (Charles) is clearly conceived as Jupiter. Shortly before, forty-eight pen drawings of mostly nude figures of the constellations had been added to the manuscript, executed rather perfunctorily on the basis of the Sicilian-Arab patterns. The man who drew them, an astronomer by profession, had learned something of the style of the first master of the royal workshop which, in 1320—30, produced an extensive and artistically valuable set of mural paintings at Strakonice castle.   :

: One half of Strakonice castle was held by the Order of St. John while the other half was occupied by a supporter of that order, Baron William III the Bavarian of Strakonice. Baron William was a blood relation of Queen Elizabeth Přemyslide and maintained close contacts with the court in Prague. It was from there that he summoned painters to his residence. The first of these painted the figures of Sts. Philip and James in the chapter hall and scenes from the life of Christ in the southern wing of the cloisters. At a final stage of his work this same painter replaced his own work on the second field by a large-sized Virgin Protectress. The painter was a disciple of the Master of Guta's tombstone, from whom he took over the type of figure and the sharp graphic drawing with a leaning towards ornamentation.   :

: The second Strakonice master made the row of apostles and St. John the Baptist in the choir loft of the church of the commandery of the Order of St. John. It is conceived as a procession and has survived in reasonably good condition. He also produced the scenes of the Passion in the frieze full of drama in the western and northern parts of the cloisters; unfortunately this has almost completely faded. The drawing of this second master resembles that engraved on the tombstone of Vojslav, abbot of the Benedictine monastery at Ostrov near Prague († 1313—16); but it is more mature and more flowing in the interpretation of the draperies. A certain similarity between the painting of this second Strakonice master and Beneš's illustrations to Kunigunde's Passional make it possible to express the belief that both these great artists may perhaps have had close contact on some joint commission for Prague castle.   :

: Both the Strakonice masters were helped in carrying out the decorations in the commandery of the Order of St. John by several younger assistants. One of them was the painter Nicholas, who, a little later, can be found in the service of an important member of the offshoot of the Přemyslide dynasty, Prince Nicholas II of Opava, the high royal official. This aristocrat was a patron of the Dominican monastery church of St. Wenceslas at Opava, consecrated in 1336. On the southern side of the choir stands a chapel which Nicholas adorned with cycles of paintings from the legends of St. John the Baptist, St. Stephen and other pictures. He expressed his self-confidence as an artist by adding his monumental self-portrait and the signature 'Nicolaus pictor'. His work shows the first signs of spatial ornamentation on pictures. He intensified the function of colour in modelling, using it as a factor almost equal to the expressively stressed line.   :

: The importance of the Strakonice-Opava workshop would probably be shown in a better light if

/27/
*Crucifix from the former convent
of the Carmelite nuns in
Prague-Hradčany. Prague,
National Gallery. Wood. Before
1350.*

/28/
The Death of the Virgin from
Košátky. Boston, Museum of Fine
Arts. Panel picture. C. 1345.

/29/
The Wrocław Trinity. Wrocław,
Muzeum śląskie. Panel picture.
Before 1353.

/31/
*The Coronation of the Virgin
with figures of the saints.
Antependium of Pirna. Meissen,
Staatliche Kunstsammlungen
(Albrechtsburg). Embroidery on
canvas. Detail. After 1340.*

the original decorations had survived both in Charles's palace at Prague castle and in the buildings that King John began to construct in Prague in 1335. The paintings in the palace, which Bishop John IV of Dražice had erected after 1329 in the Little Quarter of Prague, have also not come down to us. Chronicler Frank the Prager calls these paintings 'exceedingly beautiful' and gives a description of them. His reference to the bishop giving the painters patterns from an exemplum that he had brought from Avignon is an interesting example of how contacts with France were maintained. The Strakonice-Opava workshop dealt both with mural painting and book illustrations. It established the tradition of a linear calligraphic style, which after a time came to be used as innovation by artists such as the outstanding painter, assumed to have come from court circles, who worked in the church at Čkyně near Vimperk. This tradition left its mark even on painters who were largely under the Italian influence. :

: This Italian orientation showed most strikingly in panel painting, most of which has survived as parts of altars. Mention has already been made of the nine altars which were set up by Charles's mother, Queen Elizabeth at Zbraslav. She also founded the altar to the Slavonic Patrons, Sts. Cyril and Methodius, in St. Vitus's cathedral, where Charles himself had set up three altars. He was also concerned with the artistic decorations in the chapels of his newly founded castles Karlsburg-Tepenec in Moravia, Karlsberg-Kašperk in the Šumava mountains, Karlshausen near Hluboká-on-Vltava, Lauf near Nuremberg, Karlsfried near Žitava (Zittau), Beheimstein near Pegnitz. With the exception of Karlstein, founded in the vicinity of Prague in 1348, no painting has survived in any of these castles founded by Charles IV. :

: The courtiers followed the sovereign's example in setting up altars. Though only a small portion of the large number mentioned in historical sources has escaped destruction, the Czech Lands hold second place in Europe immediately after Italy in the number of surviving panel pictures. The knowledge of the techniques of panel painting had been proved already by the Cues globe of Přemysl II. We also hear that the daughter of that king, the Abbess

/32/
Virgin and Child. The Man of Sorrows. Karlsruhe, Staatliche Kunsthalle. Diptych. Before 1360.

Kunigunde, purchased painted panels for her Prague convent. :

: In the first half of the fourteenth century there were a large number of craftsmen living in Prague. In 1348 they founded the Brotherhood of St. Luke. Membership was open to painters, glaziers (many were painters also), carvers, gilders, and other artisans. The Latin-German-Czech minutes of that brotherhood of the years 1348 to 1527 are an invaluable source for art historians. The first list of members of the period around 1360 shows that it was an international organization, in which for example the Czech artists Václav and Ladislav and the Germans Underschick and Fridlius associated with a Frenchman called Johannes Galycus. In certain respects the statues of the Prague brotherhood bear a striking resemblance to those of the guild of painters in Siena; this would be entirely in keeping with the Italian character of the paintings produced in those years. One regulation laid down that the masters were enjoined to leave Prague from time to time; travelling was compulsory for journeymen as an essential part of their training in the arts. Another regulation forbade the journeymen to carry weapons in the workshop, which brings to mind the picture on which painter Nicholas of Opava depicted himself with a sword at the belt. Weapons were, however, essential during travel at that time. :

: A number of favourable circumstances made the journey to Italy in search of experience easier for the Prague painters. The Luxemburg signoria in Italy in the years 1330—33, the Belluno-Feltre enclave founded by Charles in 1337, mass pilgrimage of Prague craftsmen to Rome in the summer of the year of grace 1350, inn for pilgrims from Bohemia set up by Charles in Rome and then his own two visits to Rome in the years 1354—55 and 1368—69, when some artists would have moved to Italy together with the court. In addition, a constant stream of trade caravans travelled between Prague and Venice, accompanied by craftsmen and pilgrims, who used the harbour of that town on their way to the Holy Land. It is easy to picture that many a painter from Bohemia had similar adventures on his journeyings, though on a different social level, as the young Charles on the Adriatic coast. :

: Eloquent proof of this is given on the oldest sur-

/33/
The Madonna of Most. Prague.
National Gallery. Panel picture.
After 1340.

viving panels, their typology, style and, in particular, the technique of painting, which is the most reliable proof that the painters received training in southern schools. This is the case of the pictures by a master, who, after 1340, made the panel of the Death of the Virgin of Košátky (now in Boston) and about ten years later the Wrocław Trinity. This second panel was commissioned by the Silesian Prince Ludwig of Legnica-Brzeg, who was related to Charles by numerous family ties and political treaties. The picture of the Trinity has a parallel in type and style in the figure of Vratislav II in the Vyšehrad antiphonary at Vorau, which is assumed to be a copy of a painting in the palace at Prague-Vyšehrad, renovated by Charles in the years 1348—50. It might therefore be well possible that a destroyed painting by the Master of the Death of the Virgin of Košátky served the illuminator as pattern. This grandiose picture followed up in composition, types and facial expressions as well as in the deep colour scheme of icons the famous picture of the Death of the Virgin by Paolo Veneziano in Vicenza made in the year 1333. The exceptionally mature perspective composition of the Košátky panel similarly has a starting point in Venetian painting. The rhythm of lines alone is proof that the picture was the work of a central European artist, who had studied Venetian painting so thoroughly that he was able to create a work whose qualities are outstanding anywhere north of the Alps.

: The same source, though not as profound, served as inspiration for a painter who is linked with the circle of Bishop John IV of Dražice. He made the cartoon for the large-sized antependium of Pirna, embroidered in multi-coloured silk and gilt threads on canvas. The central composition of the antependium, the Coronation of the Virgin, is a subject of which Paolo Veneziano was particularly fond. It is possible that the knowledge of works such as the magnificent Veneziano antependium from the cathedral on the Yugoslav island of Krk penetrated as far as Bohemia. Today this masterpiece is in the Victoria and Albert Museum in London.

: Nothing characterizes the orientation of the Bohemian painters towards Venetian painting more clearly than their appreciation of its Byzantine roots, whereby they returned to a period of development that, in fact, was pre-Paolo Veneziano. That is the case of the Madonna of Most (before 1350), perhaps the oldest surviving Bohemian type of semi-figure of the Mother of God holding the Child playing with a goldfinch on her arm. This goldfinch had its origin in Florentine painting around 1300. Otherwise, in type and psychic expression this Madonna might be related to the work of late Greek mannerism in Venice, by the Master of the Last Judgment (today in Worcester, Mass.). The manner in which the edge of the maphorion of the Madon-

/35/
The Descent of the Holy Ghost
from the Vyšší Brod cycle. Prague,
National Gallery. Panel picture.
Probably 1347.

na of Most is serrated, the treatment of the fringes, ornaments, etc. makes an entirely Byzantine impression. The panel has a colour scheme of high quality. :

: Certain painters of panel pictures would occasionally turn to book illustrations. One of them decorated the Postil of Nicholas of Lyra, in the Jagiellon Library in Krakow, dating from c. 1350. Its simple, somewhat crude ornamentation shows that illumination was not his proper field of work. On the other hand, the modelling of the head and hand of the angel in the initial Q is of excellent quality, using light to achieve plasticity and revealing lessons learnt from Venice. The rhythm of the plastic folds of the angel's garment shows trends that were important for development: an endeavour to adapt this to the local tradition of linear rhythm. :

: This endeavour reached a grandiose synthesis on the nine panels of the Vyšší Brod altarpiece. The treble division of the life of Christ—childhood, passion and glorification—logically ensues from the set-up of the three rows of a polyptych. The majority of the panels were probably finished during the lifetime of the donor, Peter I of Rožmberk († 15 October 1347), the High Chamberlain of the Kingdom of Bohemia. In view of the status of this influential figure at Charles's court it can be assumed that the Vyšší Brod cycle—like the subsequent Třeboň altarpiece—arose in a renowned Prague workshop producing for the monarch. In iconography, typology and formal wealth the cycle was probably the work of three painters, each of whom contributed some of his personal predilections. The leading position was that of the painter who made the pictures of the Nativity, the Adoration of the Magi, the Lamentation, the Resurrection etc. It has been shown that this master was acquainted with the west European linear tradition but acquired his artistic training in the area of the Adriatic School situated on both shores of the Adriatic. His landscape with terraces of split rock cliffs, overgrown with mushroom-like trees goes back to the mosaics, which, from the twelfth century, decorated St. Mark's basilica in Venice. :

: The Christ on the picture of the Resurrection, with his attractive hieratic type of dark face and strength of expression, is a classical example of Pa-

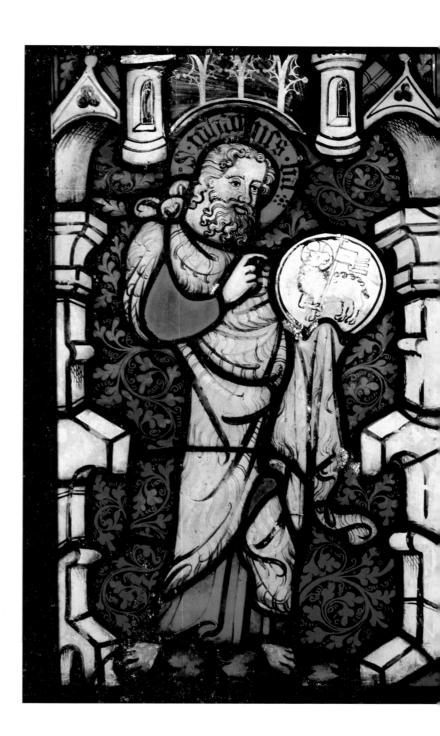

/36/
Stained glass with the figure of
St. John the Baptist from Osek.
Prague. Museum of
Applied Arts. C. 1350.

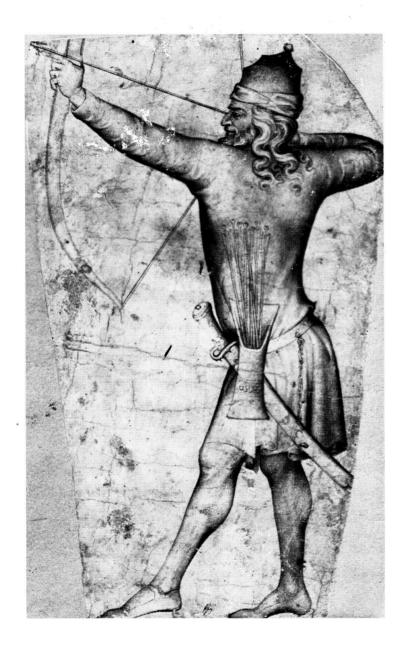

laeologus neo-Hellenism. The Siena accent of some of the lyrical details as well as the Giotto-like three-dimensional construction of the hut on the picture of the Nativity, justifies the assumption that the master must have travelled as far as Tuscany on his Italian journey. The figure of the weeping woman on the Lamentation to the left of the cross seems to be moulded out of soft material and is filled with light from within. This manner of painting anticipates the subsequent two decades. The painter of the picture of the Descent of the Holy Ghost had a different personality. He subjected Italian colour modelling as well as articulation of three-dimensional shapes to the rhythm of a calligraphically felt line. Along the edges of the raiments appear characteristic looped folds, which were frequent in the west, particularly in the Rhineland. But they can also be shown to have existed in the Czech Lands, for instance in the antiphonary of Queen Elizabeth Rycheza of c. 1320. The painter of the Vyšší Brod Descent of the Holy Ghost dealt in radical manner with the ancient problem west-south, which painters in the Czech Lands had to face over and over.
: Certain other works have more or less close relations to the Vyšší Brod cycle. One of these is the Karlsruhe diptych (after 1350). This small travelling altar was to remind its owner (perhaps a prelate at Charles's court) of famous cult pictures that might have been imported from the south. The Man of Sorrows on the second little picture belongs to the Italian type of 'Cristo passo', embodied in classical manner in the pictures by Simone Martini and Paolo Veneziano. The little Madonna is an imitation of a Byzantine Pelagonitissa, a type developed on the Balkan peninsula before the thirteenth century. It must have come to the Bohemian setting via Byzantine-Venetian pictures of the type of the Leningrad diptych. Bohemian painters successfully interpreted the complex motion of the Child (with its origin in late antiquity), but the Byzantine maphorion on the head of the Mother of God was replaced by a Gothic crown. :
: Panel painting of this stratum is very close to a stained glass window showing the figure of John the Baptist in the Cistercian monastery at Osek. For historical reasons and on account of its style its origin can be placed in the period around 1350.

/38/
The Adoration of the Magi,
The Death of the Virgin. New
York, M. Pierpont Morgan
Library. Panel picture. C. 1355.

Charles was a patron of the Osek monastery. This fact together with the outstanding quality of the work suggests that this stained glass was made by a court artist. The west European type of saint embodied, a quarter of a century earlier, on a stained glass window, now at the Schnütgen Museum in Cologne, reappears here in novel form. The architectonic setting of the figure recalls the form of the throne of the Wrocław Trinity, with which it shares a common starting point in panels by Paolo Veneziano. John's unattractive head with heavy, swollen eyelids, a knobbly nose and bloated lips, shows the maker of this stained glass window to have been affected by current Trecento art as it penetrated to Venice from the mainland.   :

: This trend found an important representative in Guariento di Arpo, on whose scenes with the history of Joseph at the Cappella dei Carraresi (Accademia) in Padua there appear similar unattractive male heads. The maker of this stained glass managed to achieve a perfect merger of all these elements of western and Italian origin, and thereby he created a new style. He gave vent to his creative vitality in broad plastic shapes and did not hesitate to use expressive deformation.   :

: The Morgan panels with the little pictures of the Adoration of the Magi and the Death of the Virgin came a little later. They are probably the remnants of a large polyptych with the life-story of the Virgin. The figure of the king in the centre of the first picture is often alleged to be Charles IV, and the figure of the apostle in the tiara on the second little panel is said to be Pope Innocent VI. This latter picture follows up some of the figures and motifs on the Death of the Virgin of Košátky. The architectural setting with its perspective construction has been omitted and a spatial effect is achieved in a more direct manner by placing the moving, plastically felt figures of the apostles one behind the other. These pictures reveal the influence of Tommaso da Modena and Guariento di Arpo. It can be detected in the fine modelling of shapes by means of light, in the formation of the long, string-like folds which alternate with the bulging volume of the bodies, the patterns adorning the Virgin's bed and particularly in the types of heads. Some of these are very similar to the head of John the Baptist on

the Osek stained glass window so that it has been suggested that they were made by the same hand. :
: It has been pointed out that there is a close relation between the little Morgan panels and the drawing of the Archer at Christ Church in Oxford. At one time a disparate view had been put forward about this outstanding drawing, probably cut out of a workshop pattern book. Among other views, it used to be considered of Sienese origin, even as the work of the Master of the Parament of Narbonne. This last attribution is faulty, since the parament was made around c. 1380, while the drawing probably dates from the period 1350—60. The southern origin (northern Italy more likely than Siena) of the Archer cannot be denied. The manner in which the wavy locks of hair are given and the rhythmical outline, however, seem to indicate that some northern artist copied this figure into his sketchbook while travelling in Italy. The softened modelling, achieved by means of dense hatching, has its closest analogy in the Morgan panels. At the same time it is indicative of the trend of development in Bohemian painting. Nor can it be overlooked that we find a reaction to this type on a later miniature in the Zagreb Bible of Purkart of Janovice, i.e. a manuscript of Bohemian origin. :
: The picture of artistic development in the Czech Lands during the 'preparatory' period before Charles' first expedition to Rome is distorted by heavy losses. Not a single building of the many under construction at the time has survived in its original form. In other fields it is possible to observe how certain aspects of the future imperial art were taking shape. In stone sculpture, for instance, monumental works were coming into being intended as glorification of the ruler's majesty. In wood carving the Paris starting point was being enriched by incorporating some of the lessons learnt from the related field of local panel painting. At the same time wood carving was under the influence of the spiritual climate of early Humanism. Painting profited more from the example of Italy, that 'teacher of nations', than from other countries without, at the same time, abandoning the tradition of west European linearism. At the same time through the mediation of Venice, Czech painting strengthened its existing relations to the great culture of Byzantium. :

/41/
Old Testament scenes. Velislav Bible. Prague, State Library of the Czech Socialist Republic. Before 1350.

Chapter V

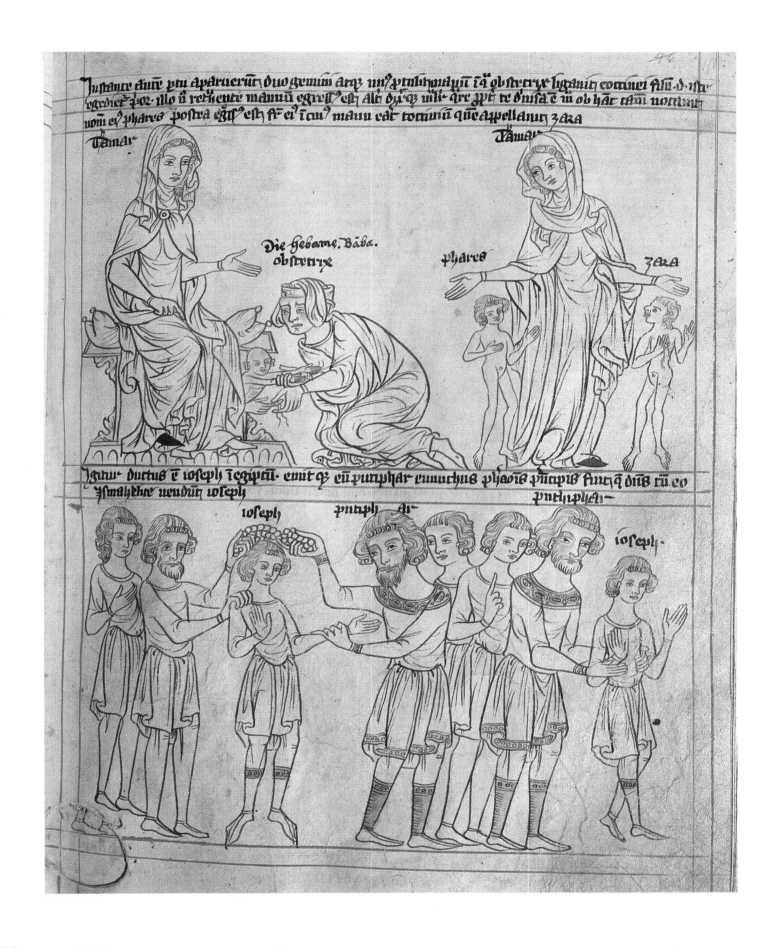

The Emperor's
Counsellors

However much energy Charles exerted personally, he could not have mastered all those immense tasks had he not managed to form a Cabinet of carefully selected, highly capable and reliable counsellors of exceptional education. Most of them simultaneously occupied leading positions in the Church. For that reason the manner whereby Charles reigned has been described as a symbiosis of 'Throne and Altar'. To this should be added that, on the one hand, Charles supported the Church through his foundations and, on the other, appointed his court officials to important offices in it. For their services to the state they received lucrative prebends and high church positions. In this manner Charles paid his ministers out of church funds. This practice speeded up the secularization of the Church, a fact that became a subject for sharp criticism during the Emperor's lifetime, for example on the part of Milíč of Kroměříž.   :

: Charles interfered in Church affairs in other ways, too; he obliged the Pope to move back to Rome after sixty-eight years of 'captivity' in Avignon; he enforced the renewal of Church Slavonic and introduced the Ambrosian liturgy in Prague. As a writer he did not limit himself to homilies but prescribed even devotional offices, to which he was certainly not entitled. While the archbishops in his imperial council were willing to assume the purely secular functions of land governors in case of need, or even command in military emergencies, Charles, on the other hand, was willing personally to involve himself in special liturgical questions. This peculiar situation can be explained by the common interests the Emperor shared with his counsellors, many of whom were his personal friends.   :

: These common interests existed also in the sphere of the arts where the Emperor and his counsellors at times gave employment to the same masters and pursued a joint programme of court art. Charles's counsellors did not accept that programme in a passive manner: they often helped to formulate it. This can be shown from a letter in which the Emperor's Chancellor Bishop John of Středa draws Charles's attention to the art of an unnamed painter whom he is sending to him with a picture representing an angel introducing the Emperor and the Pope to heaven. The wording the Chancellor used in the letter suggests that it was he who gave directives to the painter.   :

: In one important aspect the later development of art at the court of Charles IV was anticipated by a work linked with the personality of Master Velislav, the Emperor's chaplain and counsellor, protonotary, diplomat, and Deputy Chancellor for Germany. That is the well-known Velislav Bible, made before the middle of the fourteenth century, which despite the loss of certain of its parts is one of the largest pictorial codices of the Middle Ages. It contains 747 pictures drawn with a pen and coloured, with subjects drawn from the Bible, the Apocrypha, the legends of Sts. Ludmilla, Wenceslas and others as well as from a work on the Antichrist. Several open attacks on popedom indicate that, during his stay in Avignon, Velislav became acquainted with Francesco Petrarch, who was known for his sharp criticism of the local curia.   :

: The first and most mature illuminator of the Bible probably learnt his art in the region of Lake Constance. But he showed leanings towards a trend represented by the Descent of the Holy Ghost in the Vyšší Brod cycle. His illustrations are closest to it in the depiction of the cleft rocky terrain, the three-dimensional architecture and the linear design of the draperies on which, once again, there appears the motif of the loop. The majority of the illustrations are the work of an artist who made elongated figures, often with very lively movements, and in places depicted as seen from the back or from high above, strongly Sienese in type.   :

: The Velislav Bible is interesting not only for its iconographic wealth but also for the fact that its illuminators derived certain types, motifs of garments and the depiction of architecture and vegetation from Romanesque manuscripts of the eleventh and twelfth centuries. Many elements of pre-Romanesque origin still appear in the little pictures — Helios and Selene, semi-nude figures, personifications of the sources of rivers, light and shadow, day and night, ornamental motifs of waves, ovolo ornaments, caryatids, circles below the feet of the monarchs, etc. In this manner the artist tried to transport the spectator to the biblical and early Christian periods in which the events depicted took place. For the first time we are here dealing with programmed historicism, which was later to become a characteristic feature of art at Charles's court. Since Velislav was a canon of Prague cathedral and did not die until 1367, there is a possibility that his influence left a mark on Peter Parler, who in Prague cathedral also applied certain Romanesque and pre-Romanesque elements.   :

: Charles's counsellor and faithful companion Ernest of Pardubice, the first Archbishop of Prague (1344—64) and papal legate, was a fervent supporter of the arts. He saw to the artistic furnishing of nu-

/42/
*The Madonna of
Kłodzko. Berlin,
Stiftung Preussischer
Kulturbesitz,
Gemäldegalerie.
Panel picture.
C. 1350.*

merous Church institutions in his archdiocese, among others the first Bohemian monastery of the Augustinian canons. This had been founded by Bishop John IV of Dražice in 1334 at Roudnice, the town where the Prague metropolitans had their summer residence. In Prague Ernest continued the construction of the church of St. Giles founded by John IV of Dražice in 1339, completed in 1371 as a hall church with nave and aisles of even height and later rebuilt in baroque style. In St. Vitus's cathedral he had one of the gallery chapels built at his own expense and had stained glass made for its windows, the loss of which is much to be regretted. Ernest spent his youth at Kłodzko (Glatz) and it was there that he established a monastery of the Augustinian canons in 1349, located between the town and the castle; to it he presented gifts in the form of jewels, valuable chasubles and pictures. The imposing building of the monastery church was almost completely destroyed during the Thirty Years' War (1618—48).   :

: Fortunately the painting of the Madonna, which the Archbishop presented to his monastery soon after its foundation, was moved from the Augustinian church to the Franciscan church 'On the Sands' at Kłodzko. Bohuslav Balbín reports that the large-sized panel had two wings, lost today, with four scenes from the childhood of Christ. Otherwise the picture itself serves as confirmation of a report by biographer William of Lestkov that Ernest of Pardubice used to have himself depicted on stained glass and other paintings as kneeling on the ground with the archbishop's insignia lying at his feet as if he had cast them off and renounced them for 'the love of the Lord'. On the Kłodzko picture the small scale of his figure in relation to the Virgin, enthroned and wearing a crown, is an expression of humility. On it, for the first time in Bohemian panel painting, we can find the Italian type, traditional particularly in Florence and Siena. The monumental composition of the panel, its colour scheme and the depiction of the valuable fabrics all point in that direction. An analogy for the motif of the angels curiously peeping through the pierced armrests of the throne can be found in the works of Paolo Veneziano, from whom Ernest's painter might also have taken the somewhat Byzantine type of dark

/43/
The Annunciation. Full-page miniature in the manuscript Laus Mariae. Prague, Library of the National Museum. C. 1360.

/44/
The Presentation in the Temple.
Full-page miniature in the
manuscript Laus Mariae.
Prague, Library of the National
Museum. C. 1360

face of the Mother of God. The picture later passed into the ownership of the gallery in Berlin and so the only memorial to Ernest at Kłodzko is his badly damaged tombstone, the work of the Master of the archbishops' tombs. :

: Otherwise only a few illuminated manuscripts survived the first Archbishop of Prague. Two of these form part of a septipartite group of luxurious codices ornamented by illuminators of Chancellor John of Středa. The manuscript called Laus Mariae or Mariale Arnesti contains a selection of lessons from prayers to the Virgin, compiled by Conrad of Haimburg and approved in Ernest's epistle of 2 December 1356. It is decorated with filigree initials and two outstanding miniatures: the Annunciation and the Presentation in the Temple, which some scholars consider the work of the painter who made the little Morgan panels. This view can be accepted only with reservations, for the miniatures neither show the same degree of naturalism as the little panels in the depiction of the faces nor are they closely linked with the oldest part of that group of manuscripts known as the Missal of Provost Nicholas (c. 1355). It was probably commissioned by John of Středa's closest companion, Nicholas of Kroměříž, the protonotary in Charles's chancellery. The ornamentation of that missal best reflects the illuminator's Italian training, for the Tuscan type and patterns are not yet adapted to the local tradition. It has, moreover, been discovered that the miniatures in the Laus Mariae are copies. Under those circumstances they must be regarded as true copies of the lost sections of a Marian polyptych of which the Morgan panels once formed part. :

: Before 1364 a prayer book was compiled for Ernest, including meditations and popular mystic writings of the time, called Orationale Arnesti. It was adorned by the illuminators of the Missal of John of Středa, which will be discussed later. The illuminator composed his little pictures into squares of the same width as the text with short acanthus shoots and flowers at the corners. The ornamentation, to which the scribes added small initials and filigree, is not over-rich but its skilful execution shows what bibliophile demands the archbishop appears to have made. :

: By contrast, a set of hymnbooks, which Ernest presented to his cathedral shortly before his death, are of merely average standard. Six of the original nine volumes have survived. The ornamentation was done in an illuminator's workshop from which a number of manuscripts have come. Its most characteristic work is the Breviary of Grand Master Leo, dated 1356. Its ornamentation shows free adaptations of French, Sienese and Bolognese patterns. That workshop drew a good deal from the local tradition of painting. It is, therefore, possible that some of the miniatures in Ernest's hymnbooks

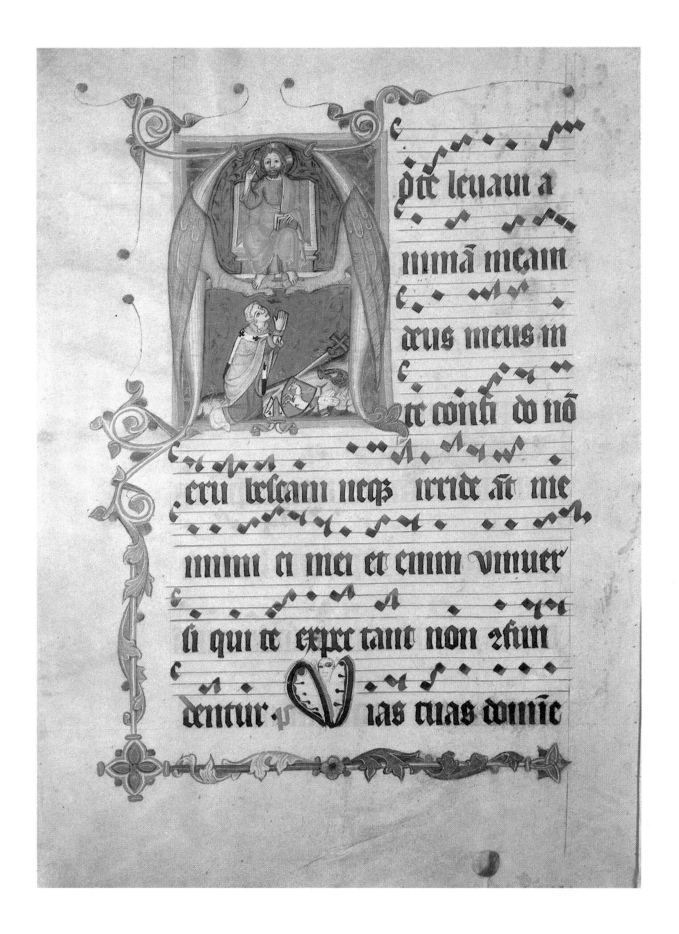

/45/
*Ernest of Pardubice Adoring God
the Father. Gradual of Ernest of
Pardubice. Prague, Chapter
Library. 1363.*

M ima xpiana · anima de gui mol
te resusitata · anima de misera s
ititure · saguine dei redempta · z li
berata · excita mentem tuam · z me
mento resusitatacionis tue. Recogi
ta redemucionem · z libiacionem tuam

/46/
God the Father Enthroned.
Orationale Arnesti. Prague,
Library of the National
Museum.
Before 1364.

(e.g. the Trinity in the St. Vitus's antiphonary) might be replicas of a lost altarpiece in the cathedral. :

: It was John of Středa who gave considerable impulse to the development of culture and art in Charles's time. For twenty-one years (1353—74) he headed the Imperial Chancellery as Chancellor. In 1353 he became Bishop of Litomyšl and after 1364 Bishop of Olomouc. He kept up a correspondence with his friend Francesco Petrarch and adopted the Ciceronean style of the early Italian Humanists. His library contained works by Seneca, Titus Livius, Valerius Maximus, Cassiodorus, Dante Alighieri, Petrarch and others. At the time of his appointment to the chancellorship he had himself depicted as donor of paintings in the sacristy of the Augustinian monastery of St. Thomas in Prague's Little Quarter; despite their bad condition they show close relations to contemporary Italianized panel painting in Bohemia. In 1356 the Chancellor founded the Augustinian monastery in Litomyšl. :

: By contrast to Charles and Ernest of Pardubice John of Středa paid his first visit to Italy only during the first Roman expedition in the years 1354—55. In one of his letters he enthusiastically hailed 'that happy day and happy hour when he turned his steps towards Italy and passed, as it were, into a golden century through the Gates of Paradise'. The triumphal procession led through towns where, apart from the new humanist enlightenment, pride was also taken in the new arts that were reviving Italy's former glory—Padua, Pisa, Siena and others as far as Rome, where the Chancellor set up an altar to St. Wenceslas in St. Peter's. The impressions he brought back from that journey roused in him a longing for art that would equal the Italian. On his return from the south he managed to attract to his scriptorium several outstanding illuminators who had been schooled in Italy. He endowed them with prebends so that they could devote themselves fully to their art as in the case of Canon Beneš of St. George's. :

: The most important of the Chancellor's illuminators was an artist whose name is not known. It was he who, in the years 1355—60, illuminated the major part of the travelling breviary known as the Liber Viaticus of John of Středa. The large number of initials with figures in that manuscript reflect changes in the spiritual life at the time of Charles. New hieratic pictures appeared, e.g. the Trinity with a semi-figure of Christ; the Man of Sorrows, on a sun disc (imago clipeata) of antique origin, or a new picture of the Virgin in Spe, where the Italian type of Virgin of Humility sitting on the ground merges with elements of the Virgin Triumphant. The pictures of Old Testament prophets, painted in monochrome in the stems of the initials, reflect the contemporary conception of the Old Testament foreshadowing events in the New Testament. :

/47/
*Head of the Virgin and Christ
on the Crucifixion in the missal
of Provost Nicholas. Brno, City
Archives, St. James's Library.
C. 1355.*

: The master of the Viaticus adopted quite a few elements from local panel painting, e.g. from the Vyšší Brod cycle. His miniatures of the Annunciation and the Death of the Virgin are variations of that theme on the Morgan panels. The figure of St. Wenceslas in the Byzantine coat of mail is based on contemporary panel paintings of the patron of Bohemia surviving in sixteenth century copies. The Master of the Viaticus enhanced the local tradition by his thorough knowledge of Italian, chiefly Sienese, painting which had reached its culmination in the works of the Lorenzetti brothers, Simone Martini and their contemporaries, the illuminators of the Maestro di Codice di S. Giorgio, Niccolò Tegliacci, Lippo Memmi, and Andrea Vanni. This explains the grandiose compositional and spatial construction of his miniatures, the plastic conception of shapes and the colour scheme with a predominance of bright, finely graded tones. The occasional use of radical bodily foreshortening and the penetrating characterization of some of the figures indicate that the master was even acquainted with manuscripts produced in the workshop of Nicolò da Bologna.

: In the Liber Viaticus acanthus is widely used, a decorative element that was popular from antiquity onwards. It is used here to create an ornamental system, which later passed into the local tradition of illuminations. In contemporary Italian manuscripts the acanthus does not appear in such naturalistic execution, but it does so on Bohemian panel paintings, where it was used as engraved drawings in the background and on the foliage patterns on the Virgin's crown. Genre scenes, e.g. a couple of equerries with horses, appear on the lower margins of the pages as in some Parisian manuscripts.   :

: The Chancellor's Liber Viaticus clearly was not the only codex of its kind. A miniature of the Resurrection was cut out of a very similar, slightly older manuscript, now lost. This miniature is today to be found in the Archbishop's Library in Olomouc. :

: The Master of the Viaticus trained a follower who, soon after 1364, made the ornaments in the Missal of John of Středa. The manuscript reveals the growing influence of the imperial iconography: Christ Enthroned is wearing imperial robes. The painter of the missal knew Italian art only from his teacher and was not greatly interested in the spatial construction of his pictures; but he had an understanding of softly painted modelling by means of inner light reflecting off the volume, of fine colouring and the decorative effect of the work as a whole.   :

: The fame of John of Středa's illuminators spread far beyond the borders of the Kingdom of Bohemia and brought commissions from abroad. The Vienna evangeliarium was made for Duke Albrecht III of Austria, a son-in-law of Charles IV since 1366. It was written and illuminated in Bohemia to serve as a ceremonial codex. Its scribe and illuminator called himself John of Opava in the explicitus of 1368, a Brno canon, parish priest of Lanškroun, known as a court scribe and illuminator from the Chancellor's correspondence. He was an outstanding painter who, in dozens of compositions of complicated New Testament scenes, alternated stocky figures in soft garments with elongated supple figures, and

69

Spm nobis dne tue.Coplenda
caitatis infunde: ut quos sacra
mentis paschalibs sacasti. tua
facias pietate concordes. P.
In die resurrectionis dni officium

quod nunc sciam sicut alia posuisti super me
tuam illa mirabilis facta est scien

/49/
Miniature of the Resurrection.
Olomouc, Archbishop's Library.
Before 1360.

who was not afraid of bold foreshortening. He derived inspiration not only from contemporary Italian book painting (Nicolò da Bologna and others) but also from the monumental works of Charles IV's court painters.

: The painter of the Missal of John of Středa made only a minor contribution to the exceptionally rich decorations of the Vienna evangeliarium. The unusual character of the commission is reflected in the fact that the text of the entire codex, written in gold, is set in coloured frames with foliated flowers at the corners. The pattern for such a layout of the pages probably derived from a late Carolingian evangeliarium of the ninth century, which Charles presented to the Prague Chapter Library, where it is deposited to this day. Of possibly even older origin was a lost Byzantine manuscript loaned to the illuminators of the Vienna evangeliarium from the imperial library. This served as a pattern for four full-page series of scenes from the lives of the Evangelists in the manner of a polyptych (twelve pictures each) as well as for the decorative motif of the spiral with acanthus flowers. The programmed historicism in the codex of the Austrian archduke appears also in the picture with the story of St. Mark, where the church is depicted as a rotunda, as in the earlier illustrations in the Velislav Bible. With its unusual painted ornamentation as well as the magnificent gold binding with motifs of lions' heads and sun-rays, ancient symbols of the ruler, this codex was intended to give an impression of great age. This must have suited the commission: the Austrian dukes laid claims to the throne on the basis of the well-known forgeries of allegedly Privilegia of Caesar and Nero issued by the ancient emperors. The distrustful Charles felt obliged to request Petrarch to investigate those privileges.

: It is likely that John of Středa's illuminators also worked on manuscripts for Charles. This is the more probable since the above-mentioned letter from the Chancellor to the Emperor about the picture he had presented to him shows that he tried to show his gratitude to his monarch in this manner. Such gifts, in fact, were common enough: Charles's nephew, King Charles V of France, received a gift of about twenty books from his librarian Gilles Malet.

/50/
The Madonna of Vyšehrad.
Prague-Vyšehrad, college church
of Sts. Peter and Paul. Panel
picture. C. 1355.

: One of Charles's counsellors and his secretary of long standing was John Očko ('The One-Eyed') of Vlašim, originally Bishop of Olomouc and after 1364 Archbishop of Prague. He was raised to the status of the first Bohemian cardinal towards the end of his life, on 17 September 1378. This outstanding statesman and enlightened humanist prelate shared Charles's grandiose ideas on foundations on the right bank of the river Vltava in Prague, where, in the years 1352—64, he had the Hospital of the Humility of the Virgin Mary built below Vyšehrad castle. It is highly likely that the Vyšehrad Madonna was made for the church of this hospital in c. 1355. It is a type of Madonna of Humility, which developed in Italy out of a Byzantine pattern (Simone Martini, Bartolomeo da Camogli, Paolo Veneziano). On pictures of this kind the Virgin does not sit enthroned as the Queen of Heaven but on the ground as a simple woman to nurse her Child. There is no agreement yet as to the attribution of the Vyšehrad Madonna. It is considered either the work of an exceptionally talented assistant of the Master of the Vyšší Brod altarpiece or a mature work of the workshop of the Master of the Death of the Virgin of Košátky. There is no doubt as to the Italian orientation of the panel and its high quality, seen particularly in the perfect modelling of the already broad main figure, in the effective contrast between warm tones of brown flesh tones and the cold blue of the Virgin's cloak, as well as in the naturalistic depiction of the vegetation. :

: John Očko set up a richly adorned chapel in Prague cathedral. In 1370 as archbishop he had a 'new chapel' consecrated in his palace in the Little Quarter of Prague in the presence of Charles IV and King Wenceslas. This 'he had recently furnished as a remarkable and beautiful and magnificent piece of work . . . in honour of the arms of Christ'. :

: While this chapel has vanished without a trace, the well-known votive panel, today in the National Gallery in Prague, comes from another chapel at the archbishop's castle in Roudnice, consecrated in 1371. By its division into two strips, it is reminiscent of the tympanum of the church of Our Lady of the Snows, where the increasingly large scale of the two kneeling donors anticipates Očko's panel, on which the heavenly beings and the mortals are of

/52/
Votive panel of John Očko of Vlašim with a portrait of the Emperor Charles IV. Prague, National Gallery. Panel picture. 1371.

73

/53—54/
*Scenes from the lives of
the Evangelists. The
Vienna evangeliarium of John of
Opava. Vienna,
Österreichische
Nationalbibliothek.
1368.*

*(In the scene from the life
of St. Luke there is one of
the oldest depictions of
a painter's studio.)*

equal size. On the upper strip Charles IV and Wenceslas IV are kneeling before the throne of the Mother of God with the Child; on the lower strip the archbishop is kneeling in front of St. Adalbert. The remaining patrons of Bohemia, Sts. Sigismund, Wenceslas, Procopius, Vitus and Ludmilla, are present in both scenes. The painter of the panel came from the circle of Charles's court painters working on mural paintings at the turn of the 1350s and 1360s; from these in particular he adopted the portraiture. But his picture shows certain leanings towards Gothic, strengthened probably under the influence of such west European works as the little Bargello panels, made in France, probably in Paris, at about the same time.

: Očko's votive panel shows the archbishop's close links with the ruling dynasty and his respect for the traditions of the Bohemian state. The archbishop expressed this by presenting to his chapter two lectionaries with pictures of the kings of Bohemia and the Prague metropolitans. Both codices are now lost, but there must have been a clear iconographical relationship between the first of them and the miniature of Vratislav II in the Vyšehrad antiphonary at Vorau and with the depiction of the Czech kings (respectively Margraves of Moravia) in some later manuscripts. These cycles of books are based on monumental art. The recent discovery of a Přemyslide cycle in the church at Zahrádka (c. 1340) on the estate of the Vyšehrad chapter proves that the iconographical programme incorporated in the paintings in the rotunda at Znojmo (c. 1134) was not entirely forgotten in later ages. John Očko used statues or pictures in his Little Quarter residence as patterns for the depiction of his predecessors in his second lectionary. The original works had been made on order of Bishop John IV of Dražice.

: Another of Charles's counsellors and diplomats was his friend Albrecht of Sternberg, who was Bishop of Schwerin, Litomyšl and Magdeburg and papal legate. After studying in Bologna and Paris he became associated with the early Humanists and with Augustinianism, which development he supported by founding a canonry in his birthplace at Sternberg in Moravia in 1372.

: The monastery, surviving only as a torso, was finished before 27 February 1376, together with the still surviving chapel at Sternberg castle. It is a single-naved chapel with two compartments of cross vaulting and a polygonal choir built by the masonic lodge of Matthias of Arras, which remained active in the Czech Lands long after the death of that court builder († 1352). The stone sculpture of an old man on one console, showing an influence of Peter Parler, may well represent the man who built the chapel. The successor to one of the greatest of Charles IV's painters, the Master of the Emmaus Cycle, painted scenes of the Annunciation and the Nativity on the walls.

: In the bishop's Krakow Bible from the years 1371—78 the Emperor is depicted worshipping Christ Enthroned together with the man who commissioned the work. A similar double portrait is contained in the richly illuminated Pontifical of Albrecht of Sternberg of the year 1376. These two manuscripts were decorated by a craftsman-illuminator, who adopted some of the principles of court painting of the 1360s.

: As can be seen, Charles's counsellors among the Church prelates contributed greatly to the development of court art. Thanks to them the new art did not remain limited only to the Emperor's Prague court and castles but spread to other country residences and to the monasteries. This brought the leading artists a number of commissions, and they likewise gained numerous stimuli for their work from Charles's counsellors.

/55/
Coronation of a Queen.
Pontifical of Albrecht of
Sternberg. Prague-Strahov,
Museum of
National Literature.
1376.

/56/
Odo of Metz: Interior of the palace chapel of Charlemagne. Aachen. 796—814.

Chapter VI

Passionate Collector
and Generous Benefactor

Charles IV was one of the major collectors since antiquity. This very fact brought a strong influence to bear on the development of art at his court, for the objects the Emperor collected required either architectural, goldsmith or bejewelled receptacles, artistic book bindings, etc., or they themselves were valuable materials, out of which new works were fashioned. Moreover, the Emperor's collections gave his artists inspiration and a measure of quality and served as patterns. Charles's collections centred around two main spheres: with some licence, the first can be termed archeological and the second involved the natural sciences. Both these spheres interlinked with the cult of relics, i.e. sacred mementos of Christ's life and martyrdom on earth and of the saints. The period belief in the supernatural power of these mementos was shared by Charles as much as the conviction that they were symbols of the ruler's legitimacy. It is clear that he tried in every way to strengthen the cult of the relics of Christ's Passion, which were a major part of the treasure of the kings of Rome, for this treasure was in his possession from 1350 onwards. Further, Charles encouraged the veneration of relics of his own personal patrons, his dynastic ancestors and his predecessors on the throne of Bohemia and the imperial throne: St. Wenceslas and St. Charlemagne, and among other rulers St. Sigismund, the patron of Burgundy, where the last remnants of the former imperial sovereignty had to be stubbornly defended. When Charles managed to acquire the entire skeleton of St. Vitus in Pavia in 1355, he was able to make the cathedral on the grounds of his castle in Prague the sole centre of that saint's cult, acknowledged and worshipped internationally as the first martyr. Similarly the relics of numerous other saints were to link the new seat of the Emperor with all corners of his empire, both symbolically and otherwise, through the processions of pilgrims who made their way to Prague to worship them.   :

: Charles collected relics whose authenticity was, in the eyes of his contemporaries, sufficiently guaranteed by the personality of the previous owner. For instance, the Emperor of Constantinople, John V on his request sent him the bones of the patriarchs Abraham, Isaac and Jacob. Louis the Great of Hungary gave him the table-cloth used at the Last Supper. The French dauphin, later King Charles V, handed over to him two thorns from Christ's crown. The Emperor was given part of Christ's loin cloth by Pope Urban VI personally. In addition, Charles often travelled through ancient seats of cults, where relics were kept, whose genuineness could not be doubted, for they had been worshipped there since ancient days. He exerted pressure to have the tombs of saints and sacred receptacles opened, often he would take away part of the contents. Charles's procession through Germany in 1354 has rightly been called a 'real raid on sacred relics, collected with true insatiability'. The result of all that collecting was that numerous local cults became gradually concentrated in Prague.   :

: The most mighty cult centre of western Christianity was Rome, for it owned the largest number of relics. For long centuries processions of devout and curious pilgrims had made their way there which, in years of grace, became a considerable source of income for the papal curia. It is interesting that Charles intervened even there but only superficially. Before his coronation as Emperor in St. Peter's at Easter 1355 he went clothed as a simple pilgrim to look at the Roman mirabilia. Among others he also visited the church of Pope Marcello. An old stone slab suddenly began to move under his foot and to his inquiry he was told that this was the spot where once Christians were beheaded. He had the slab raised from the ground and a protective grating made for it.   :

: The Emperor placed a good many of the objects he collected at the disposal of the public. Only a few of the relics which he brought to Prague had repositaries of their own. For the majority of the relics he had reliquaries made in the form of crosses, busts, arms, little towers, etc., before handing them over to the sanctuaries. The activity Charles undertook in this sphere has no like in scope in the history of medieval art. He was able to make use of the wealth of the Kutná Hora silver mines and the high standard of the Prague goldsmiths, who established a guild of their own as early as 1324. He made contact with them in 1333 when he ordered silver statues of the apostles for the tomb of St. Wenceslas. He gave the goldsmiths and jewellers who worked for him whole collections of pearls and precious minerals for their use. The works made to his order are the more remarkable for the quality and quantity of the antique and Byzantine cameos with engraved reliefs set in them. It has already been mentioned that Charles became acquainted with glyptics in his childhood in Paris, where, in all likelihood, the basis of his later collections was laid. As time passed, the property of his ancestors became part of his own possessions, including rings with cameos that had belonged to the Emperor Henry VII and to King John of Luxemburg. Works of this kind came to Moravia in the ninth century; many were of outstanding quality, e. g. a sardonyx cameo with a portrait of the Greek sculptor Pheidias. Other cameos will have found their way to Bohemia in the twelfth century among the Byzantine treasures which King Vladislav II brought back in waggonloads. A letter from an agent who was looking for cameos for a Bohemian ruler does not refer, as recent research has shown, to Wenceslas IV but to Charles. Italy offered the most likely chances of acquisition. The Imperial Chancellor John of Středa wrote to Prague from the first Roman expedition requesting camels and horses to be sent after them for the transport of gold, precious stones, pearls and 'other precious objects'. :

: From 1350 on Charles had the old coronation treasure of the kings of Rome exhibited on the Cattle Market—today's Charles Square—in Prague every year at Easter and with it reliquaries made on his orders. The people who came to see these treasures were able to buy cast metal badges: one of them, accidentally surviving, represents the Pope with the key of St. Peter, Charles with the Longinus's lance and their coats of arms. In 1369 the number of visitors from the whole of Europe was estimated at about one hundred thousand. This led to an immense growth in the power and international repute of Charles's imperial residence. Nor was the economic effect of those Prague pilgrimages negligible. :

: By degrees Charles gave a considerable portion of his best acquisitions to Prague cathedral without in so doing renouncing the right to dispose in his will of the objects so presented. The St. Vitus's inventory of 1378 gives detailed information of the cathedral treasure shortly after the Emperor's death. Thanks to him the number of imported precious textiles had grown to more than three hundred and the number of gold bejewelled works to one hundred and fifty. Among these were thirteen silver reliquary statues and twenty-seven gold and silver busts of saints. The chapter library owned some two hundred manuscripts at the time and most of them were illuminated. The major advantage of the St. Vitus's inventories for the years 1354—78 rests in some of the objects being described in regard to age and style. Thanks to this we can deduce, despite all

/57/
Pilgrim's badge with the figures of Charles IV and the Pope. Prague, Museum of the City of Prague. Cast metal. 3rd quarter of 14th century.

the losses, that the cathedral treasure, apart from more or less 'modern' Gothic works, comprised objects of 'pagan' origin, that is antique Greek, Byzantine Greek, and Roman as well as those of oriental origin marked as 'Tartar'. The inventory reveals that the number of antique and Byzantine cameos in Charles's collections alone amounted to hundreds and that there must have been a great wealth of pearls and other precious gems.

: The most valuable part of the cathedral treasure was the tomb of St. Wenceslas itself. It was built in the saint's chapel in 1357 to a pattern of the tomb of Charlemagne, which the Emperor had seen at Saint-Denis in his childhood. The tomb with the gold statue of St. Wenceslas at the head stood on a pedestal incrusted with polished gemstones, and its sides were covered with eighteen gold and silver reliquaries. No less than nine hundred and thirty-five gems, four hundred and forty-eight pearls and thirty-seven cameos were used to decorate the tomb. The two largest cameos represented the Emperor and the Empress, whose crowns were adorned with forty precious stones and as many pearls. It would, of course, not be possible to attach such a large number of gems and pearls to the ancient wreaths on the profile busts of the emperors, usually found on classical cameos of sardonyx. It must therefore be deduced that these two cameos were made to ancient patterns by one of the Emperor's artists, who, on them, depicted his noble master and his wife Anne of Świdnica. The ornamentations on Wenceslas's tomb and a number of other precious works in the grounds of Prague castle were taken away by King Sigismund at the beginning of the Hussite Wars, as he was in urgent need of funds to pay his soldiers.

: It was at that time that the original sceptre, orb and ring in the coronation treasure of the kings of Bohemia were lost. But the magnificent crown, called the St. Wenceslas crown, escaped all dangers without the least blemish. Charles had it made of pure gold in 1346 to the pattern of the Přemyslide crown. This explains its intentionally historical shape corresponding to the type prevailing in the 11th—12th century. Four noble fleurs-de-lis emerge from the quadripartite headband of the crown. On the crossing of the arches a small particle of the

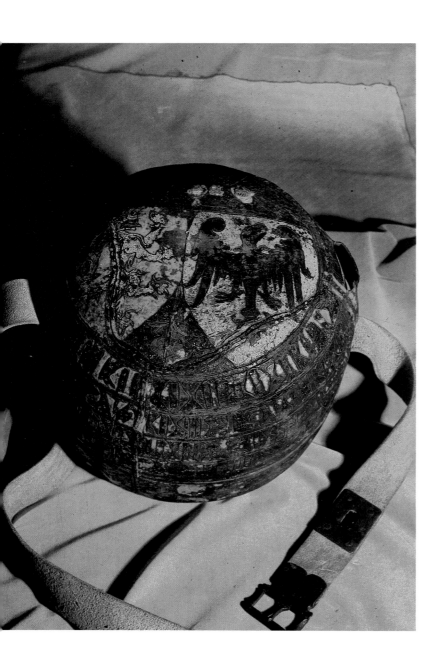

/58/
Leather case for the royal crown of Bohemia. Prague, treasure of St. Vitus's cathedral. 1347.

/59/
The royal crown of Bohemia,
called St. Wenceslas crown.
Prague, treasure of St. Vitus's
cathedral. 1346.

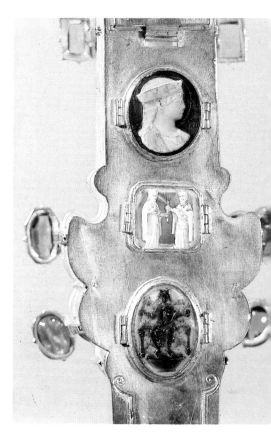

/60/
Reliquary cross with cameos.
Prague, treasure of St. Vitus's
cathedral. Full picture and
detail. Probably 1349.

/61/
Onyx goblet presented by Charles IV. Prague, treasure of St. Vitus's cathedral. 1350.

/62/
Rock-crystal dish in a silver mount. Prague, treasure of St. Vitus's cathedral. After 1353.

Crown of Thorns is affixed below a Byzantine sapphire cameo with a relief of the Crucifixion (13th century). The St. Wenceslas crown is set with twenty pearls, and ninety-one solitaires — sapphires, emeralds, rubies and spinels of inestimable value. In 1347 Charles had a receptacle made for it of wrought, incised and coloured leather with the coats of arms of the Czech Lands and with foliage ornamentation. He dedicated it to St. Wenceslas, on whose skull, hidden in a gilded and wrought bust, it rested from the year 1358 until the arrival of King Sigismund in Prague.

The St. Vitus's treasure contains a gold reliquary Greek cross which Charles had made some time before 1349. It was probably intended as a coronation cross for the kings of Rome, for its fleurs-de-lis correspond to those on the royal crown of Rome, kept in the cathedral treasure at Aachen. This cross is decorated with nine antique and Byzantine cameos. A Roman onyx cameo from the third century A.D. is a particularly valuable glyptic work of art; it has a profile bust of a ruler of the type of Alexander of Macedonia. The value of the work is increased by pearls, sapphires and emeralds set in it.

There are other surviving works whereby the founder enriched the treasure of Prague cathedral.

One can cite a receptacle of transparent violet, white-grained onyx from Venice, which Charles had set in a gilded silver and partly enamelled mounting. Its stem bears the coats of arms of the empire and Bohemia with an inscription of dedication dated 1350. From Venice came a crystal cross, a thirteenth century work, which must be considered a gift from the Emperor in view of its huge value. The Emperor was certainly the donor in the case of another work of the same origin, material and age: a crystal dish with lid in which a fragment of byssus material was kept (allegedly the veil of the Virgin Mary), which Charles acquired in Trier in 1354.

: Even more valuable is a large, pearl-shaped twelve-sided jug perfectly bored and polished out of a single large piece of crystal. It probably dates from the 11th century and may have come from Italy or from Egypt. Some time before 3 February 1349 Charles had this magnificent work of art set in a gilded silver mounting and adorned with pearls, malachites, sapphires and emeralds and fitted out to hold the cloth from the table of the Last Supper.

: Entirely different in character is a gold reliquary cross in the St. Vitus's treasure. On its front, below a crystal lens, a fragment of linen material is affixed, allegedly Christ's loin cloth which Charles was given by Pope Urban V. This cross, too, is set with sapphires and spinels, but its decorations proper are made of incised drawings filled with black enamel. Its vertical bar depicts scenes of the Crucifixion and the handing over of the loin cloth. Its horizontal beam has a portrait of the kneeling Pope Urban V, Cardinal Pietro de Bellifortis, Charles IV and Wenceslas IV. The fact that the meeting between the Emperor and the Pope took place during the second Roman expedition and that Wenceslas is not marked as king of Rome allows one to date the cross to the years 1368—76. The mature engraving, on which hatching is widely used, points to a goldsmith trained in Italy who, in the scene of handing over the relic, followed up similar scenes at Karlstein castle.

: The same goldsmith decorated two reliquaries in a similar technique, and these later found their way into the Weltliche Schatzkammer in Vienna. On the first of these, intended for the fetters of the apostles, he engraved busts of Charles and Pope Ur-

/64/
Binding of a Carolingian evangeliarium with a late Roman consular diptych. Prague, Chapter Library. Made about the middle of the 14th century.

/66/
Scenes from the life of
St. John the Evangelist.
Lid of a case for the
tunic of the saint. Gold
and black enamel.
Vienna, Weltliche
Schatzkammer.
1368 — 76.

/67/
Case for the fetters of
the apostles with
engraved figures of Sts.
John, Peter and Paul
on the lid and Pope
Urban V and Charles
IV on the front. Gold,
black enamel. Vienna,
Weltliche
Schatzkammer.
1368 — 76.

/65/
Reliquary cross, said to belong to
Pope Urban V. Prague, treasure
of St. Vitus's cathedral.
1368 — 76.

ban V as well as the figures of the chained Sts. John, Peter and Paul. The other, in which St. John's tunic used to be kept, has eight complex compositions with scenes of the saint's life. As in the case of the Velislav Bible and the Vienna evangeliarium, the ancient setting of the scenes is expressed by means of Romanesque architectonic motifs.   :

: With his gifts Charles enlarged not only the treasure of St. Vitus's cathedral but also those of other church institutions in Bohemia and Germany. The abbey of the Augustinian canons (formerly Benedictines) at Herrieden in Bavaria, in the diocese of Eichstädt, was presented with a particle of the bones of St. Vitus', kept in a charming reliquary of gilded silver. The base of the reliquary, marked with the donor's coat of arms and an inscription of dedication, forms the architectural motif of a rotunda reminiscent of that Prince Wenceslas built for the saint at Prague castle. The figure of the young St. Vitus, with a slightly antiquated contraposte, in the tower-shaped crystal receptacle with a picture of the Crucifixion on the top of the reliquary gives an idea of the figural work made by Prague goldsmiths at the time of Charles IV.   :

: Naturally Charles's generosity was also bestowed upon the treasure of the ancient cathedral at Aachen, where on 24 July 1349 his second wife, Anne of the Palatinate, was crowned. At that time he accepted the crown of the king of Rome for the second time, for his preceding coronation, which had taken place three years previously at Bonn, was considered valid but lacking that truly dignified setting which Charlemagne's Aachen palace chapel of the years 796—814 alone could provide. Charles visited Aachen seven times altogether. The character of the Aachen cathedral treasure — one of the most important of its kind — left a mark on his own collecting. It was there that the Emperor saw the marble Roman sarcophagus with a relief of the Rape of Persephone (2nd cent. A.D.), a Roman bronze bear of the same period and a number of other antique, Byzantine and early medieval works. He added to the treasure by making a gift of three spired reliquaries of gilded silver and rock-crystal that hold the rope from the scourging of Christ, Christ's belt and that of the Virgin Mary. The decorations of these reliquaries include pearls, gemstones and enamel-work apart from six ancient and medieval cameos. The most valuable of these, adorning the base of the reliquary with the belt of Christ, is cut out of an Indian sardonyx. It shows portraits of the royal couple in profile, each crowned with a laurel wreath.

In about 1376 Charles commissioned a wrought silver, partly gilded and enamelled reliquary bust to hold the skull of Charlemagne, again adorned with gemstones and cameos. Its monumental conception, the perfection of the shape of the head, with stress on the anatomy of the face and the neck muscles, recalls the head of Christ of the Pietà in the church of St. Thomas in Old Brno dating from around 1385. (The historicism of the marlstone bust of Wenceslas of Radeč in the St. Vitus's triforium belongs likewise to this radical proto-Renaissance trend.) On the bust of Charlemagne rested the golden crown which Charles commissioned to be made for his own coronation at Aachen in the year 1349. The crown was set with gems, three large pearls and seven cameos on Charles's orders. Together with Gallo-Roman cameos of chalcedony, there appeared also older and superior quality cameos of two-layered sardonyx. A classical cameo showing Psyche and four putti in particular shows what outstanding works of antique glyptics Charles had in his collection. :

: There can be no doubt that his taste became refined thanks to his close contacts with the Italian Humanists. It has been wrongly suggested that there existed a contrast between Charles's collecting linked closely to the cult of relics and that of the Italian Humanists. It is sometimes overlooked that the latter, too, attributed cult and magic significance to the remnants of the Roman Empire and, furthermore, assigned them importance in regard to politics. Petrarch's letter 'To Laelius' of 25 February 1355 contains a fascinating report on the poet's stay in Mantua on Charles's invitation. 'I gave him several gold and silver coins with portraits of our rulers inscribed with tiny and ancient lettering', Petrarch writes. 'He showed great pleasure in those faces and it seemed as if he had never accepted a gift with greater delight.' By studying the biographies of the Roman Emperors twenty years later Charles reached the conviction that one of those coins, on which a bust of a young man and a triumphal arch were minted, could not represent Julius Caesar, as Petrarch had told him. To dispel his doubts Petrarch's pupil and tutor to Charles's younger son Sigismund, Niccolò Beccari, wrote a letter. It is interesting that it was not the Italian Humanists but Charles who was right, for this coin—as has been discovered on the basis of the description of it in our own century—was a silver denarius of Augustus dating from the years 29—27 B.C. :

: It is pleasant to think that Charles gave the poet something in return for his gift. At the end of his letter of June 1355, full of reproaches that the Emperor was leaving Italy for a 'barbarian country', Petrarch mentions that Laelius had brought greetings to him from Charles and 'Caesar's portrait, an ancient work'. In another letter, dated Milan, 21 March 1362, he thanked Charles for his gift: 'a most highly valuable goblet of pure gold with engraved ornaments'. :

: Charles's attitude to the art of imperial Rome (whose monuments he had seen in Trier and in Rome) is also shown on the little panel of the consular diptych made of ivory at the end of the 5th

/68/
The Madonna of Brno.
Constantinople icon from the
12th century, given by Charles
IV. Brno, former Augustinian
monastery of St. Thomas.

century A.D., which he had affixed to the front panel of a late Carolingian evangeliarium, now in the Prague Chapter Library. Originally the relief represented a sitting consul organizing a race in the circus, dressed in a tunic, dalmatic and toga with a mappa in his right hand and a consul's sceptre in his left. Some time in the 11th century it was slightly damaged by adaptations whereby the figure was changed to represent St. Peter. :

: Two hunting horns of ebony, which Charles originally took to Karlstein castle and which, in 1645, came to the St. Vitus's treasure, were considered to date from a still earlier period. Although it is fairly late Sicilian-Moorish work of the 11th century, they show certain ancient motifs, chariot races in the hippodrome. :

: Charles showed a preference for Byzantine works in his collecting. He was the only medieval west European ruler who had himself depicted in a Byzantine coat of mail of ancient origin (thórax lepidotós) on the seal of the first central European university, which he founded in Prague in 1347—48. The mail collar on his statue as king on the Old Town bridge tower can be confronted with the report that Wenceslas II appeared at his coronation in 1292 in a cloak of gold mail, probably made for him by his court goldsmith John of Greece. On the first reliquary scene at Karlstein castle Charles is depicted in a valuable robe with a pattern of trees and two parrots. A strikingly similar pattern adorns the Byzantine brocade from the 10th—11th century, found in the royal tomb in Prague cathedral. The Byzantine cameos in Charles's collection have already been mentioned. The Emperor's predilection for Byzantine magnificence was understood by his son-in-law, the Hungarian King Louis the Great, who in 1353 gave him a silver pectoral cross with Greek lettering. :

: At this point some remarkable examples of Charles's interest in the art of the Orient should be mentioned. They cannot be considered mere chance, for the Bohemian Chronicle, which the learned Franciscan bishop and papal legate Giovanni Marignolli wrote for Charles, contains a description of that famous traveller's journeys to China and India, and a large part of it is devoted to matters of the arts. The value of the late Carolingian New Testament in the Prague Chapter Library is greatly increased by Charles having precious Persian material of the Sassanid period (5th—6th cent.) with hunting scenes attached to its inner covers. :

: In the royal tomb in St. Vitus's cathedral two pieces of brocade with vine leaves and shoots, woven in China in the 14th century, were discovered among other materials. Some of the textiles are marked as 'Tartar in origin' in the inventories of the St. Vitus's treasure, which must refer to Oriental fabrics as such. In his Majestas Carolina Charles forbad the persecution of Saracen marchants coming to Bohemia; he even settled some 'Orientals' in Prague below Petřín Hill, where they lived in tents and wove carpets. :

: The scattered remnants of Charles's private collections show how great was his liking for variety and diversity. It was perhaps from his visit to Venice in 1337 that Charles brought back an ivory jewel box, the oldest surviving 'cofanetto' from the workshop of the Embriachi family. In 1376 he placed in it the relics of St. Sigismund, although the reliefs of the erotic scenes on the little box cannot be considered at all suitable for such sacred objects. He brought back an alabaster statue of the Virgin from France, perhaps from Avignon; today it is to be found at Karlstein castle. The broad head and the relatively large figure show that it came into existence shortly before the middle of the 14th century. :

: As heir to the Přemyslide treasure, Charles was able in 1356 to give to his brother John Henry, Margrave of Moravia, a very precious picture for the monastery of the Augustinian hermits of St. Thomas in Brno, which he had founded, a 12th century Byzantine icon, today known as the Madonna of Brno. This icon with its strict expression and outstanding qualities as a painting, bearing the Greek inscription MP ØV (Mother of God), was at the time considered a work by St. Luke in person. On the other hand, however, Charles acquired pictures which we today would regard as avantgarde, among them a signed diptych and a triptych by Tommaso da Modena in Karlstein castle. :

: The Emperor's collections reflect his interest in the natural sciences. Apart from precious minerals and pearls it contained all manner of natural rari-

/69/
Aachen, cathedral. Carolingian
palace chapel with a Gothic
choir, added in 1355—1414.

/70/
Three spired reliquaries given by Charles IV. Aachen, cathedral treasure. Third quarter of 14th century.

/71/
Bust of Charlemagne, given by Charles IV. Aachen, cathedral treasure. Wrought silver. Probably 1376 (crown 1349).

ties. This can be deduced from the report that in 1354 Charles contributed a coral tree for the ornamentation of the tomb of St. Wenceslas and had the skeleton of a dragon taken to Karlstein castle, probably that of a crocodile. As time passed, he had opportunities to broaden the inherited collection of astronomical instruments and manuscripts of the kings of Bohemia, today in the hospital library of Nicholas Cusanius. Its most valuable part is a star globe of King Přemysl II. Charles's interest in astronomy was known to and shared by his nephew, King Charles V of France, who expressed it by a diplomatic gift. When at the beginning of the year 1378 the Emperor was returning from France, he sent after him a 'golden goblet of great weight adorned with gems on the foot and lid, very finely enamelled, depicting the heavenly spheres with the zodiac signs, planets and fixed stars'. This gift together with other valuable objects was handed over to Charles, accompanied by his son Wenceslas IV,

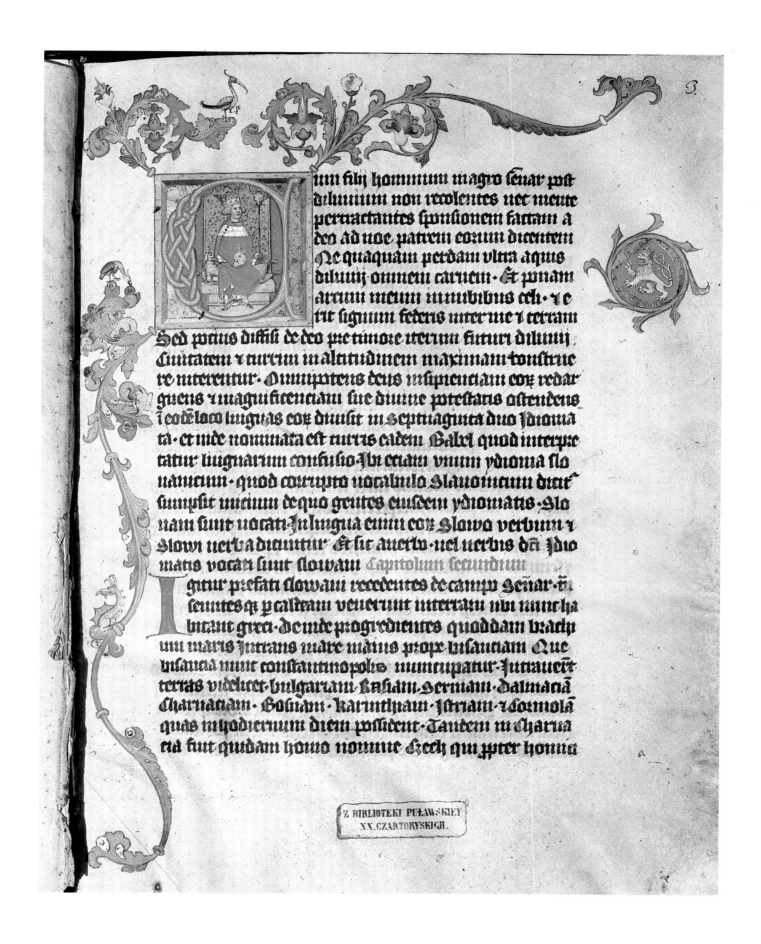

/72/
Wenceslas IV Enthroned.
Chronicle of Přibík Pulkava of
Radenín. Krakow, Muzeum
Narodowe, Biblioteka
Czartoryskich.
C. 1374.

/73/
*Archer-Centaur. Al-Sufí's Atlas
of the Constellations.
Prague-Strahov,
Museum of National Literature.
Venice or Padua. C. middle of
14th century.*

by the king's brother, the Duke Jean de Berry, as can be seen on one of the miniatures in the official report on the Emperor's visit included in the Grandes Chroniques de France.   :
: Charles availed himself of every chance of making acquisitions and obtaining possession of books. A characteristic detail is recorded in the Grandes Chroniques: King Charles V of France showed his imperial uncle two Books of Hours for him to choose that which he liked best. He selected . . . both of them! His efforts in acquiring objects turned mainly towards unique bibliophile editions. In 1354 he sent part of the 6th century manuscript of St. Mark to Prague from Aquileia; it was at that time thought to be the work of the evangelist himself. The fragment, in which the Emperor made a handwritten note on acquiring the object, is today to be found in the Prague Chapter Library; unfortunately it no longer has the magnificent covers which cost the giver 2,000 gold coins. A late Carolingian evangeliarium from around 870 A.D., whose valuable cover has already been mentioned, can also be considered a gift from Charles to the same library. While the full-page miniatures in the evangelia-

/74/
*Wolf-Lupus. Al-Sufí's Atlas of
the Constellations.
Prague-Strahov,
Museum of National Literature.
Venice or Padua. C. middle of
the 14th century.*

N prefentauttos chofes
a denifees dift ledit duit de
Berry alempererur quole
Roy le faluoiret lui enuoi
oit deses iouautx cert que

/75/
Charles IV accepts gifts from
Charles V. Illustration in
Grandes Chroniques de France.
Paris, Bibliothèque Nationale.
1378—80.

rium still exemplify illusionism or early Byzantine patterns, its rich initials are done in Frankish-Saxon style. Charles handed over to the Slavonic abbey in Prague Church Slavonic Cyrillic pericopes, which were believed to have been written by the leading Bohemian representative of the eastern liturgy, St. Procopius of Sázava. The manuscript, later bound together with the Church Slavonic Glagolian offices as the Rheims evangeliarium, is decorated with simple plaited ornaments. It was made in the 11th century in Russia.   :

: The selection of books in Charles's personal library reflects his liking for exotic things. The Astronomical Compendium, which he inherited from the kings of Bohemia and which later passed into the property of the library of Cardinal Nicholas Cusanius, includes astrological elucidations of the birth of Christ, Mohammed, etc. The Emperor borrowed a Koran from the Prague Chapter Library and never returned it. He was greatly interested in alchemy. He possessed 'black books'. Among his most valuable acquisitions was the Al-Sufi's Star Atlas with a Jewish-Arab thesis on the magic effects of precious stones and cameos, today to be found in the library of the Museum of National Literature at Prague-Strahov. The atlas was illuminated in the middle of the 14th century in northern Italy, probably in Venetian Murano or in nearby Padua. The painter who made the outstanding full-page pictures used lost antique patterns as well as Arab sources. This explains why some of the constellations (Heracles, Pegasus, etc.) are reminiscent of Pompeian painting.   :

: Later these miniatures served as patterns for the figures of the constellations in the Munich Compendium of Wenceslas IV. Charles laid the foundations of his son's enormous library by having the Krakow manuscript of Pulkava's Chronicle copied for him shortly before 1374 and personally correcting it. This book contains copies of two of the Emperor's own writings: the coronation order of the kings of Bohemia and prayers for the queen. The title page with a miniature of the young Wenceslas on the throne follows up the work of the illuminators of Chancellor John of Středa.   :

: Abroad Charles gave precious books as official presents. He had occasion to do so in 1378 when he and his son Wenceslas IV were liberally entertained by King Charles V of France. The Emperor acknowledged the valuable gifts he received from his French nephew by giving him the Ottonian evangeliarium, illuminated around the year 1000 in the workshop of the Master of the Registrum Gregorii at Trier. (In 1379 Charles V had a magnificent gold binding made for this evangeliarium and presented it to Sainte-Chapelle.) It is highly likely that the Emperor took possession of this evangeliarium, together with other treasures in Trier, after the death of his great uncle, the Archbishop and Elector Balduin, who died on 21 January 1354.   :

: Another exchange of gifts included mementos of the patron of the goldsmiths, St. Eligius, who worked at Saint-Denis under the Merovingian King Dagobert. The Emperor was given his mitre by King Charles V and that very year (1378) he presented it to the Prague guild of goldsmiths. With this gift he expressed his acknowledgement to the representatives of the craft which he encouraged by many commissions. In the Old Town of Prague alone there were fifty goldsmiths at the time, some of whom served as aldermen. The Prague goldsmiths made a cover for their patron's mitre with a gilded silver frame in the shape of the mitre and set with crystals. In return for the mitre the Emperor sent Charles V a manuscript with the legend and office of St. Eligius, today in the Bibliothèque historique de la ville de Paris. The ostentatiously adorned codex fills in some of the gaps that existed in the development of Bohemian book painting between the Krakow manuscript of Pulkava's Chronicle and Wenceslas's Willehalm of the year 1387.   :

: The few examples that survive and the sparse reports show how Charles IV's collecting stimulated a lively circulation of cultural, artistic and material values. Though largely centred on the early medieval cult of relics, it went far beyond this framework. In more than one regard Charles was a predecessor of the collectors of the Renaissance and Mannerist periods, who built up their 'Kunstkammer', 'camerae raritatis', and libraries as a universal picture of the world and thereby laid the foundations of our modern museums.   :

: Thanks to Charles the cultural and artistic horizon broadened in a territorial and chronological sense. For the Emperor collected objects the origin of which went far beyond the borders of the western Christian world and extended to the middle of the second millenium of the past. In confrontation with the Emperor's collections the Gothic style lost its normative validity. Its limited possibilities were felt when it became necessary to give expression to the historical traditions on which the Emperor based his claims as monarch. Without the Emperor's collections the programmed historicism of art at Charles's court cannot be imagined.   :

/76/
Reliquary for the mitre of St. Eligius. Prague, National Museum. 1378.

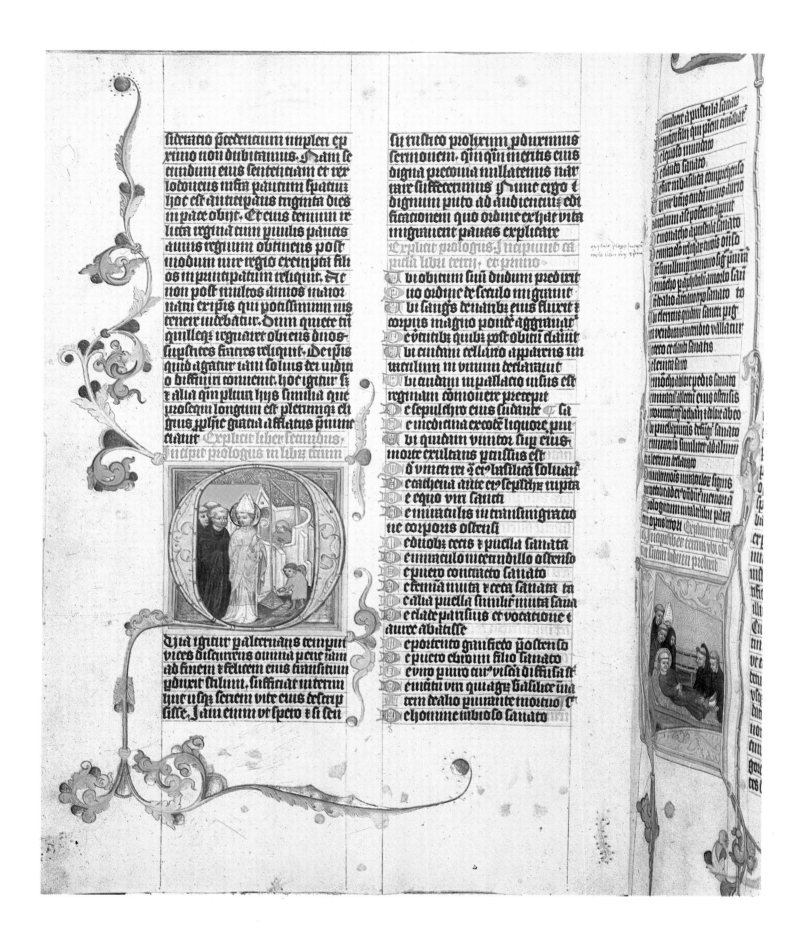

/77/
The Office of St. Eligius. Paris, Bibliothèque historique de la ville de Paris. 1378.

/78/
Karlstein castle. 1348—67.

Chapter VII

Karlstein Castle

Charles IV had a great number of castles built or reconstructed, among all of which Karlstein castle ranks as the most important. It so happens that this castle is one of the best preserved medieval castles in general, although it suffered from the tooth of ages and from later adaptations. It was built 30 km south-west of Prague on a steep limestone spur near the river Berounka. The foundation stone was laid by Archbishop Ernest of Pardubice on behalf of his friend Charles IV on 10 June 1348 in the presence of many persons of importance. (Charles was at that time engaged in diplomatic negotiations with Archduke Albrecht II of Austria at Seefeld castle.) He had selected for Karlstein castle the strategically most important site available — the geometrical centre of an approximate square with sides measuring some 250 km, formed by the natural frontiers of Bohemia. Construction work went on at a great pace so that by autumn 1357 the basic work was finished.   :

: It is not known who drew up the plans for Karlstein castle. It must have been an eminent builder of fortifications, who was able to put into practice the wishes of the man who commissioned the work. There was nothing in the whole of Europe to compare with the complex layout of the castle buildings, making perfect use of the configuration of the rocky spur. The broadly designed outer bailey is formed by two entrance gates, the northern bastion, the burgrave's house with courtyard, a defence system along the periphery of the castle and finally, much lower on the south-west slope lies the well tower of pear-shaped ground-plan. These structures are surrounded by a strong outer wall. In height and architectonically, this outer bailey is intentionally kept low, following the central European tradition. This gives even more grandeur to the dynamic crescendo of the main part of the castle surrounded by an inner wall. The profile of its elevation rises from the square palace with a semi-circular tower at its eastern side and a narrower transverse wing past the square central tower to the Great Tower in the north. The building reaches its climax in its mighty prism rising high into the sky. The two towers were not only separate units of fortifications but also served as residential buildings with several storeys, each with a number of rooms and their own chapels. In their exceptionally large size they differ from the many smaller towers of the period that served purely defence purposes. They are more like the residential keeps that were built in the tenth to thirteenth centuries in western Europe and in southern Italy. The use of this older type of structure can be explained by Karlstein castle serving as seat of the imperial court from time to time, and from 1357 it had a permanent chapter. While other castles had one or at most two chapels, there were five chapels at Karlstein.   :

: The architectural form was determined by Charles's express wish that the sacred content of the two square towers should remain untouched even if the rest of the castle should fall into enemy hands. The big four-storey tower with its mass of thousands of tons of ashlar heaped on top of the rocky spur gives an impression of complete impregnability: its north wall is almost seven metres thick. The smooth walls stressed only slightly by cornices underline the terse appearance. The wooden casing of the tower is the result of pseudo-Gothic renovation of the castle in the years 1887—1904.   :

: The three-storeyed central tower with walls more than three metres thick is called the church of the Virgin Mary. In view of this the hipped, shingle-covered roof culminates in a sanctus tower, in which a bell hung. The slim bell tower adds to the monumental silhouette of the castle a more intimate scale as do the little polygonal oriels with tall tent roofs on the southern wall on the third floor of the palace.   :

: The entire wealth of artistic decorations of Karlstein castle was concentrated in its interior. The living quarters in the palace with rooms laid out in the current scheme of 'thoroughfare', fulfilled every demand for comfort. The larger part of the first floor of the palace was taken up by the Vassals Hall, reconstructed last century from the former White Hall. The windows here are set in deep recesses in the main southern wall and have seats along the sides. The carved beams and octagonal columns holding the flat wooden ceiling were originally brightly coloured. In its general appearance and in the details this room corresponds to the Rittersaal in the imperial castle at Nuremberg, which Charles from 1347 frequently used as his residence.   :

: Next to the White Hall was the chapel of St. Nicholas. Its nave covered with a beamed ceiling opened through a pointed triumphal arch with narrowing sides into the presbytery located in the eastern, semi-circular tower and ending in a conch. Only the triumphal arch has survived of the original chapel adorned with Italian geometrical ornaments. Today it is deposited in the castle stone collection on the ground floor of the Great Tower. The rest of the mural paintings in the chapel dating from 1353 were destroyed in the sixteenth century. According

/80/
Madonna of alabaster. Karlstein castle, former imperial palace. Before the middle of 14th century.

/81/
Madonna, the Man of Sorrows, angels. Diptych by Tommaso da Modena. Karlstein castle, former imperial palace. C. 1355.

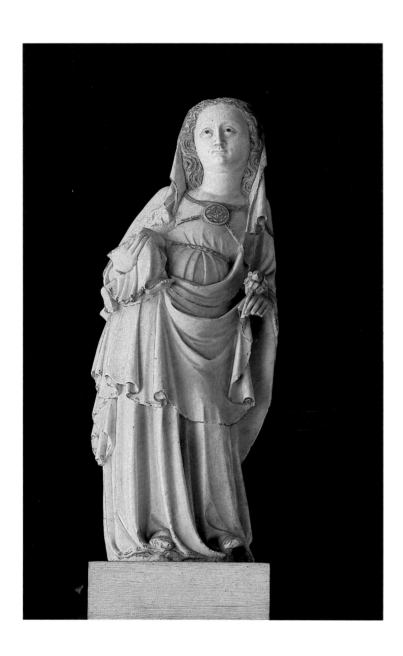

to Giovanni Marignolli's chronicle they represented the Miracle with the Finger of St. Nicholas, which happened to Charles in the St. Francis monastery in Prague. Charles's personality was enhanced at Karlstein castle not only by the castle bearing the Emperor's name, as did other imperial castles, but also by numerous portraits of him.

: The requirements of representing the person of the Emperor and his dynasty form the guideline of the decorations in the Great Hall on the second floor of the Karlstein palace. There the Emperor's family tree on his father's side was painted on the walls. In the third quarter of the sixteenth century this painting was completely destroyed, but the names and titles of fifty-seven or fifty-eight persons depicted on it have survived at least on a copy entitled Linea Caroli IV.

: The family tree began with Noah who, in Charles's words, 'spiritually means Christ'. Then followed the patriarchs of the Bible, Ham, Cush, Nimrod, persons from the Greek mythology, Belos and Ninus, and they in turn were succeeded by antique gods and heroes, Saturn, Jupiter, Dardanus, Herictonius, Ilus and Priam. From there as far as the thirty-sixth figure, that of the French King Louis II, the Karlstein family tree was identical with the genealogy of the Capetians. The most important place, in this part, was set aside for Emperor St. Charlemagne. The link between the French kings and the Luxemburgs was provided by dukes and counts of Lorrain and Brabant, from whose line Charles's grandmother Margaret, the wife of Emperor Henry

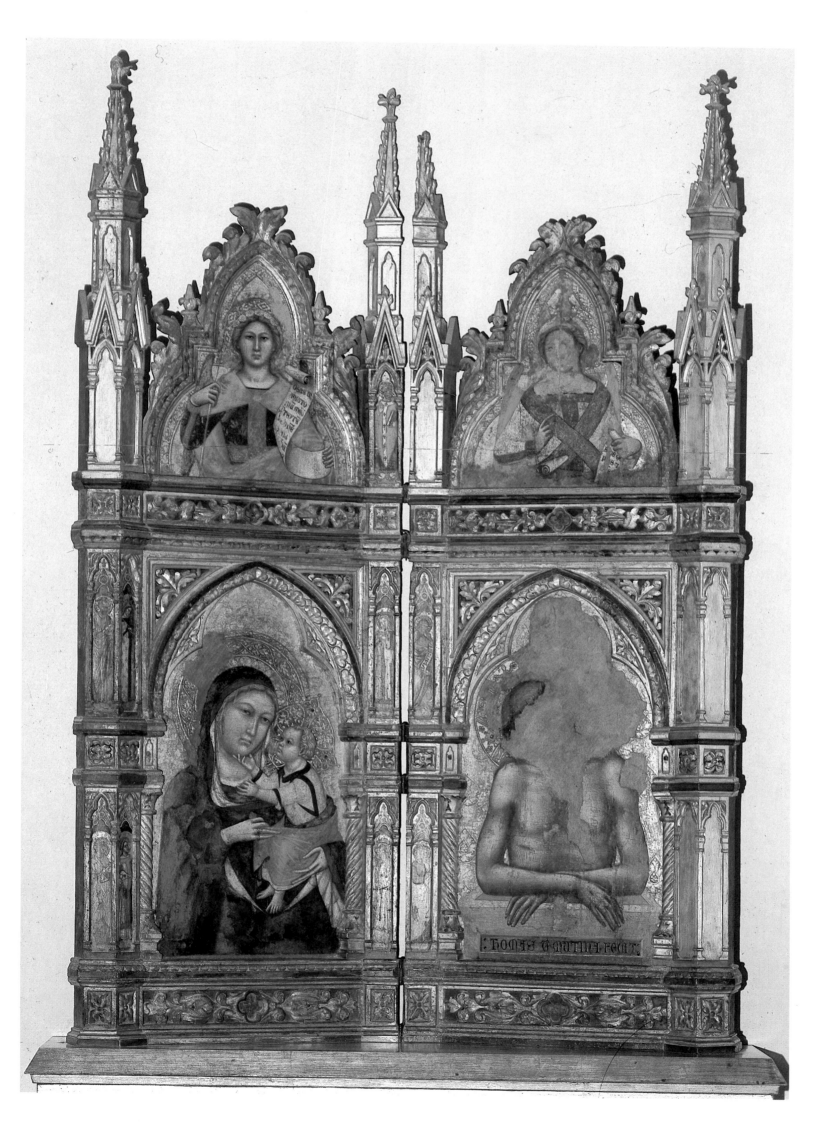

VII, had descended. After the figures of that imperial couple the family tree continued with the portraits of King John of Luxemburg and Elizabeth Přemyslide, who in the inscription was given as daughter of the Czech King Wenceslas II. The entire set reached its culmination in the portraits of Emperor Charles IV and his three (respectively four) wives.   :

: The text of the Linea Caroli IV is copied in antique capitals on the late Renaissance pedestals and plinths of the thrones on the well-known genealogical series contained in the compendium of Emperor Maxmilian II. It was made in the years 1574—75 by the Czech engineer Matthew Ptáček-Ornys of Lindperk as a proposal for the renewal of the Karlstein family tree, then already irrevocably damaged. His miniatures are full of drastic mistakes of fact, but are still Gothic in character, for apart from numerous Renaissance patterns Ornys also used an old workshop pattern-book of the years 1370—1400. Out of these patterns he assembled a remarkable mannerist composition.   :

: More important are the miniatures in the Latin Emmaus Bible, the second part of the Vyšehrad antiphonary of the years 1360—61 and other manuscripts from the same workshop, for instance the Bible of scribe Nicholas. Apart from numerous counterparts of surviving mural paintings in the Slavonic abbey and at Karlstein castle, these miniatures include the figures of monarchs seated on the throne or standing. Some of them show a striking typological relation to figures of the Hapsburgs on the stained glass windows in St. Stephen's cathedral in Vienna. It is assumed that their makers derived their knowledge from the Karlstein genealogy. One can deduce from this affinity that the figures depicted in the hall of the imperial palace at Karlstein castle were comparatively large-sized, agile figures of monarchs, each seated on a throne with a richly carved seat or a baldaquin constructed in perspective. Some dukes were armed with swords and shields. On the genealogy great importance was clearly attributed to the depiction of coats of arms.   :

: Charles had his work cabinet and audience chamber next to the hall with the family tree. Its southern wall, originally with an oriel, was decorated with paintings, of which the overpainted coats of arms and the inscriptions 'SPQR' and 'Roma caput mundi regit orbis frena rotundi' are still visible. The ceiling is held by two mighty carved girders and the walls are covered in richly carved, painted and gilded coffer panelling.   :

: The neighbouring room, also with panelling, was by tradition known as the Emperor's bedroom. Through a triumphal arch this room opened into the area of the eastern semi-circular tower, where the monarch's chapel was located.   :

: Of the original decorations of Karlstein palace

there remains, apart from a French alabaster statue of the Virgin, only a signed work by one of the greatest painters of the Trecento. That is the little altar by Tommaso da Modena with semi-figures of the Virgin, the Man of Sorrows and angels in a richly carved frame. The magnificent painting has outstanding plastic qualities and forms enveloped in soft light. It is in no way surprising that the Emperor commissioned Tommaso to make him an altar for his private chapel. The workshop of that great Modena artist was, at that time, working not only in Treviso, i.e. in the immediate neighbourhood of Charles's Belluno-Feltre enclave, but actually in the parish church at Feltre. In October 1354 Charles had himself and his wife Anne of Świdnica depicted in the local convent of St. Victor and St. Corona. The commission for the little altar and other works by Tommaso da Modena might, of course, have been negotiated after the Emperor's return from the first Roman expedition by the Bishop of Belluno-Feltre, Jacob of Brno.   :

: The decorations of the rooms in the central tower, linked to the palace by a drawbridge, have survived in far better condition. The original plan counted on this keep also being used as a dwelling. Its entire second floor was taken up by one large hall. But when Charles set up the Karlstein chapter by the Document of Foundation and Consecration of 27 March 1357, this hall was changed into the church of the Virgin Mary. At that time all its profane furnishings were removed. The beamed ceiling, which could not be changed into vaulting, was adapted to the new function of the room by being painted with semi-figures of angels. To this day the statue of the Virgin Enthroned survives in the chapter church, having once, in accordance with its consecration, adorned the altar. It is carved in wood, coloured and gilded. The solidity of the statue, the overall conception of form and the loose design of the draperies reveal the affinity to the early stone works made in Peter Parler's masonic lodge.   :

: The chapter church of the Virgin Mary came into being as a provisional adaptation of a secular hall and is not of any great value as regards its architecture. This is not true of a room entered through a pointed portal at the south-west corner of the church. At the end of a narrow linking corridor

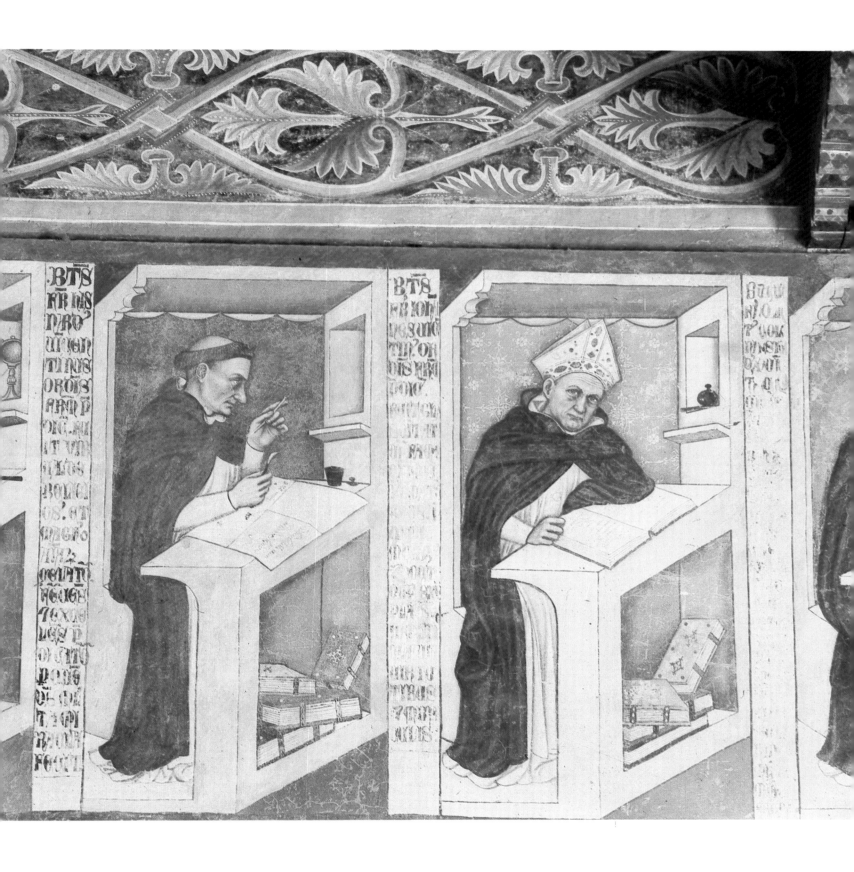

/82/
*Tommaso da Modena: Cycle of
Famous Members of the
Dominican Order. Treviso, mural
painting in the chapter hall of
the Dominican monastery. 1352.*

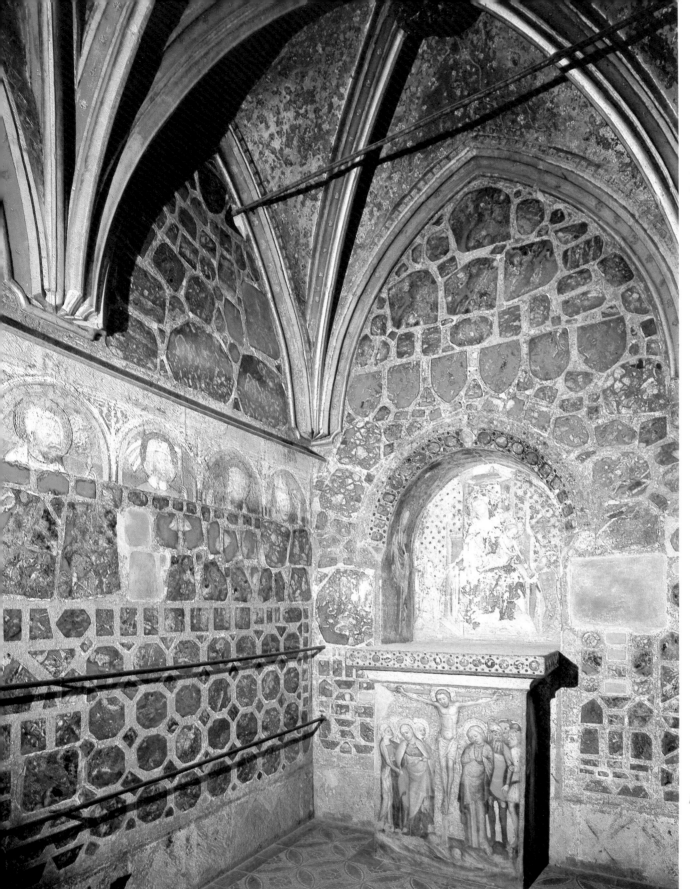

/84/
Gallo-Roman
cameo with the head
of the Medusa (3rd
to 4th century A. D.)
on the boss of
the imperial oratory,
called St. Catherine's
chapel.

/85/
Christ and the
Virgin grant
Charles IV and
Anne of Świdnica
the rule of the world.
The Crucifixion.
Mural painting on
the altar wall of the
imperial oratory.
After 1355.

/83/
The imperial oratory, called St.
Catherine's chapel. Interior. After
1348; incrustation of walls with
semi-precious stones. C. 1367.

there opens up through a richly profiled, shouldered portal with the original painted ironwork door, a sanctuary known as the Emperor's oratory. : : This truly miniature sanctuary, only 3.92 by 2.33 m, is carved out of the thickness of the southern wall of the tower. It is a true architectural jewel. It is lit by two Gothic windows with tracery and has two compartments of cross vaulting. The vaulting ribs with elaborate profiles belong to post-classical Gothic but spring from flat imposts, a trend typical of high Gothic. The boss of the eastern vaulting compartment was not made by a stone-cutter but by a jeweller. It takes the form of a circular target of gold foil set with thirty-nine amethysts, cornelians and chrysoprases. In the centre there is an exceptionally large gem of blueish-white chalcedony with a Gorgonian head of the Me-

dusa—Gallo-Roman work of the third to fourth century. The value of the room was enhanced in 1360s, when its vaults and ribs were gilded and the walls set with polished semi-precious stones. On the right side of the altar table there is a painting of St. Catherine, whom Charles venerated greatly; for it was on her saint's day in 1332 that he won his first battle near the fortress of San Felice. This painting has been the reason why in the sixteenth century the chapel came to be known as St. Catherine's. :
: The importance of this room on the second floor of the central, or church tower at Karlstein castle derives primarily from its exceptionally rich mural decorations. The paintings are done in tempera technique on a secco-fresco base. The full mastery of tempera shows that the painters were acquainted with the technique of panel painting. They will have devoted themselves to that in the winter months when it was not possible to paint the walls. (It is known that medieval painters in Italy worked in these two spheres simultaneously.) :
: The surviving paintings in the church tower were made in several stages by four of Charles's court painters. In about 1356 the oldest master painted the altar recess and lintel in the Emperor's oratory. In the recess below the picture of the Veraicon there is a painting of the Virgin Enthroned, Charles IV kneeling and his wife Anne of Świdnica, both in

imperial robes. The Christchild is grasping the folded hands of the Emperor and Mary holds the Empress's folded hands in her right hand. This gesture as an expression of homage, the promise of a vassal's faithfulness, sets out to say that the Emperor derived his power directly from Christ. It is in exact conformity with the Golden Bull of 1356, in which Charles IV laid down by law that state power be independent of the Pope. The meaning of the scene is stressed by having the painted figures of the apostolic princes Peter and Paul present as witnesses to this homage on the jambs of the recess. The decoration of the recess must be taken as a glorification of Ektheosis, of imperial dignity in the spirit of the tradition of Constantine the Great, with whom Charles IV is often compared. :
: This idea is further elaborated in the lintel of the oratory, which holds busts of the Emperor and Em-

/86/
Emperor Charles IV and Anne of Świdnica raising the Cross. Mural painting on the lintel of the imperial oratory. After 1355.

/88/
Stained glass with the Crucifixion in the imperial oratory. Now in the former imperial palace. C. 1367.

/87/
St. Procopius. Mural painting on the northern wall of the imperial oratory. After 1355.

press with a large gold cross in their hands. A pattern for this can be found in the iconographic type of 'Constantine and Helena Raising the Cross', developed in Constantinople before the ninth century and widely known especially in Orthodox churches in the Balkan peninsula. It was also frequently to be found in Byzantine crafts, e.g. in cameos and coins, through which it might well have reached Charles's court.   :

: Of the two works by this painter, known as Master A, only the decorations in the recess have survived intact. These slim, agile figures wrapped in decoratively gathered draperies make a timeless impression within the framework of Bohemian painting of that period, which aimed at solid figures. They are far closer to the work of the Parisian illuminators who, in the years 1348—52, decorated several manuscripts, mainly the Bible moralisée of Charles's brother-in-law, the French King Jean II le Bon. The well-known portrait of that monarch in the Louvre shows likewise a relation to the portraiture of Master A. It is, however, possible that the situation was similar to that of Bohemian wood sculpture of the first half of the fourteenth century when the accomplishments of Parisian art were transmitted to the Czech Lands via Strasbourg. In such a case Master A would be identical with the imperial painter Nicholas Wurmser of Strasbourg.

Documents exist to show that by 5 July 1357 he had settled in Bohemia and was married to Agnes of Žatec. He owned a farmstead in the village of Mořina near Karlstein. The head of the Virgin of the altar recess, however, is not of western origin but purely Sienese in type. The court painters, who were expected to have broad education in the arts, usually derived stimuli from several centres of the arts.

: A different problem arises in the case of a painter who, shortly after 27 March 1357, painted the figures of the seven patrons of Bohemia on the northern wall of the Emperor's oratory. Only the damaged heads remained when the chapel was inlaid with polished gemstones. In the narrow strip above the incrustation, where the painting was covered by a relic board, the brilliant Italian colour scheme has survived in its fullness.

: The heads of those saints have a certain analogy in the Liber Viaticus of John of Středa. There is a special closer relationship to the stained glass with the figure of John the Baptist at Osek and with the Morgan panels. These relationships suggest the person of the court painter known as the Master of the Emmaus Cycle in view of his decisive share in painting the cloisters of the Slavonic abbey in Prague. A stained glass window with a dramatic Crucifixion also came from his workshop. This was placed in the window of the Emperor's little Karlstein chapel at the end of the 1360s. The glass in reminiscent of the stained glass at Osek.

: The scene of the Crucifixion at the head of the altar table in the Emperor's oratory and the figure of St. Catherine on its right side are the work of yet another painter. He adapted his work to the ornaments on the altar recess by using outline drawing of slim figures garbed in decoratively flowing draperies. But he differed by using a warmer colour scheme, more plastic and softer modelling of shapes as well as looser brushwork. The figure of an angel steeped in light and holding an incense burner on the northern gable end of the little corridor linking the oratory with the church can also be ascribed to the same painter. As he also made the majority of the apocalyptical scenes in that church, he has been given the name of the Master of the Karlstein Apocalypse.

: The layout of paintings in the church of the Virgin Mary unfavourably reflects the fact that this sanctuary was created out of a secular hall that had, partly at least, been decorated previously. The entire upper strip of the oldest paintings below the ceiling was destroyed. Inscriptions that relate to these destroyed paintings reveal that, among others, there were pictures of Charles IV and Queen Blanche worshipping the Holy Trinity and two other of Charles's wives; Queen Anne of the Palatinate and Empress Anne of Świdnica in the company of pro-

phets and apostles. Here, too, must have been true portraiture like that applied by Master A in the neighbouring Emperor's oratory. To this master, probably to be identified with Nicholas Wurmser of Strasbourg, can also be ascribed the well-known relic scenes on the right half of the southern wall of the Marian church. There are three scenes set in a relatively shallow space of a church interior. The first depicts Charles IV at the moment when he accepts as a gift from his nephew, the Dauphin of France, two thorns from the crown of Christ, which had been kept in the Sainte-Chapelle in Paris. This scene is based on a historical event that took place in the Imperial Diet at Metz at the turn of the year 1356—7. The Dauphin is dressed in his favourite gown as a university Master as in numerous illuminations in his manuscripts, e.g. the miniature by Jean Bondolf of Bruges in the Hague Bible of the years 1371—2. An even closer similarity is provided by the parament at Narbonne. It is likely that a portrait of the Dauphin existed at the court of Prague, and that the imperial painter used this as a pattern. Charles V of France is wearing a royal crown in this picture, although he was not entitled to this until 1364. This crown is Renaissance in character and must have been added during the first restoration of the painting, which probably took place when the church tower was repaired in 1508.

: The same is true of the crown of the ruler who, in the second relic scene, is handing the Emperor a small object. One can therefore agree with the explanation that this latter ruler is the Duke of Mantua, Margrave Luigi I Gonzaga. At the end of 1354 Charles acquired another relic in Mantua, part of the sponge from Christ's crucifixion. He had it placed, together with the two thorns and part of the wood from the cross, in a gold receptacle shaped like a cross, which is today in the Weltliche Schatzkammer in Vienna.

: The reliquary is depicted in the third relic scene where the Emperor is about to place it in the ostensory, 'a famous new cross of pure gold, covered with the most precious of pearls'. This ostensory cross, about which Charles wrote to the Pope on 21 December 1357, has unfortunately not survived. At the time when the relic scenes were painted it must have been kept nearby. According to the

founder's original plan, the second floor of the church tower was to serve as 'Schatzkammer'. :

: The relic scenes will have been made in the spring months of the year 1358. They involved a break in the sequence of the apocalyptical scenes. They are painted across the apostolic crosses of consecration, which acquired that they were made after the consecration of the chapel on 27 March 1357. Today all later overpaintings have been removed, so that a number of empty spaces remain in the original. :

: In particularly bad condition is the picture of the four Apocalyptical Riders on the left side of the southern wall. The best surviving figure of the Rider with a Sword is an authentic work by the Master of the Emmaus Cycle. :

: The scenes inspired by the ninth to twelfth chapters of the Revelation of St. John are different in character. They were applied by the Master of the Karlstein Apocalypse to cover the eastern wall of the church of the Virgin Mary. (A picture of nine angelic choirs and two guardian knights on the left half of the western wall can be ascribed to the same master.) With their small scale and lack of monumentality these scenes recall book painting. Close relations in style link them to miniatures made by the illuminator of the Breviary of Grand Master Leo in the year 1356. The breviary originated in a workshop that was working for the prelates at Charles's court, e.g. Ernest of Pardubice. An early work by this workshop, with a Sienese-Bolognese orientation, is the psalter of the Karlstein chapter, which was originally made for the St. George's convent at Prague castle. It is typical of the exceptional receptiveness of the illuminator of that manuscript that he adopted certain scenes from Canon Beneš's illustrations in the Passional of Abbess Kunigunde. The manuscripts made in that workshop included certain Byzantine-Italian schemes of movement, also to be found in the church of the Virgin Mary. The similarity in the conception of the figures, often puppet-like, their childish naive expressions and comical grimaces are truly striking. They make it possible to put forward the view that the Master of the Karlstein Apocalypse can be identified with the illuminator of the Breviary of Grand Master Leo.

: Despite all the charm of his brushwork the paint-

/9/
*Relic scene. Charles accepts a relic
from the Dauphin of France
(Charles V), and Luigi I
Gonzaga, the Margrave of
Mantua (?) and places it in
a reliquary cross. Church of the
Virgin Mary, southern wall.
Mural painting. 1357—8.*

/92/
*Mask of the Demon of Storm
and a town destroyed by an
earthquake. Detail from the
Apocalyptical Cycle on the eastern
wall of the church of the Virgin
Mary. After 1357.*

er was not a man of great invention. It must, therefore, be assumed that he owed certain exceptional motifs to the quality of his patterns. The picture of the town in the right half of the central strip shows that a knowledge of Sienese vedutas had reached him. What is even more remarkable is the town in the middle of the third strip. Its buildings in the midst of an earthquake are brightly lit by crossing strokes of lightning. The mask of an antique demon floats in the sky hurling streams of water from his mouth. The masks of 'voices from space' on the neighbouring scene are closer to their antique prototypes than the illustrations in western European manuscripts of Terence's comedies dating from the ninth to twelfth centuries. The master probably used an Early Byzantine manuscript in Charles's library. One of the masks painted in the chiaroscuro technique recalls by its colour, light effects and type the Gallo-Roman cameo with a Gorgonian head of the Medusa on the boss in the adjoining Emperor's oratory.   :

: The right half of the western wall is covered by two monumental apocalyptical scenes representing the Woman Fleeing from the Dragon into the Wilderness and the Woman Clothed in the Sun. The second picture is conceived as a Virgin and Child with regard to the Marian consecration of the church on 27 March 1357. It is followed up by the miniature of the Virgin and the Saints in the Vyšehrad antiphonary of the years 1360—1, which sets the upper limit of its time of origin. With their drawn outlines both the pictures correspond to the paintings of Master A, but their execution is closer to that of the art of the Master of the Karlstein Apocalypse. This ambivalence perhaps explains itself if one assumes that the latter painter finished off the picture begun by Master A, who was not able to do so as, in the meantime, he had been set another task, namely to decorate the southern wing of the cloisters in the Slavonic abbey in Prague.   :

: As the pictures vary in subject-matter and quality, one of the painters tried to unify the decorations of the church of the Virgin Mary by painting a socle. It is made up of a console cornice, arched frieze, coffer ceiling, hanging draperies and illusively painted marble coffers. The architectonic motifs appearing on this socle are Hellenistic-Roman in origin. They

survived throughout the Middle Ages in Italy. This knowledge must have been brought to the Karlstein painters by Roman artists, who around 1300 worked in the upper church of St. Francis at Assisi. The triple arcaded loggia below the relic scenes is also Italian in character.   :

: About the year 1360 five scenes were painted in the window recess cut into the western wall shortly beforehand. Two of them, Christ in Limbo, and the Resurrection, have themes related to the tomb of Christ, which is shown here by a figure in polished gemstones. The selection of the remaining three scenes, with the Virgin Mary as central figure — the Descent of the Holy Ghost, the Death, and the Coronation of the Virgin—derive logically from the consecration of the sanctuary. The scenes are in poor condition. By their suppressed outline draw-

117

/94/
Angels Battling with Devils.
Scene from the Apocalyptical
Cycle on the eastern wall of the
church of the Virgin Mary. After
1357.

ing, subdued range of colours and the advanced use of colour steeped in light, they coincide with the fragments of the original paintings removed from the walls of the spiral staircase in the Great Tower at Karlstein castle. Part of these fragments are today exhibited on the first floor of the palace.

: This spiral staircase, built in a special annex to the southern wall of the Great Tower, leads to the chapel on its second floor. It is divided by landings into twelve sections spanned by segmented vaulting with strips, and sparsely lit by seven oblong windows set in narrowing jambs. The outer walls are covered by twenty-eight scenes of the story of St. Wenceslas beginning at the foot and unwinding as one moves up; the inner wall shows nine scenes from the life of St. Ludmilla, arranged in the opposite order. The pictures were, in places, lightly overpainted in the years 1608—9 and then more thoroughly in 1897—8. At that time whole sections were painted on to new plaster with the aid of tracing paper and copies. A comparison of the original fragments and those tracings and copies enables one to get a fairly reliable idea of the original appearance of the two cycles.

: The discovery of a walled-in document dates

/95/
Angels Battling with Devils.
Detail of the Apocalyptical Cycle
on the eastern wall of the church
of the Virgin Mary. After 1357.

/96/
Detail of the Crucifixion in the
missal of the Olomouc Chapter
Library (No. 137.) C. 1360.

them to the years 1360—1. That same year the Vy-šehrad antiphonary was made and its semi-figure of an angel playing an instrument is copied from the vaulting of the staircase. The dating seems to be confirmed by the scenes on the right of the entrance to the tower chapel. On it Charles IV is placing some relic into a reliquary cross, which is the same as the cross on the third relic scene. The event is witnessed by prelates and three of the Emperor's wives. The picture must have been made during the lifetime of Anne of Świdnica who died on 11 July 1362 or, at the latest, prior to the Emperor's marriage to his fourth wife, Elizabeth of Pomerania, on 21 May 1363.

: The pictures of the life of Prince Wenceslas and his grandmother St. Ludmilla at Karlstein are conceived as a history of the Přemyslides, from whose dynasty the Emperor's mother Elizabeth had descended. A depiction of the members of the Přemyslide dynasty, both men and women, was added to the two cycles in front of the entrance. This part is the most badly damaged section of all the decorations on the staircase. It forms a pendant to Charles's family tree on his father's side on the second floor of the palace.

: The St. Ludmila cycle is, at the same time, a glorification of the apostle of the Slavs, St. Methodius of Salonica, Archbishop of Velehrad in Moravia (died 885). The first scene of the story of St. Ludmilla represents a feast in his metropolis where this outstanding Greek scholar is making a prophesy for Prince Bořivoj, which Charles might well have related to himself: 'Thou shalt be Lord of thy Lords and all thy enemies shall be subject to thy might...'

: On the fourth scene of the legend Emperor Henry the Fowler throws himself at the feet of Prince Wenceslas, who appears as Elector at the Imperial Diet at Regensburg in the company of two angels. It is natural that Charles himself is depicted in the figure of the Emperor doing homage to Wenceslas.

: Of all surviving paintings the staircase cycle is most closely related to Charles. The Emperor himself, in honour of his baptismal patron, composed a famous prayer in which the story of the saint is incorporated. He gave new meaning to material that had been treated many times before in the Church Slavonic and the Latin tongues. He gave even greater poignancy to the basic contradiction between light—good and dark—evil in the spirit of the neo-Platonic Augustinian cosmology. Cosmological significance is attributed to the numbers applied in the architecture of the staircase and in the whole design of the two cycles: 7 — 9 — 12 — 28.

: The last number, 28, represents the number of scenes in the story of St. Wenceslas which, in turn, is connected with the alleged date of the saint's death by martyrdom on 28 September 928. It is also an expression of the four phases of the moon. Among the old Slavs the moon corresponded in the social hierarchy to the status of prince (cf. Polish 'księżyc' meaning 'moon' and 'książe' meaning 'prince'). The St. Vitus's inventory of the year 1354 includes a reliquary statue of St. Wenceslas standing on a moon.

: In the staircase cycle the saint accomplishes

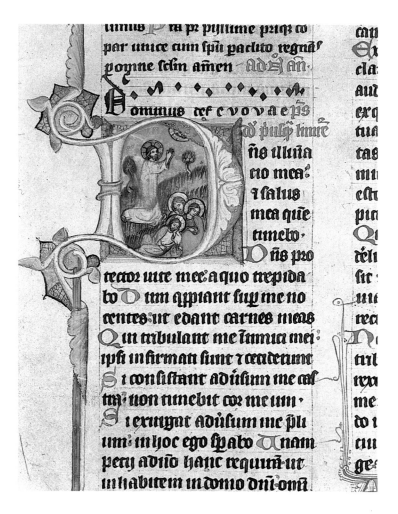

/97/
Christ on the Mount of Olives.
Psalter of the Karlstein chapter.
Prague, Library of the National
Museum. Before 1350.

twelve deeds: he works on the fields, in the vineyard and in the forest in the manner of figures depicted on calendars ever since the ninth century. Legend, however, has it that he did all his work at night.   :

: The exceptional wealth of subject-matter in the St. Ludmilla and St. Wenceslas cycles gave the Emperor's painter sufficient opportunity to develop his advanced art. This painter, who used to be known as the Master of the Staircase Cycle, is today a personality of some repute. Apart from his modest share in the typological cycle in the cloisters of the Slavonic abbey, paintings in the St. Wenceslas and the Vlašim chapels in Prague cathedral have been attributed to him, dating from the seventies of the fourteenth century. At that time the only painter recorded in the cathedral was Master Oswald, to whom a total of eight sources refer. As late as 7 February 1383 he took part in a financial dispute representing the interests of the St. Vitus chapter. He had close relations with Peter Parler. This can be shown, among other examples on the Stockholm drawing of the Virgin with St. Wenceslas, which can be ascribed to him. A stone crab is sketched on the right hand margin of the sheet. In the Czech Lands the name of Oswald was very rare at the time, but it existed widely in southern Germany. It can therefore be assumed that the master came from there to Prague as a relatively young artist, perhaps with Peter Parler in 1356.   :

: Before coming to Karlstein Oswald must have visited Italy. This can be deduced from the nature of the exceptionally rich painted architecture on his cycles. This architecture follows the rising rhythm of the staircase in harmonious lines and creates a spatial setting for the scenes. Here again appear elements of Italian architecture similar to those making up the socle in the neighbouring church of the Virgin Mary. The master enriched it with certain Parlerian motifs such as shouldered portals, suspended bosses, and porches with semi-circular portals. This leads one to the belief that he must have had access to as yet unexecuted plans of Peter Parler. A typical feature of his stereometric feeling for form is the twisting of architectonic elements with their edge to the front. Similar artistic principles can be found in the case of the rich architec-

/98/
*Woman Clothed in the Sun.
Western wall of the church of the
Virgin Mary. After 1357.*

tural frame on the little altar by Tommaso da Modena in the Karlstein palace. Oswald was also the first painter who took Tommaso's principles of multi-figural compositions to the north, naturally set in complex architecture. His advanced manner of soft plastic modelling by means of light has also its starting point in the work of Tommaso.   :

: In the depiction of horses twisting their heads as they jump, Oswald used the scheme of movement used in antiquity, which survived in Byzantine painting. This would have come to him via Venice (The Conversion of St. Paul on the Berlin predella by Lorenzo Veneziano). Some scenes on the Karlstein staircase take place in a landscape laid out in several planes with the spatial effect heightened by avenues of trees. These landscapes show the influence of the Sienese vedutas by Ambrogio Lorenzetti.   :

: In his cycles Oswald adhered to the programmed historicism of art under Charles IV. On the eleventh scene of the St. Wenceslas legend he depicted a well observed rotunda; elsewhere he painted a Romanesque conch and arched friezes. An ancient and yet surprisingly modern feature are the landscapes painted in the staircase window recesses. They are steeply terraced with cleft rocky cliffs and only sparse signs of vegetation. The impression of desolation of inhospitable regions which they arouse is intensified by the expressive colour scheme and the sharp light. This type of landscape of antique origin survived in Byzantium for many ages and was handed on to Italian painting. The distinctive character of the Karlstein landscapes rests in the absence of figures, fauna or architecture. For the first time since the end of antiquity the landscape here became an independent and self-sufficient subject of depiction.   :

: The entire second floor of the Great Tower is taken up by a chapel which, according to the Document of Foundation and Consecration of 27 March 1357, was consecrated to the 'Most Glorious Suffering of Christ the Lord and its Symbols'. It is known as the chapel of the Holy Rood.   :

: The greatest attention was devoted to the construction of this sanctuary from the very beginning, for it was to be the most important part of Karlstein castle, indeed the very reason for the foundation and construction of the castle. The chapel derives its ground-plan from the fortified character of the Great Tower: it is a rectangle broadened by two deep window recesses on the eastern side and one on the western side. A fourth recess was broken through for the window above the shouldered portal at its southern end. For security reasons the pointed windows with tracery are very narrow. The chapel is spanned by two compartments of cross vaulting, the pear-shaped ribs of which run straight into polygonal pillars with pyramidical ends.   :

: This sanctuary, relatively simple architecturally, was given the most costly decorations. The aim of Charles in so doing is shown in the words of the chronicler Beneš Krabice:

> 'The Emperor set up a large chapel in the upper tower (of Karlstein), the walls of which he had inlaid with pure gold and valuable gemstones and he beautified it both with relics of the Saints and with chasubles for (the chapter) . . . and adorned it with very precious pictures. In the whole wide world there is no castle, no chapel as magnificently fitted out and that is right, because the Emperor keeps the Imperial Jewels and the Treasure of the entire Kingdom there.'

: In the eyes of his contemporaries it was his ownership of the Imperial Coronation Treasure that made Charles legally Emperor of the Holy Roman Empire. For that reason he had them deposited in the chapel of the impregnable Great Tower. The most valuable part of the treasure was the gold Coronation Cross of the first half of the eleventh century set with pearls and gems. It contained a particle of the wood from Christ's Cross with a nail and part of the lance. Charles added to this his own new ostensory cross, which he had painted on the third relic scene and on the scene on the staircase of the Great Tower, as related above.   :

: This painting also depicts a historical event: the transfer of the particle of the wood of the cross from the old coronation cross to the new ostensory. A lance made in the Rhineland in the eighth century also formed part of the imperial treasure, and legend related it originally to St. Constantine the Great and later to St. Longinus. The Imperial Crown of small enamelled plates set with gems with one arch was made for Emperor Otto I in the eleventh century according to a Byzantine pattern. Tradition, however, ascribed it to St. Charlemagne — like the eastern European sabre from the second half of the ninth century and the majority of valuable garments made in the second half of the twelfth century in Palermo. The treasure included a number of other relics and works of art.   :

: In the Holly Rood chapel it was to be guarded by the 'Heavenly Host', which is mentioned in the Document of Foundation and Consecration of

27 March 1357. This Heavenly Host is represented by pictures with semi-figures of saints.   :
: In 1357 the chapel had only provisional decorations. It is not certain whether a signed triptych by Tommaso da Modena formed part of it, though it later came to be placed on the altar wall. This outstanding work of art would, in its subject-matter, have fitted better into the neighbouring church of the Virgin Mary. Its central panel represents the broad semi-figure of the Virgin and Child. St. Wen-

ceslas is depicted in the cap of a Venetian doge on the left wing of the triptych. The right wing represents St. Palmatius, whose relics Charles acquired in Trier in 1356. That same year he founded a little church to that saint in the settlement below Karlstein castle. The elegant figures of the two holy knights show that Tommaso himself was strongly influenced by northern Gothic.   :
: Some time before 1360 the Master of the Emmaus Cycle began to work in the chapel. He used a brush to draw the busts of five saints on the wall. They were to constitute a synopsis for the originally planned mural decorations. At the same time they were to give Charles some idea of the proposed design. Some of those busts, such as those of St. John the Baptist and St. Andrew, give a remarkable impression of the work of almost Michelangelo in the mightiness of the human form. No wonder that the drawings were for a long time wrongly considered the work of a Renaissance artist of the sixteenth century. The differentiation of the heads shows that

/100/
Master Oswald: St. Wenceslas
Baking Wafers and Taking
them into the Rotunda. Scene
from the St. Wenceslas cycle on
the staircase of the Great Tower.
1360—1.

the master had command of a broad range of types.

: He was able to apply this on a large-sized painting of the Twenty-Four Elders Worshipping the Apocalyptical Lamb, which he did on the southern half of the wall in the western window recess. In its basic triple harmony of bright yellow, red and blue pigments, the crescendo of colour tones and the strong outline drawing of this picture of grandiose conception recalls the stained glass at Osek. But it shows at the same time that the master was approaching a softer conception of form in conformity with the general development of Bohemian painting of the time. The drawing of the lines, the aesthetic effect of which is increased by numerous pentimenti, is becoming looser. Along the hems of the cloaks decorative loop folds are modestly applied; these were a favourite of Master A who came from the west, but they were not unknown in Bohemian paintings beginning with the antiphonary of Queen Rycheza. The tufts of hair and the beards alone are painted in paste, otherwise the painting has a wealth of glazes to model the pale and the dark flesh tones. It is typical of the Emperor's liking for the exotic that negroes appear side by side with oriental types.

: As on the Morgan panels, space is achieved by the solid figures ranged in several strata one behind the

/101/
Master Oswald: Drawing of the Madonna with St. Wenceslas. Stockholm, Royal Library. After 1360.

/102/
St. John the Baptist. Sketched drawing on the northern wall of the Holy Rood chapel. Detail. Before 1360.

125

/103/
Holy Rood chapel. Interior by candle-light. Before 1367.

it possible to trace his activity up to the year 1368. Theodoric painted the monumental figure of the Apocalyptical Lord in the northern half of the western window recess. He decorated the wall of the north-eastern window recess with scenes of the Annunciation, the Visitation of the Virgin and the Adoration of the Magi. In the figure of King Balthazar he depicted Charles IV, who already during his lifetime was compared to the patriarchs of the Bible. In his near monochrome paintings Theodoric outdid the mighty physical shapes of the Master of

other. The picture gains dramatic effect by the gradation of the actions of worship and kneeling in several phases and the twisting of the heads at various angles, including lost profiles. The spatial impression is heightened by the stereometric form of the richly carved throne behind the figures in the lowest rows.   :

: The depiction of musical instruments is of great value to musicology. Each instrument is given with equal precision as in the still-lifes of the famous Dominican cycle by Tommaso da Modena at Treviso made in the year 1352. The old man in the second row (second from the left) is holding a musical instrument called 'ala bohemica' (Bohemian wing), which forty years earlier was depicted by Canon Beneš in the Passional of the Abbess Kunigunde. Nowhere else in Europe is there any other documentary proof of that instrument.   :

: After completing this picture the Master of the Emmaus Cycle began to paint the opposite wall of the recess where remnants of his strong outline drawing have been found. He could not finish this painting, however, for the only entrance to the chapel was blocked by scaffolding on which Oswald was painting the staircase cycle.   :

: It was not until the scaffolding was removed some time in the early 1360s that Master Theodoric, called Zelo, could take up work on decorating the Holy Rood chapel. Documents exist to show that Theodoric was imperial painter and owner of a house in Prague Hradčany in 1359. At that time he was Head ('First Master') of the Prague Brotherhood of Painters. A total of six written reports make

/104/
Tommaso da Modena: Triptych (The Virgin with St. Wenceslas and St. Palmatius). Detail. Holy Rood chapel. Probably 1356.

/ 105 /
Master of the
Emmaus Cycle:
The Worship of the Apocalyptical
Lamb. Mural painting in the
western window recess. Holy
Rood chapel. Before 1367.

the Emmaus Cycle, and he used more light to surpass Oswald in the use of colour. His figures are
immobile, spiritual in the extreme and have a special stiffness of expression.   :
: These features are also characteristic of the panel
paintings from Theodoric's workshop, which differ
from the master's murals by their broad range of
colour. He made an enormous set of one hundred
and thirty panels, the largest that is known and survived from any medieval painter. Apart from the
large-sized scene of the Crucifixion and the tripartite picture of Christ in the Tomb with Angels and
the Three Marys, these pictures represent larger-
than-lifesize semi-figures of apostles, holy virgins,
widows, knihgts, monarchs, abbots, bishops, popes,
Church fathers, prophets and angels. In type and
basic compositional design Theodoric was able to
follow the brush drawing of his predecessors.
A comparison with certain panels, e.g. St. Philip and

St. Matthew with John the Baptist on the fifteen years older stained glass at Osek, shows a broad relationship in the down-to-earth physiognomy. This might mean that Theodoric was a disciple of the Master of the Emmaus Cycle.
: A document dated 28 April 1367 is of considerable importance in assessing Theodoric's art. In it Charles IV remunerated the master for having decorated the Holy Rood chapel 'so ingeniously and artistically'. It follows from this document and other texts that Theodoric carried out the entire layout of the chapel according to the Emperor's directives. :
: On the vaulting and in the background of the mural paintings gilded covers of thin-walled Venetian glass were affixed to represent the sun, the moon, the planets and the fixed stars. On the figure of the angel in the Annunciation, painting is combined with squares of gold foil to imitate a mosaic. The recess above the altar, where the imperial coronation treasure was kept, the sanctuary, the ribs of the jambs and the tracery in the windows as well as the frames of the panel pictures were covered with thick layers of gilded stucco. This is hallmarked in the same way as the richly stuccoed and gilded applications on the pictures. The four foliated capitals on the corners of the window recesses are similarly

treated with gilded stucco. The knowledge of this age-old technique, which was of Persian origin, was kept alive throughout the Middle Ages by the Arabs.
:
: The lower strip of the walls is incrusted with little polished slabs of jasper, chalcedony, onyx, agate, amethyst and cornelian brought from the rich deposits around Dresden. Polished gemstones are suspended on the gilded ironwork grille, which is probably the work of smith Wenceslas in Peter Parler's lodge. The grille divides the nave of the chapel from the presbytery, the floor of which was covered with green and red glazed tiles.
:
: The lower part of the windows had infills in the form of mosaics of yellowish semi-precious stones and quartz of purple hue, and there was probably stained glass in the upper parts, perhaps destroyed during the Hussite siege to the castle in 1422. The main source of light in the chapel were four crystal lamps and more than five hundred and seventy candles, affixed on iron spikes on the walls. The polished gemstones and the gilded glass lids scattered their light in innumerable reflections. The small patches of gilded stucco with their hallmarks would glitter in such a light. Charles's writings show that the Emperor was interested in the neo-Platonic Au-

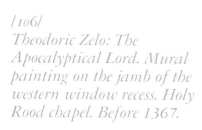

/106/
Theodoric Zelo: The Apocalyptical Lord. Mural painting on the jamb of the western window recess. Holy Rood chapel. Before 1367.

/107/
Theodoric Zelo: The Adoration of the Magi. Mural painting on the jamb of the north-eastern window recess. Holy Rood chapel. Before 1367.

/108/
Theodoric Zelo: The Crucifixion.
Panel picture. Holy Rood chapel.
Before 1367.

gustinian metaphysics of light. It was his intention that the lighting of the Holy Rood chapel should enhance the 'splendour of the Empire'. :

: With its ostentatious magnificence this chapel recalls Early Christian and Byzantine interiors adorned with mosaics and incrustation of polished gemstones. An example of this is the basilica at Parenzo (Poreč) in Istria, which Charles passed on his journey in 1337. Later Theodoric followed in his footsteps. He would have visited Venice, where he must have seen certain Byzantine elements and principles of art. ⸱ :

: The panels on the walls of the Karlstein Holy Rood chapel fulfil a function different from that of the pictures in the western Christian regions. They serve as reliquaries. Following the eastern custom their frames held relics covered with crystals or cameos. Furthermore, Theodoric's panels form a pictorial wall in the manner of the iconostasis such as Charles and his painter might have seen at St. Mark's in Venice or in the cathedral on Torcello Island. :

: A characteristic feature of Theodoric's painting is the treatment by which the haloes and parts of the figure overlap the frame. This treatment was unknown in the west, but it can be found on Byzantine and Russian icons of that period. Up to the Hussite wars the Karlstein pictures of the Holy Rulers were partly covered with gold or silver shields. A pattern for this combination of goldsmithing with painting was provided by the gold and silver covers of Byzantine icons. One of these, the Madonna Nicopeia, is kept in St. Mark's to this day.

: Some of Theodoric's saints of strict appearance, with eyes open as if in a trance, follow the semi-figures of the apostles made by the Master of Caorle. This eminent Venetian artist stands out for the somewhat Macedonian character of his works. Following the pattern of Paolo Veneziano, Theodoric often covered large areas with almost non-articulated draperies. His close relation to the region of Veneto is shown also by still-lifes with scribes' tools on the pictures of the Church Fathers. Here the Prague master came up to the standard of Tommaso da Modena's still-lifes on his Dominican cycle at Treviso. :

: The plan of decoration at Karlstein was later applied in different versions elsewhere. Historical reports speak of the decorations of the imperial castle at Tangermünde in Brandenburg made not long after 1373. The great hall of that castle was adorned with pictures of Charles IV and the electors and a scene of a tournament. There were, further, pictures of the kings of Bohemia. At Tangermünde as at Karlstein castle gemstones and gilded glass lids were used to decorate the interior. Similar decorations can be assumed to have existed also in some other of Charles's castles where unfortunately they have vanished without trace. :

/109/
Theodoric Zelo: St. Theodorus.
Panel picture (painter's
self-portrait?). Holy Rood chapel.
Before 1367.

/111/
*Prague castle with Charles
Bridge. Bridge founded in 1357.*

Chapter VIII

Prague
as the Residential Town
of the Empire

One of the causes of the decline of imperial authority in the culminating Middle Ages lay in the fact that no emperor was personally able to deal with all the acute problems that arose simultaneously in various parts of the enormous territory of the Holy Roman Empire. Not even Charles was able to do this although he spent a great deal of his life in the saddle. His friend Francesco Petrarch bitterly complained that he did not stay in Rome to rule the world from there as Augustus had done. Later complaints were voiced that Charles, to whom the Archbishop of Prague gave in memoriam the proud title of the ancient emperors 'pater patriae', father of the country, was, in fact, stepfather of the empire, for he neglected German affairs. It would equally be possible to complain that after his coronation at Arles in 1365 Charles spent little time in the Kingdom of Arles, which also formed part of the Roman Empire. But if we look into his itineraries, we discover that he traversed and retraversed the whole of Germany.   :

: In his journeying he stayed most frequently at the imperial castle in Nuremberg. Not far from Nuremberg, in the little town of Lauf on the river Pegnitz, he set up a Bohemian mint and built a fortress. In it have been found about one hundred and thirty coats of arms of the Bohemian Estates at the court of Charles, engraved into sandstone.   :

: In 1349 Charles ordered the Nuremberg Council to build the main market place—the Hauptmarktplatz—on the site of the ghetto which had been laid waste during a pogrom. Its dominating feature is the church of Our Lady and St. Wenceslas, today's Frauenkirche. The building, consecrated in 1358, is the old type with square nave and aisles, three times three vaulting compartments, a pentagonal choir and an ostentatious porch. The statues in the choir, made by Nuremberg stone-cutters, included one of St. Wenceslas. The slightly later and in style more advanced stone work in the nave and porch of the church were made in Parler's masonic lodge. An astronomical clock was installed in the porch. It depicted Charles IV on the throne and to him at noon every day the Electors paid their respects as they passed in solemn procession while trumpeters set their instruments to their lips. Such mechanisms existed already in antiquity. There was an alle-

/112/
Nuremberg. Imperial castle.
Founded in the 12th century. One
of the residences of Charles IV.

gory of Charles and his son Wenceslas, who was born in Nuremberg on 26 February 1361, on a painting, today destroyed, in the St. Maurice chapel of the St. Sebald church. The scene of Charles's betrothal to Anne of Świdnica was shown even in this sacred setting as a gallant scene in the garden of love. Records exist to show that the Emperor rewarded the Nuremberg painter Sebald Weinschrötter in 1360 for work done. :
: By the time of his two coronations as King of Rome (Bonn 1346, Aachen 1349) Charles had already decided to make Prague his residence. For it was not only the capital of the Kingdom of Bohemia, but also the centre of a strategical triangle formed by his three minor domains: Luxemburg, Mazovia near the Lithuanian border and Belluno-Feltre outside Venice. (The eastern Silesian border of Charles's state reached almost to the outskirts of Krakow, the residential town of the Kings of Poland.) As the 'first merchant on the imperial throne' Charles was aware that the capital of Bohemia lay at an

equal distance from the Rhine, the Vistula, the North Sea, the Baltic Sea and the Adriatic Sea. The old trade route from Venice to Gdansk, Riga and Novgorod passed through Prague and to ensure its safety the Emperor had Wrocław castle built in 1359 and the city's suburbs enlarged and fortified. This route linked the waterways of the river Vltava and the Elbe between Prague and Hamburg and other Hanseatic towns. One of these was Tangermünde in Brandenburg on the lower Elbe where, in 1374, Charles began extensive work on fortifications. Even when he was improving the layout of Nuremberg he must have had Prague in mind, for Nuremberg provided protection for the trade route linking it with Frankfurt and Cologne. Trade with distant places brought numerous foreign merchants and their servants to Prague, among them even Saracens. By raising the Prague bishopric to the status of archbishopric in 1344, Charles speeded up the concentration of priests and church schools. Apart from the old metropolitan 'studium particulare'

/113/
View of Prague. Woodcut in the
Chronicle of the World by
H. Schedel. Nuremberg 1493.

Prague had three colleges and twenty-nine parish schools. This provided suitable prerequisites for the development of higher education when, in 1347—8, on pattern of Paris and Bologna, Charles established a university in Prague. The number of students from the whole of Europe enrolled at Prague university ranged from ten to thirty-four thousand. Many magnates and princes, usually accompanied by their entire courts, came to visit Charles. The Elector of Saxony took up permanent residence in Prague from 1346.

: Prague's international significance rose in 1350 when the imperial crown jewels were brought there from Germany. They were known as 'das Riche', i.e. the Empire, and were identified with the Holy Roman Empire. For their safekeeping Charles had Karlstein castle built. The very act of transferring the jewels was a bold break with tradition, but to some extent it merely reproduced the example of the Holy Emperor Constantine the Great, who moved the imperial residence from Rome into the new geographical and ethnic setting of Constantinople. Charles was always stressing the continuity of the Empire from its Roman beginnings. He believed that he had inherited the blood of the Emperors Diocletian and Maximian through his mother Elizabeth Přemyslide. Both emperors were considered of Slavonic origin, as natives of Dalmatia. Charles showed a lively interest in the biographies of the Roman emperors and he collected their portraits. After his return from his first Roman expedition in August 1355, the Great Hall of Prague castle was adorned with some 120 panel paintings representing Ninus, Alexander of Macedonia, Tolus, Romulus, and Roman and Constantinople emperors. Inscriptions referring to these pictures have partly survived.

: In 1370 the Emperor had the roofs of the two towers of Prague castle gilded 'for them to shine and reflect the sun over a great distance'. In this manner he endeavoured to make Prague resemble 'golden Rome' ('aurea Roma') and Constantinople. Prague came to rival these cities in consequence of the revolutionary changes that Charles introduced in its layout. The territory inside its fortifications rose to 7.5 square kilometres and the number of inhabitants grew to an estimated 85,000.

: In the Document of Foundation of the New Town of Prague, dated 28 March 1348, Charles called his residence 'a town of birth and education... which town We took a liking to in Our young days'. He states that the houses and buildings in this town 'cannot in any manner accommodate their inhabitants comfortably', the less so 'the nations of different regions and parts of the world... and the crowds of people that no one can count...' For that reason he had with foresight availed himself of the fact that the town lies in a fertile landscape in the geologically highly advantageous Prague basin, with its ample supplies of spring water. He purchased land on the right bank of the river Vltava, which surrounds the Old Town in the south-eastern section like a large ring stretching from the river below Vyšehrad castle as far as the river at Poříčí. (On that land there had been, up to that time, some scattered parishes and a total of fifteen churches.) In the years 1348—50 Charles had the outer side of that ring surrounded by fortifications with towers and gates over a total length of 3,430 m. For this he needed more than 100,000 cubic metres of stone. The remains of the fortifications and later depictions of the system bring to mind the third ring of fortifications in Florence. The houses built on this land are similarly of the southern Mediterranean type. They were placed at the disposal of the inhabitants. According to a rough estimate 1,450 houses were built in the New Town in the years 1348 to 1367. At the same time construction work began on five new monasteries, four churches, two hospitals, a town hall and a market hall.

: In the whole of contemporary Europe there was no other town where such extensive building activity was undertaken over an area of 2.4 square kilometres. While in other medieval towns the width of the streets ranged from 3.5 to 7 metres, in the New Town of Prague the streets were laid out to a width of 18 to 27 metres. The largest of the three market places, the Cattle Market (today's Charles Square) is 80,550 square metres in size, an area not even approached by the Place de la Concorde in Paris, the largest 18th century square. The area occupied by private houses, courtyards, cemeteries and gardens was also exceptionally large. The advantages of this environment appear the more striking if compared with the Prague Jewish Town, where some 12,000 inhabitants lived crowded together on 0,32 square kilometres of built-up area. The entire New Town was built to a consummate plan which followed the age-old practices of the Roman surveyors-agricensors, applying a knowledge of astronomy. :

: Charles's intention to link up his New Town with the Old Town into a single unit can be seen in the manner in which the eastern Hill Route (today's Hybernská Street) leads straight into Celetná Street, the way to the Old Town Square. The axis of the New Town, the Horse Market (today's Wenceslas Square) with a length of 750 metres, was laid out at right angles to the south-eastern section of the Old Town fortifications. When these fortifications were taken down on Charles's orders in 1367 and the moat was filled in, there arose a place called 'Můs-tek', 'Little Bridge'—to this day the busiest cross-roads in the whole of Prague. It is highly likely that the plan that provided for the exceptional size of the Cattle Market catered for annual exhibitions of the imperial crown jewels and Charles's reliquaries. The square was to be the grandiose meeting place for tens of thousands of pilgrims.   :

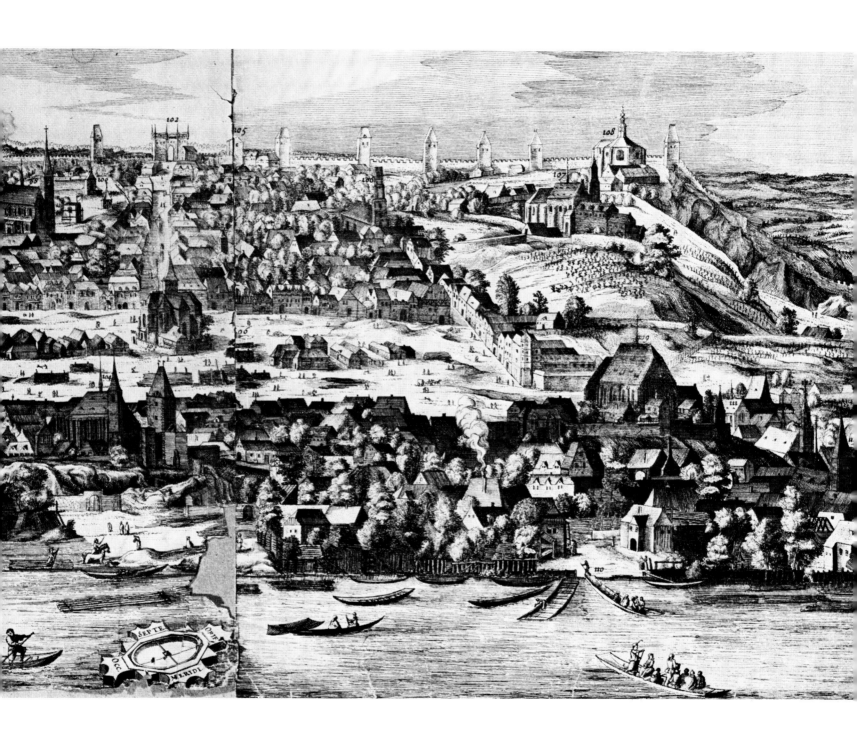

/114/
View of Prague. Detail. Cattle Market (now Charles Square) in the New Town. Drawn by Philip van den Bossche, engraved by John Wechter. Published by Aegidius Sadeler in 1606.

/115/
The monastery church of Our Lady and St. Charlemagne in the New Town, at Karlov. Founded in 1350. (Renovated in the 18th century).

: A very interesting layout of ecclesiastical buildings occurred on the rising terrace at the upper or south-eastern part of the New Town. Here the east-west link of the Slavonic abbey with that of the Karlov monastery and the north-south link of the church of Our Lady on the Grass with St. Catherine's form an exact cross. The centre point of its arms is the church of St. Apollinaris. The foundation of city units in the form of a cross follows the old conviction that in this manner the town becomes a likeness of the heavenly Jerusalem and enjoys special protection. Inside the fortifications the plan left ample space for subsequent building work undertaken by Wenceslas IV and this space proved sufficient for the growth of the town for the best part of five hundred years. :

: It has rightly been said that in the case of the New Town of Prague one cannot properly speak of 'a medieval town at all', for 'in its functional ground-plan the Middle Ages had long finished'. We are dealing here with a 'work anticipating the new era, a rebirth—renaissance—of humanist principles'. But there was only one way to this new era—via

antiquity. Only in that way can one explain the non-medieval dimensions of the network of streets in the New Town. In front of St. Gallus's church in the Old Town a building literally antique-Renaissance in type and function was erected in the years 1359 to 1361—a textile store called 'Booths', in the form of a low basilica with transept, almost 200 metres long and 22.6 metres wide. This building served its purpose until 1891 when it had to give way to the headquarters of a savings bank. In the recent period the remarkable discovery was made that the manner in which the New Town was founded corresponded to the requirements formulated by Vitruvius, the Roman theoretician of architecture. His work was copied in one of the manuscripts in the Prague Chapter Library from about the middle of the fourteenth century. :

: Among others, Vitruvius recommended that '... the sacred temples of the gods whose protection the community enjoys most... should be given sites on the highest points from where the major part of the town can be viewed'. On the left bank of the river Vltava such a place was taken up by the

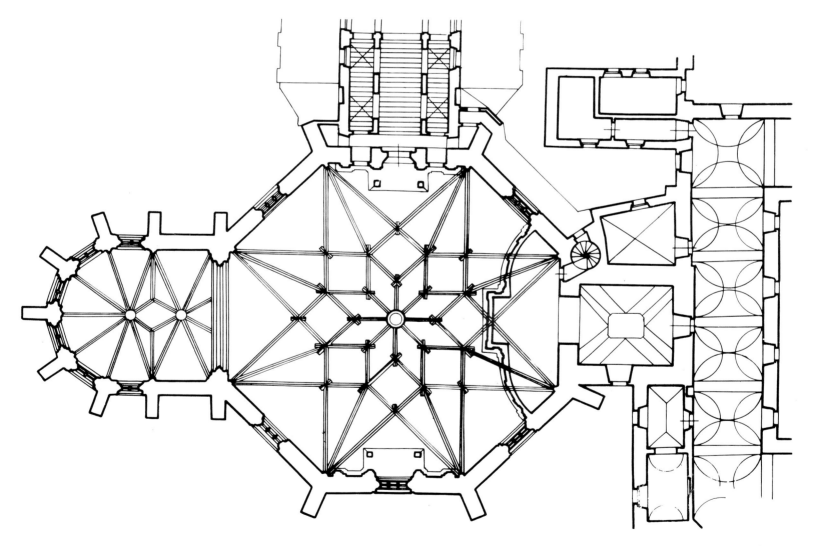

/116/
Ground-plan of the monastery church of Our Lady and St. Charlemagne in the New Town, at Karlov. Founded in 1350.

tomb of St. Wenceslas, above which Prague cathedral was built.

: The highest point in the New Town at its furthest south-eastern end by the tower of painters and gable-makers used to be known as 'Mons Caroli'. It was at this point that, in 1350, Charles founded the monastery of the Lateran Augustinian canons, consecrated to his other saintly ancestor, the Emperor Charlemagne. The elongated presbytery of the monastery church leads into an octagonal nave, which probably was to have been roofed over by a vault on four piers. In ground-plan this church was to remind its founder of his coronation as King of Rome in the Aachen palace chapel of Charlemagne in 1349.

: At the lower, northern end of the New Town stands the parish church consecrated to the last Ottonian emperor St. Henry, another link in the imperial tradition. This church is a hall type with nave and aisles of equal height and has three times four vaulting compartments. Its only tower rises out of the southern square at its western façade. One of its characteristic features is the contrast between the comparatively low, broadly spread interior and the high tent-shaped roof rising to a slim sanctus tower.

: To St. Catherine, to whom he owed his first victory near San Felice, Charles built a votive convent of the Augustinian nuns in 1355—67. It was the only nunnery in the New Town. On the western façade of the convent church stood a tall tower, the only part that has survived. It is reminiscent of the tower on the façade of the little church of Our Lady on the Grass (Na slupi) in the upper New Town, part of the former monastery of the Servites whom Charles called from Florence in 1360. This miniature structure is effective through the intimacy of its square nave with a vault resting on one slim column. The character of the little church, like the exclusiveness of the order, prevented it leaving any great influence on the wider public. The very foundation was private in character.

: The church of Our Lady of the Snows ('On the Sands') leaves an entirely different impression. It stood at the lower end of today's Wenceslas Square. It belonged to the monastery of the bare-footed Carmelites whom Charles summoned from the Rhineland in 1347. Originally this church was to have been built as a large three-naved basilica, roughly one hundred metres long and thirty-three metres high. This suggests that the order had great ambitions and at the beginning enjoyed the Emperor's support. The slim compound piers on which the walls of the long choir rest have sharp profiles. This suggests a certain relationship to the masonic lodge of court builder Matthias of Arras. The choir was consecrated as late as 1397 but construction did not continue. The Emperor seems to have lost interest in the Carmelites, and they did not succeed in obtaining funds elsewhere.

: Construction work did go ahead at great speed at the north-eastern end of the New Town at the monastery of the Benedictine Ambrosians from Milan. With its unusual liturgy the monastery was to remind Charles that on 5 January 1355 he was crowned King of Lombardy at Sant' Ambrogio in Milan. About 1502 the monastery was completely destroyed.

: Charles's greatest monastic foundation is the monastery of the Croatian Benedictines, the Glagolians, known as the Slavonic abbey (Na Slovanech). History has left so much evidence on this that a separate chapter is devoted to it.

: A bridge across the little river Botič linked the New Town on the southern side with Vyšehrad castle. On the site of its Romanesque hill fort, Charles had a stronghold built from 1348 on with new fortifications, the mighty Tábor Gate and a royal palace. Apart from the castle itself the grounds of Vyšehrad had four and a half hectares of buildings. Its dominant feature was the Romanesque chapter church of Sts. Peter and Paul, whose reconstruction continued after the Emperor's death. The castle and the church suffered bad damage during the battle of Prague in 1420.

: On the left bank of the river Vltava Charles did not limit himself to the construction of Prague castle and the cathedral. Here, too, he undertook major construction work essential to the extension and maintenance of the town fortifications. In 1358—60 he had a mighty line of fortifications set up, leading from the walls of the Premonstratensian monastery at Strahov across Petřín Hill down to the river, almost two kilometres in length. This provided protection from the south-west for the densely settled area of the Little Quarter and the parishes of Nebovidy and Újezd. A part of these fortifications, called the 'Hunger Wall' has survived to this day. On the north-western side, the towns of Hradčany, Pohořelec and the New World were surrounded with city walls. This completed the unification of Prague into one town where it had previously been split up into a number of quarters and parish settlements of various sizes.

: The whole of Prague was now divided only by the

/117/
*Prague, New Town. Church of
Our Lady of the Snows.
1347—97.*

river Vltava. On 9 July 1357 Charles solemnly laid the foundation stone for a new stone bridge across the river, to take the place of the Romanesque Judith Bridge, which had collapsed during the floods in 1342. The new bridge was built to a plan by Peter Parler, aided by Little Quarter stone-mason and councillor Jan Otlín. The bridge is 516 metres long and 9.5 metres wide. Its sixteen arches resting on sixteen mighty pillars form large semi-circular curves which, towards the centre of the bridge, rise to a complete semi-circle. At the same time its axis curves slightly in a gentle arch towards the water. :

: It has been pointed out that there is a similarity between Charles Bridge and the stone bridge that was built across the Mosel by Charles's great-uncle, the Archbishop—Elector Balduin in his residential town of Koblenz in 1343. The joint inspiration of the two bridges is revealed by two bridge arches below the statue of St. Vitus on the façade of the Old Town bridge tower. These arches faithfully reproduce the ancient Roman bridge across the Mosel in Balduin's main residence (and the one-time residence of Constantine the Great) at Trier. Charles used the ancient title of 'Augustus' in certain documents. By building a stone bridge he assumed another status of the ancient emperors 'pontifex', the bridge builder. He had another bridge built in 1370, crossing the Oder at Fürstenberg near Wrocław. :

: The very conception of the majestic statues of Charles and Wenceslas IV on the façade of the bridge tower is linked to all this. The statues express the joint reign of the last two years of Charles's life. Like Charlemagne, who had his son Louis the Pious crowned at Aachen in 813, Charles had his son Wenceslas crowned on 6 July 1376. Niccolò Beccari, in a letter to the Emperor, compared their reign to the joint triumph of the Emperor Vespasian and his son Titus. In a manuscript of the year 1400, containing the Golden Bull, this letter is accompanied by a miniature, which is a copy of the two statues on the façade of the Old Town bridge tower. :

/118/
Typological cycle in the cloisters of the Slavonic abbey: Israelites Gathering Manna. (Compartment XIV 2.) C. 1360.

Chapter IX

The Slavonic Abbey

At the beginning of 1346 Charles IV, the then Margrave of Moravia, went to Avignon to visit his former Parisian teacher, now Pope Clement VI. He spoke to him of the many things he had seen and learned during his travels about Europe: in Slavonia and in many other regions of the south the canons spoke the same language during church service as many schismatics in the countries surrounding the Kingdom of Bohemia. Charles was referring to the population of the Lithuanian-Russian region that bordered on the most easterly of the Luxemburg territories, Mazovia. On that occasion he requested the Pope to be allowed to select several suitable places and settle the south Slavonic monks there. The sceptical Pope granted him permission to set up only one monastery with the Church Slavonic liturgy, which Charles then established in Prague. On 28 December 1359 Pope Innocent VI conceded that the monks of that monastery might serve mass according to their rites even in other places, on condition that the Emperor was present. Not until two years after Charles's death, at the time of the dual popedom, was Prince Conrad II able to summon some of the south Slavonic monks from Prague to Silesia. He settled them at Oleśnica, on the important trade route that led from Venice to Riga and Novgorod. Ten years later King Jagello called monks from Prague to establish a subsidiary Slavonic monastery at Krakow on the crossroads with the no less important trade route linking the North Sea with Kiev and Constantinople. Both these foundations continued Charles's programme but its implementation was slowed down by obstacles raised on the part of the Popes.

: One of the striking features about Charles is that he was indefatigable in seeing that these two trade routes were kept in operation without interruption. His interests in eastern Europe were also due to the fact that Galicia was colonized from Silesia after 1349 as one of the lands of the Crown of Bohemia. While in Poland Charles tried openly to continue the policy of expansion initiated by Wenceslas II; but his plans for Russia remained somewhat obscure. He had an interesting passage inserted into the Pulkava's Chronicle: King Vratislav II and his successors were to be subject to the Margrave of Moravia for all time, together with Poland and with Russia, and the other dukedoms that had once belonged to the Great Moravian Empire.

: There can be little doubt that the development of Charles's European policy was hampered by the fatal consequences of the split in the Church, which divided the Christian world at the end of the eleventh century. Charles had personal interests in overcoming this schism. A proof of this can be found in a letter he sent on 19 February 1355 from Pisa to Stephen Dushan, the powerful 'Czar of the Serbs and Greeks', during his siege on Constantinople. In the letter Charles expressed pleasure at the fact that the addressee spoke the same 'noble Slavonic tongue'. The disagreements between Catholicism and the Orthodox Church were overcome, or at least lessened, by the monks of the Slavonic monasteries along the shores of the Mediterranean. For they kept up their age-old contacts with the Orthodox Balkan peninsula and with Russia but ac-

/119/
*Pašman Island near Zadar,
from where Charles summoned
Croatian Benedictines of the
Church Slavonic liturgy to
Prague in 1347.*

knowledged the Pope as the Head of the Church. Their literature contained translations both from Greek and from Latin.

: In 1347 some of these monks came to Prague, the majority from the ancient Benedictine abbey at Tkon on Pašman Island near Zadar on the Dalmatian coast. A few came from Senj, where Charles had been in 1337 and where his chaplain and counsellor, John Protiva of Dlouhá Ves, became bishop through Charles's intervention. The monks owed their exceptionally favourable position within the Bohemian Church organization to the legend that protected them from the attacks of the Latin clergy: the Church Slavonic liturgy with the Glagolitic script, it said, was formed by their famous ancestor St. Jerome, who was born in Stridon in Dalmatia. By chance, according to the Dalimil Chronicle, the original home of the Czechs also stretched along the shores of the Mediterranean Sea. For that reason the liturgical language of the south Slavonic monks (the Croatian version of Church Slavonic) was considered the language of the 'Old Czechs'.

: Charles announced in an epistle published on 21 November 1347 in Nuremberg that he was founding a new monastery in Prague 'in memory of St. Jerome, the eminent doctor of Stridon and renowned commentator and translator of the Holy Script from Hebrew to Latin and to the Slavonic tongue, from which the Slavonic speech of Our Kingdom of Bohemia surely derives'. For that reason it was his desire that the saint 'be given back to his nation and homeland'. In a document of 1 November 1352 he again thanked the south Slavonic monks that 'through them the Czech tongue is being adorned with the brilliance of greater honour'.

: In medieval sources Charles's greatest monastic foundation is called the 'monastery of St. Jerome the Slav' or 'Monasterium Slavorum'. The name 'Emmaus', by which it is known today, arose only in the seventeenth century. The monastery was consecrated by Archbishop John Očko of Vlašim on Easter Monday, 29 March 1372 in honour of the Virgin Mary, Sts. Jerome, Cyril, Methodius, Adalbert and Procopius. The Emperor took part in the celebrations with his son Wenceslas IV and the company of the entire court, at which, as usual,

Wenceslas, the Elector of Saxony, was residing. The Emperor's relatives who participated in the festivities included Wenceslas, Duke of Luxemburg and Brabant and Elector Jean de Ligne, Archbishop of Mainz. The Pope sent his legate, the Patriarch of Alexandria, while the King of Hungary was represented by Archbishop Thomas of Esztergom and the high royal official Vladislav of Opole, the King of France by his counsellor Aimeric de Maignac, Bishop of Paris. The presence of mitres and banners of numerous other archbishops and bishops as well

/120/
Pašman near Zadar, Benedictine monastery church. Detail of the façade. 14th—15th century.

147

as princes from all corners of Europe stressed the importance of the event. :
: The monastery was erected in the New Town of Prague, in the settlement of Podskalí on the territory of the Vyšehrad chapter. The latter linked it with a local tradition of Slavonic divine services, St. Methodius of Salonica and St. Procopius having once resided at Vyšehrad. Below this acropolis there was a church consecrated to St. Adalbert to whom, at the time, the 10th century Church Slavonic hymn 'O Lord, be merciful' was ascribed. In selecting a site for the monastery regard would have been paid to the fact that here stood the Romanesque parish church of Sts. Cosmas and Damian, whose consecration was identical to that of the old monastery on Pašman Island. The church in Senj had the same consecration. The Vyšehrad chapter transferred this church at Podskalí to the south Slavonic monks together with the neighbouring church of St. Nicholas and certain outbuildings. :
: Beneš Krabice, the chronicler, speaks of a 'work admirably built' when referring to the new monastery, which Charles built for the south Slavonic monks on an area of four hectares. Although the building was disfigured by baroque alterations, neo-Gothic adaptations and an air-raid on 14 February 1945, its original appearance dating back to the years 1348—72 has basically survived. :

: The main part is formed by the church of Our Lady and the Slavonic patrons. It was the largest church in Prague that was completed during the Emperor's lifetime. On its southern side its stability is ensured by a system of cathedral buttresses. The church had no towers on the western side and was entirely covered by a saddleback roof. The top of the slim sanctus tower in the centre of the roof ridge reached a height of almost fifty metres. Red and green glazed tiles were used as roof cover to contrast with the white walls. Since the church stood on a raised terrace above the right bank of the river Vltava, it was visible from afar. The interior can be reached through two original portals on the northern side and a renovated one on the western side. It was brightly lit by eighteen windows and could hold some 2,500 visitors. The nave and aisles

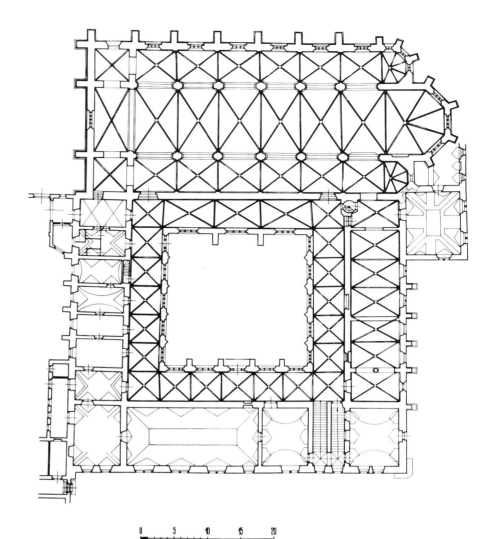

each have seven bays of cross vaulting and a pentagonal choir. The width of the two side aisles is half that of the nave, but they are identical in height. In other words, the church is a hall type and has the considerable length of fifty-four metres.

: In principle, that is the type that developed from the antique pattern of the Mediterranean area, especially in south-western France in the eleventh century. It was known to the Greek builders of St. Bartholomew's chapel at Paderborn, finished in 1017. In Bohemia and Moravia different versions of this type can be found, ranging from the Premonstratensian monastery church at Teplá, founded in 1193, to the nave of St. Barbara's at Kutná Hora, consecrated in 1548. This three-naved hall type appeared only sporadically at the beginning as compared with the predominant basilicas. In 1304 preference was given to it, as against the basilica type, in the foundation of St. Stephen's cathedral in Vienna, and this fact imprinted its mark upon the development of medieval architecture in central Europe. The Emmaus hall derived certain characteristics from the Danube basin. The shallow niches of its three choirs open along one level direct into the naves without triumphal arches and form part of them. Furthermore, the two side choirs lie parallel the main choir. An identical layout can be found in the brick-built hall of the church of Our Lady on the Sands at Wrocław founded in 1334. This similarity in design is hardly chance, for another Wrocław hall church, the Augustinian church of St. Dorothy, was founded by Charles IV.

: Two builders were in charge of the construction of the Slavonic church. The first, who built the choirs of the three naves, was somewhat conservative and used traditional cylindrical piers with geometrical and foliated capitals. Around 1367 another architect took over, and he proved far more progressive. Like the builder of the sacristy of the Augustinian church at Litomyšl he, too, rejected all traditional architectonic detail. He raised the arches of the arcades direct from twelve octagonal pillars. The ribs running out of the slanting springers on the piers and the outer walls plunge into flat moulding attached to the cornice below the windows.

/123/
Abbey church of Our Lady and the Slavonic Patrons. View of the vaulting. 1348 — 72.

: One can deduce from this that the second builder of the church made every effort to construct a unified, clear-cut and acoustically good interior, in which the specific features of the Slavonic liturgy could find full expression and where its words and songs could resound fully.   :

: On the southern side the original single-storeyed monasterial building (today two storeys high) lies alongside the entire length of the church. It was finished before 1367. It is built on the customary square ground-plan with a cloister garth in the centre. The ground floor of the entire eastern wing is taken up by one room with seven bays of cross vaulting. The monumental portal on its western side shows that at the time when the church of the Slavonic patrons was under construction, this room served as a sanctuary. Later it was changed into the chapter hall and imperial chapel. It escaped subsequent alterations by contrast to the refectory in the southern wing. The cloisters, built in 1353, have twenty-two compartments of cross vaulting and are lit by eighteen windows with pointed arches and renovated tracery. On the eastern and western side of the cloister garth there appears the picturesque motif of the two-sided buttress, used likewise by Peter Parler on the Golden Gate of Prague cathedral. In size the monasterial building corresponds to that of a well-furnished abbey and this tallies with the report that there were about one hundred monks. This unusually large number can be explained by the fact that the Pope did not permit Charles to set up another Church Slavonic monastery.   :

: The stone ornamentation in the abbey is modest on the whole. This is due to the intentional reduction of architectural elements. On the southern side of the main chancel of the abbey church a right-angled tripartite sedile dating from about 1350 has survived. The two dragon-like monsters upholding its pointed arches are worked somewhat superficially. But the two relief coats of arms above them are very fine. As a pendant to the Czech lion the Byzantine motif of the two-headed eagle appeared here for the first time in Bohemia. The same stone-cutter made the figural consoles supporting the tympanums of the two portals along the northern side of the church as well as the consoles and keystones in the cloisters. On one of the consoles foliage hides a mask of a demon with branches growing out of his mouth. It represents a creature which in medieval Bohemian sources is called 'faunus'. These sculptures give the impression of improvization on the part of the sculptor. Both have typical contrasts of volume modelled softly, as though of mud, and sharp edges giving decorative outlines.   :

: The main ornamentation in the monastery was carried out in the form of mural painting. Before 1353 an unknown master covered the jambs of the portals to the imperial chapel with painted coats of arms, showing the royal lion of Bohemia and the imperial eagle. The emblems are composed as trefoils with an illusive plastic conception and a clear colour scheme that points to a painter of Italian orientation. Later, but certainly before 1372, the coats of arms of the lands ruled over by Charles were painted on the eastern side of the vaulting in the nave of the monastery church. A total of eight of these have survived, though in very poor condition. These paintings show Charles's liking for heraldry and the representation of his majesty as a reigning monarch.   :

: The world fame of the Slavonic monastery is based on its cycle of paintings. Originally this covered the outer peripheral wall of all four wings of

/124/
Sedile in the main choir of the church with the coats of arms of the Emperor and the Kingdom of Bohemia. C. 1350.

the cloisters, making a total length of 130 metres. It consisted of eighty-five scenes designed as two strips in each compartment. About one third were destroyed during an air-raid on 14 February 1945 and exist only on older photographs. Some of the pictures suffered damage so badly that this could not be made good even by post-war restoration work. In the course of this work most of the paintings were conserved after the over-painting had been removed. Although the cycle is a mere torso today, it is one of the most extensive and artistically most valuable sets of mural paintings north of the Alps.   :

: The iconographic composition of the cycle, in which scenes of the Old Testament are confronted with those in the New Testament, is based on the method of typological parallelism. This is basically contained already in the Bible and early Christian art and theologically elaborated in the writings of the Church fathers. In the Czech Lands this approach can already be found in the illuminations of the Vyšehrad evangeliarium of King Vratislav II dated 1080. In decorating the cloisters of the Slavonic monastery, this old method was chosen since it best corresponded to the cult of the main patron, the greatest biblicist, St. Jerome. This same biblicism found expression in the Latin Emmaus Bible, the oldest Bohemian Bible of Leskovice or Dresden (of the sixties of the 14th century), and in the Bohemian Glagolitic Bible of the year 1416. To this can be added the Glagolitic manuscript of Czech and Croatian translations of Bible commentaries.   :

: Though the iconographical pattern for the Emmaus cycle can be found in contemporary typological compendiums (Speculum humanae salvationis, Biblia pauperum, etc.) its set cannot be regarded as a mere compilation. The endeavour to express complex symbolical content can be seen in frequent deviations from the iconographical tradition, even from the literal wording of the Bible. For instance, the scene of the stoning of Christ does not take place in the Temple (St. John, 10,23) but in a vineyard so that, at the same time, it represents the parable of the wicked husbandmen (St. Matthew, 21,23).   :

: A highly original scene is to be found in the sixth compartment, based on the Apocrypha, where the Sibyl shows the Emperor Augustus a woman in the sun. Here the Sibyl is not depicted in the customary manner as an old woman but as a beautiful young woman on a throne holding the attributes of a monarch. This picture is succeeded by a mural on the same subject at Libiš (c. 1390), one of the villages whose name was derived in the Middle Ages from the original matriarch of the Přemyslides, Princess Libuše. In Bohemia the Sibyl used to be identified with Libuše and the Queen of Sheba. According to the 'Prophecy of the Sibyl Libuše' popular at the

time, which Marignolli included in his chronicle, Charles's mother Elizabeth was to give birth to a son 'who will shine like the sun and reign over many kingdoms'.   :

: It is significant for dating the Emmaus cycle that a number of the scenes represent the multiplication and the consumption of manna, bread, fishes, oil and wine as well as the raising of the dead, healing of the lepers and clearing of infested waters. This must be regarded as a reflection of the famine and

pestilence that befell Bohemia in the years 1358—62. It was at that time that Charles had the Hunger Wall built and Archbishop Ernest of Pardubice had corn distributed among the people. It can further be shown that the cycle originated at that time since some of its scenes and figures became patterns for the illuminators of the Vyšehrad antiphonary, made in the years 1360—1, and of the Latin Emmaus Bible.   :

: The cycle is important to us since its major part was made by three of Charles's court painters. Furthermore, they signed their work but in the specific medieval manner: with the aid of three different types of architectonic elements that divide the two Old Testament scenes in the lower strip of the individual fields.   :

: The first painter used painted Gothic piers at this point. This artist illustrated the major part of the southern wing of the cloisters (compartments IV-VII) and painted three pictures in the XXIInd compartment, the last but one in the eastern wing. His painting is flat in conception and has a calmly balanced design. Even the scenes where he was forced to depict a larger number of people have all the heads on the same level. But he more often used isolated figures surrounded by large empty patches of a blue background. The pictures are worked to a strictly geometrical plan with symmetry, with the triangle and diagonals as determining elements. The characteristic features of the naturalistically conceived male heads and the pleasant women's faces make it possible to identify this painter with Master A, who, around 1357, was working on the paintings on the second floor of the church tower at Karlstein castle.   :

: The Woman Clothed in the Sun, which this painter painted in the VIth compartment of the cloisters has an interesting typological precedent on an enamel medallion in the Arts and Crafts Museum in West Berlin. The amulet came into existence around 1340 in the Upper Rhineland, probably as a miniaturized copy of some venerated west German picture or statue. A comparison also arises with certain illustrations in the Strasbourg manuscript of Heinrich Seuso's Exemplar, although they were made at a slightly later date (c. 1365) and do not attain the quality of the work of Charles's painter. Both these comparisons seem to suggest that Master A was identical with Nicholas Wurmser of Strasbourg. The village of Mořina near Karlstein castle, where this imperial painter owned a farmstead before 21 November 1359, is included in the registry of the Slavonic abbey for the years 1352—65.   :

: In a document dated Karlstein castle, 17 July 1359 Charles settled certain of the Emmaus affairs. It may well have been that he sent Wurmser to Prague at that time to decorate the abbey cloisters.

It is strange that after that initial picture in the southern wing of the cloisters the master interrupted his work and returned to it only towards the end of the whole cycle. During this period a document was issued at Avignon, dated 20 January 1360. In it the Pope permitted the confessor to grant Wurmser absolution 'in articulo mortis'. The painter had either fallen ill or he was afraid of being infected with the plague.   :

: In an imperial document of 26 December 1360 there is no mention of the fact that Wurmser was to exert greater efforts in painting 'places and castles to which he is to be sent' as in an older document of 21 November 1359, but only of his preceding 'multiple merits'. From this one might deduce that Wurmser had done his chief work for Charles before 1360. This makes Master A the oldest of a whole group of imperial painters of mural pictures.   :

: The pictures that this master made in the cloisters of the Slavonic abbey show that he had been trained in Paris and Siena. He kept in touch with the development of French art. The woman standing on a serpent, which he painted in the Vth compartment of the cloisters, represents the 'pelerin' type of Madonna. This type was only just appearing on the Ile-de-France.   :

: An important relationship, iconographically and partly also in style, links the attuned panel painting of Annunciation with a picture on the same subject now in the Sachs Collection in Cleveland, Ohio. That picture was made in a French, probably Parisian, workshop under the influence of Italian masters at Avignon, especially Matteo Giovanetti. The Prague painting, however, is closer to the Gothic art of Simone Martini, whose angel in the famous Antwerp Annunciation can be considered the prototype of the Emmaus Angel. To this should be added the relatively complex architectonic background in the IVth compartment, where the town in the left-hand upper section gives the impression of the veduta on the picture of the Good Government by Ambrogio Lorenzetti in the Siena town hall, made in the years 1337—9.   :

: Master A, who painted the head of the Lord in the IVth compartment, used a rare Byzantine motif of a polygonal halo. The original layout of the scenes

/126/
Typological cycle in the cloisters of the Slavonic abbey: Crowned Sibyl on the Throne. Detail. (Compartment VI.) C. 1360. (Condition before the abbey was bombed on 14 February 1945.)

/127/
Typological cycle in the cloisters of the Slavonic abbey. The Annunciation. (Compartment VII a.) C. 1360.

in this field is an interpretation of the Good Friday Matins hymn of the eastern liturgy (Makarismoi), contained in the Prague Glagolitic Fragments.

Far more advanced in style of painting are the pictures along the entire western and north-western wings of the cloisters (compartments VIIb—XVIIa), to which the final scenes on compartment Ia belong. The pictures along the lower strip of these compartments are divided by unusual antiquated pilasters with fluting and low capitals. These features distinguish it from the preceding group of paintings. As the second part of the cycle is the most important in scope and artistic value, the artist who made it is known as the Master of the Emmaus Cycle. The parts of the scenes that survive in best condition are identical in style, colour and technical execution with those that he made on the second floor of the church tower and in the Holy Rood chapel at Karlstein castle in the years 1357—9. It is possible to trace even older works by the same master. The Christ on the Emmaus Raising of the Young Man of Naim recalls St. John the Baptist on the stained glass at Osek. The two figures are identical in their posture, the broad shoulders, and wavy outline of the pliant draperies. Some of the heads, bent forwards or backwards, in the cycle have no less close analogies on the Morgan panels.

In a number of his highly narrative scenes, the artist intentionally rejected the principle of flat symmetry which had been binding for his predecessor. He managed to rouse a dramatic effect by means of irregular caesuras. He never hesitated to place figures on two or more spatial planes. Sometimes he placed them along the edge of an ellipse —on the picture of the Gathering of Manna even along the margins of two intertwined ellipses. By movements in opposite directions and by overlaying these figures he creates the impression of spatial depth. Some scenes include architectural interiors in depth and advanced landscape motifs, such as trees with large crowns which did not fit into the area of the picture.

The Master of the Emmaus Cycle owed much to north Italian painting. From Tommaso da Modena, who painted at Treviso and on Charles's personal fiefdom at Feltre, he adopted pre-Renaissance analytical realism. Examples of this can be found in the

similarity in type of the unconventional heads depicted at various angles. The Gathering of Manna is a simplified version of the principles applied on Tommaso's Martyrdom of St. Ursula at Treviso. :
: The painter found an even more important example in the work of the great Paduan-Venetian artist Guariento di Arpo. In his cycle of the History of Abraham in the Cappella dei Carraresi at Padua, the crowds of agile figures are linked with steep rocky cliffs and three dimensional but slightly undersized architecture in a similar manner as in the Slavonic abbey. Some of the male heads of the Master of the Emmaus Cycle likewise follow up the painting of Guariento and his Venetian disciple Nicoletto Semitecolo. The latter has been identified as the artist who made the cartoon for the mosaic on the Golden Gate of Prague cathedral. :

: The outlook of the abbey in general explains why the Master of the Emmaus Cycle applied certain motifs and types of Byzantine origin in his work. These can be found on the scene of Christ Feeding the Five Thousand, along the upper edge of which the persons eating are reclining on an ancient triclinium. The master might well have come across this motif—unique in its kind—on the mosaic with the History of Joseph in the narthex of St. Mark's. :
: The viner Nabot on another Emmaus scene corresponds by the exceptionally complex position of his limbs to the Child on the Byzantine Pelagonitissa by the Venetian Master of the Leningrad Diptych. This type of picture served as pattern for the Bohemian painter of the Karlsruhe diptych. :
: Around the middle of the fourteenth century Venetian illuminators of the History of Troy used the pattern of the famous Greeco-Syrian manuscript of the Vienna Genesis from the 6th century, which was then in the possession of the Doge. In it we can find the prototype of some of the Emmaus figures, e.g. the Pharisees in the dramatic Stoning of Christ. Such patterns might have found their way into the master's pattern-book—and from there to the walls of the cloisters, through the mediation of Venice. But the possibility exists that the master had access to a similar early Byzantine manuscript in Charles's library. :

: Of the paintings that the third important master contributed to the decorations of the cloisters, only the heads of four angels have survived. They are to be found on compartment Ia and there are a few dilapidated fragments in parts of the southern wing (compartments XVIIb to XXI). The fragments of little pillars dividing the pictures in the lower strip are again different in form and colour from the architectonic features used by the two preceding masters.   :

: The fragments are only partly identifiable. Mannneristically elongated figures can be distinguished in the Scourging of Christ contrasting with the

mighty figures of mercenaries on the Resurrection depicted in radical foreshortening. The brushwork is characteristic of Master Oswald, who made the cycle of St. Ludmilla and St. Wenceslas on the staircase of the Great Tower at Karlstein castle. This would give a firm basis for dating the two cycles. Oswald must have begun the ornamentation of the Emmaus cloisters in compartment Ia before 1360. Then he interrupted the work for a long time, obviously because he had been summoned to do the decorations on the Karlstein staircase. When that task was completed, he returned to the Slavonic abbey, probably in 1361.   :

: All these three painters were outstanding artists. Master A, probably to be identified with Nicholas Wurmser of Strasbourg, used the western European tradition of the calligraphic line. The Master of the Emmaus Cycle became known for the robustness and agility of his figures. Oswald cultivated light plastic modelling by means of light. Their cooperation in decorating Karlstein castle, the Emmaus cloisters and undoubtedly other buildings which have not come down to our days, did not take place without certain mutual influences. There may well have been some interchange of workshop pattern-books. Only in this manner can one explain, for instance, the identical depiction of the tall oak forest on the Emmaus Flight to Egypt and on the 17th scene of the St. Wenceslas cycle. The architecture of both these cycles reveals Parlerian motifs.

/132/
The Ascension of Christ.
Vyšehrad antiphonary. Vorau,
Chorherrenstift. 1360—61.

Similarly, they made use of certain common types and schemes of movement.

The rest of the abbey furnishings suffered from the tooth of ages even more than did the cycle of paintings in the cloisters. The extensive library was scattered during the attack of the Passau soldiers in 1611 and all that remains are some fragments and manuscripts dispersed to various places. They show that the actual purpose of the institution was the teaching of language, which was to complement studies at the Latin university for educated persons of the time. The Stockholm Abecedarium made for Diviš, the abbot of the main Benedictine monastery at Břevnov near Prague, is a type of special textbook. It contains the Hebrew, Greek, Latin, Glagolitic and Cyrillic alphabets with explanatory notes.

The Strahov fragment of a Church Slavonic missal, written parallel in Croatian Glagolitic and the Latin script was to serve as workbook for the priests with a Latin education. The writings of a number of medieval scholars show that their authors had attended language courses at the Slavonic abbey. For instance, the Glossary of Master Bartholomew of Chlumec (said Klaret) in which the Emperor himself participated as author contains Greek words translated by Church Slavonic expressions.

It was the Emmaus monks who recognized the origin of the eleventh century Cyrillic pericope which the founder presented to their monastery as an alleged autograph by St. Procopius of Sázava.

/133/
Philosopher and Astronomer.
Drawing cut out of a workshop
pattern-book. Erlangen,
Universitätsbibliothek. C. 1370.

They correctly ascertained that the pericopes were written 'to the Russian law', 'in Russian lettering', (i.e. in Cyrillic). That is what is said in the Czech-Glagolitic colophon of the illuminated Church Slavonic offices, which in 1395 were bound with the pericopes as the Rheims evangeliarium. In 1452 a Hussite deputation took the codex as a gift to Constantinople and from there it was later taken to Rheims. It was used there when the kings of France took the oath during their coronations. Its Cyrillic part was not deciphered until Tsar Peter I did so during his visit to France. Around 1370 the Tursko fragment of a Glagolitic psalter came into existence with a badly damaged miniature. It depicts the Slavonic Abbot Paul I the Bear, worshipping Christ Enthroned.   :

: A picture of St. Jerome Healing the Lion, of Venetian-Dalmatian origin, probably stood on the high altar of the abbey church as a number of works in the Czech Lands refer to it. The Emmaus Crucifixion came from the abbot's chapel of the Slavonic abbey. The master who painted that outstanding panel dating from c. 1370 knew the work of the artists who made the cycle in the cloisters. But he was even more strongly influenced by Master Theodoric.   :

: To the same workshop must be ascribed brush drawings at Erlangen and Dessau. The drawings in the same style formed part of an older strata of workshop pattern-books from the years 1370—1400, which were used in 1375 together with several Renaissance patterns by Matthew Ptáček-Ornys in his design for a new Karlstein family tree.   :

: A close connection to the Emmaus Crucifixion exists in the case of an older layer of paintings recently discovered by means of X-ray photographs below the later overpaintings on the Madonna of the Krakow Order of St. Augustine. The Madonna was made around 1370 for the monastery of that order at Roudnice. A pattern for it has been discovered in the western Ukrainian icon of the type of the Volhynian Mother of God. Such an icon was probably brought to Prague by Russian priests who served mass in the Slavonic tongue at the court of Wenceslas II. It is highly probable that Charles presented it to the Slavonic abbey where it was destroyed when the altar was laid waste in 1611.   :

/135/
*View of the vaulting of the
ambulatory of St. Vitus's
cathedral. 1344—85.*

Chapter X

Prague Cathedral

The culmination of Charles's efforts as a building entrepreneur and donor is St. Vitus's cathedral in Prague of which he and his father King John of Luxemburg laid the foundation stone on 3 March 1344. Charles did not live to see the completion of the building but there can be no doubt that he personally took the decisions as to its general artistic conception and that he approved the preliminary plans for each individual part according to which building work continued over many decades. :

: Continuity in the work was ensured by the second builder, Peter Parler, who as the Master of the King's Works headed the St. Vitus Masonic Lodge in the years 1356 to 1397. He then passed on the charge to his sons Wenceslas, John and Peter. In that sense the personality of Charles IV can be associated not only with the part of the building that came into existence during his lifetime, but with all that was built up to the year 1420: the choir, the southern façade of the transept with the Golden Gate and the big tower. The Renaissance choir by Boniface Wohlmut dates from the years 1559—61 as does the northern section of the transept. The long nave and the western façade of the cathedral with the two towers is the result of pseudo-Gothic construction work done in the 19th and 20th centuries. :

: In principle St. Vitus's cathedral was to use a traditional type of nave with side aisles with transept, chevet and a system of flying buttresses current in the west. The general conditions, however, made it necessary to introduce a number of specific features both on the inside and the outside of the building. They distinguish Prague cathedral from other cathedrals of the same type. :

: The first cathedrals, as is well known, came into existence from the twelfth century on in France and England in towns where bishops resided and chapters existed. The endeavour to lift them above the town as its dominant feature led to these buildings being raised to a great height. The record was reached with the tower of the cathedral at Beauvais, 153 metres high. :

: The construction of the greatly oversized big tower of Prague cathedral was interrupted by the Hussite wars at roughly half its planned height. (Its Renaissance spire dates from the years 1552—61.) The tower is 100 metres high. If St. Vitus's cathedral stood on the Old Town Square, it would rise above all the medieval buildings on the right bank of the river Vltava. In this it conforms to every other cathedral. :

: A special feature of Prague cathedral is its unusual site. It forms part of the building complex of Prague castle on the top of a steep terrace above the left bank of the river. The relatively great distance from the compact town on the opposite bank meant that there existed the danger that the cathedral would be cut off from it as an independent ideological and artistic unit, like the Romanesque church of St. George in its immediate vicinity. The danger was all the greater in that like that church, the cathedral stands exceptionally high above the town: its foundations were laid 75 metres above the level of the river so that the peak of the big tower rises 175 metres above the water. The roof ridge of the New Town church with the highest interior, Our Lady of the Snows, is about 120 metres lower than the top of the St. Vitus tower. :

: To achieve an artistic link between the cathedral and the town under those circumstances it was necessary to make radical changes in the traditional layout of the cathedral exterior. Prague cathedral is not organized in a simple manner from west to east as elsewhere but it is turned south, in the direction of the opposite bank of the river. The southern porch, the Golden Gate, faces in that direction with its large-sized mosaic; so, too, does the large tower and the huge window in the southern transept with its rich flamboyant tracery. The fact that the technically demanding and expensive construction of the tower was given priority over the completion of the transept and the nave confirms that the cathedral was planned to be viewed from the right bank. :

: In the Middle Ages Prague cathedral looked different from what it does today when only its roof and the upper part of the tower is visible behind the tall Theresian castle complex built by Nicolo Pacassi. Charles's palace, lower than its Jagiellon reconstruction, stood in front of the eastern part of the cathedral choir and the western parts of St. George's church. It hid the lower parts of the cathedral when viewed from the east. But it did not obstruct the view from the upper New Town and from Vyše-

/136/
Henry Parler the Elder and Peter
Parler: Holy Rood church.
Founded c. 1330, choir 1351, in
Schwäbisch Gmünd.

/137/
Relief of the Last Judgment on
the southern portal of the Holy
Rood church in Schwäbisch
Gmünd. After 1351.

165

hrad. Such a panorama was first depicted on a woodcut in Schedel's World Chronicle (Nuremberg, 1493). The person who made the woodcut noticed one of the characteristic features to be found also on later vedutas: the window arch of the unfinished southern transept hangs high in the air like lace suspended between the apse and the big tower. Speaking figuratively, one might describe the relation of Prague cathedral to the town by comparing it to the sculptural decorations on the northern façade of the church at Mühlhausen in Thuringia where an illusively conceived Charles IV is graciously acknowledging from a balcony the homage paid by an admiring crowd.

: St. Vitus's cathedral gave Charles's Prague a dominant feature in its proportions corresponding to its non-medieval size. It gave rise to new dimensions in town planning, which were later made full use of by the architects of Prague baroque. The baroque churches, palaces and gardens on the left bank of the river Vltava took the dominating location of the cathedral into account and created an artistically effective base and setting for it. Such a gradation of buildings impressed upon the Hradčany panorama its typical inner dynamics and is one of the reasons why many visitors consider Prague one of the most beautiful cities in Europe.

: The relation of St. Vitus's cathedral to the town was naturally conditioned and determined by the choice of the site. Its special character required certain anomalies in ground-plan. While the Gothic canon required a clearcut relation between chancel and transept, this was suppressed in Prague as the outside walls of a large square chapel with an area of 100 square metres project into the area of the southern section of the transept, and, at the same time this chapel projects considerably beyond the ground-plan of the chancel. It forms, as it were, a church within a church.

: The demanding artistic decorations in this chapel fully conform to the purpose of protecting the tomb of St. Wenceslas, to whom the chapel is consecrated. This tomb has remained in its place without change ever since 936, although three churches have in turn encompassed it.

: The first church was a Carolingian rotunda with four apses, consecrated to St. Vitus and founded by St. Wenceslas. In the years 1060 to 1092 Spytihněv built a basilica in its place, in substance still an Ottonian building with two choirs, a western transept and threee crypts. This continued to fulfil its functions for twenty-five years after the foundation stone of the cathedral was laid before the new building encompassed it, having been begun 40 metres to the north-east. Then the basilica was gradually taken down but its altar and other works of art were transferred to the new cathedral.

: Prague cathedral continues some of the functions of Wenceslas's rotunda. It is a typical ruler's church such as the feudal barons built for themselves, their families and their retinue in their residences during the early Middle Ages. They considered the church their exclusive property, placed priests in it as they thought fit and regarded the church treasure as their financial reserve. John of Luxemburg and Sigismund professed this same attitude to the St. Vitus's treasure.

: In the case of Charles IV it is not easy to draw the dividing line between his residence in the palace and the adjacent cathedral. For the cathedral was the place where the coronation ceremony took place as he himself laid down in his Coronation Order. At the same time it served as jewel house for the Bohemian crown jewels. Charles also directed the use of the reliquaries in the cathedral treasure. The cathedral was the burial place of his ancestors, members of his family, leading courtiers and artists and as well a gallery for their sculptured and painted portraits. Charles's sense of ownership towards the cathedral completely smothered its function as a metropolitan cathedral, the more so as the Prague archbishops and canons were also the Emperor's ministers and officials.

: Charles had a decisive influence over the artistic decorations of the cathedral by entrusting its construction by stages to two builders of different training and talent. The first of these, Matthias of Arras, took up the work in 1344 when there were ample funds, for King John had three years earlier allocated to it the tithe of the silver mines at Kutná Hora. The master brought a masonic lodge with him, which continued work in the Czech Lands after Matthias's death in 1352 until the end of the century.

: Matthias of Arras built the entire eastern part of the St. Vitus's choir with five apsidal chapels, between which the external flying buttresses were placed. Along the northern side of the ambulatory he built one chapel, on the opposite side two chapels and half of a third. Under his supervision the nine piers of the nave were constructed with the apsidal wall above the arcades, and this was raised to the height of the triforium.

: Characteristic features of this part of the cathedral include the formal purity of post-classical linear

profiles on the slim concave shapes. Though the builder came from Arras in northern France, his art shows a closer relation to a group of cathedral chevets in the south of France (for example the cathedral at Narbonne, begun in 1272 and especially that at Rodez, founded in 1277). On both buildings the participation of Jean Deschamps, trained at Amiens, is on record. The chevet in the cathedral at Limoges is ascribed to him, and this leaves an impression that is very similar to the termination of the choir in Prague. :

: The manner in which Matthias dealt with his task has rightly been termed traditionalist and outdated in development. (In Bohemia, for example, there is the spatial layout of the choir at Sedlec.) It appears that Charles wished the St. Vitus's cathedral to follow the tradition of French cathedrals that he had known in his youth. Matthias's architectural style, however, did include certain elements that were no

longer part of that tradition and led towards late Gothic, for example, on the big chevet buttresses the finials penetrate the roof at the height of the balustrade. :

: The second builder of the cathedral, Peter Parler of Schwäbisch Gmünd, was a builder of different artistic type. He belonged to a widely scattered family, in which the trade of builder and stone-mason was handed on from father to son. The family came from the western part of Germany and its members worked in the whole of central Europe during the fourteenth and the fifteenth centuries. Peter Parler spent his years of apprenticeship at the masonic lodge of his father Henry, who was in charge of construction work on the Holy Rood church in Schwäbisch Gmünd (founded c. 1330). Prior to that he had worked as 'parlier' or foreman in his birthplace, Cologne, where from 1248 the construction of the famous cathedral was going ahead. :

: These two churches were of entirely different character. The church at Gmünd is a civic hall from the beginning of late Gothic with reduced buttresses and an ingenious straddled placing of the oval piers in the choir ambulatory. The church has a wealth of sculptured decorations, which anticipate later development in Parlerian sculpture in the Czech Lands. Thanks to Cologne cathedral central Europe became acquainted with French Gothic. The Cistercian church at Sedlec in Bohemia follows it in its ground-plan but without the buttresses. In

Cologne these buttresses show by their great wealth of forms that the builder had full mastery of the building material. :

: There is a seeming contradiction between the opinion that Charles became acquainted with the young Parler on his travels in southern Germany towards the end of the summer of 1353 when he was passing not far from Schwäbisch Gmünd, and the wording of the somewhat doubtful inscription on the builder's bust in the St. Vitus's triforium. According to this the Emperor brought the twenty-three year old master to Prague in 1356. But this apparent contradiction can be surmounted. Charles probably did make Parler's acquaintance in 1353. But as in the meantime the Matthias of Arras's masonic lodge was continuing work according to the plans that the late Matthias had left, he put the younger master in charge of the construction of the Frauenkirche in Nuremberg. The Parlerian character of that building as well as of its rich sculptural decorations was recognized only recently. :

: What is clear is that Peter Parler came to Prague no later than in 1356 as a young, yet well experienced builder who had travelled widely and had gained a breadth of outlook. With his arrival construction work speeded up considerably. We are well informed of the course of the work as well as of the life of Peter Parler thanks to an unusually large number of sources. Of prime importance among these are the building plans of the St. Vitus's masonic lodge, today kept in Vienna. :

: Apart from the late Gothic copy of the ground-plan of the cathedral in Rodez in southern France, which Matthias of Arras must have brought with him, the original plans of St. Vitus's cathedral on parchment have survived. They show the transverse section of the northern side of the St. Vitus's choir, the ground-plan of the southern arm of the transept, the ground-plan of the big tower and a sketch of its two lower floors. On the basis of a drawing or model by Parler, the smith of the lodge, Wenceslas or Vaněk, cast the metal sanctus spire in St. Wenceslas's chapel in 1373—5; this can be considered one version of the planned top of the big tower which was, however, not executed. :

: The most important epigraphic document is a memorial inscription engraved on a stone tablet

/139/
Prague, St. Vitus's cathedral. Drawn by Philip van den Bossche, engraved by John Wechter, published in Prague by Aegidius Sadeler 1606.

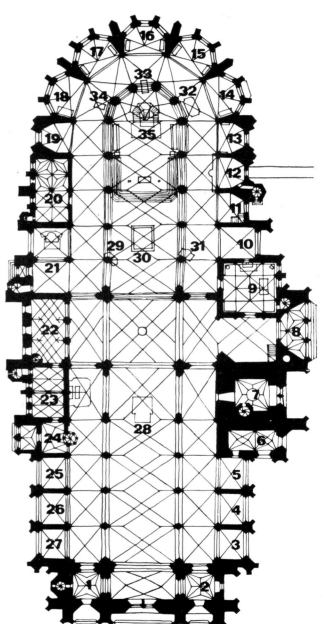

on the façade of the Golden Gate which recapitu-
lates the building history of the years 1344—96.   :
: Around 1400 three carved tombstones were made
in identical style for Matthias of Arras, Peter Parler
and the Emperor's painter Oswald, who were all
buried in the cathedral. The inscription on Parler's
tomb shows that the builder died in Prague on 13
July 1399. A number of data, though factually not
entirely correct, are contained in the epigraphs written additionally by brush above the busts in the
triforium (1387—92).   :
: In his chronicle Canon Beneš Krabice (died
1375), one of the directors of the Board of Works,
devotes a good deal of space to the work of the St.
Vitus's masonic lodge.   :
: The surviving weekly accounts of the lodge for
the years 1372—8 represent another unique source
of information. They contain all the fees paid out in
those years by the chapter as well as by the treasurer
in charge of the funds set aside for the cathedral
construction. Even the names of the stone-masons
who built it are given. There are no obvious French
names among them, which means that Arras's ma-

sonic lodge had moved on to another building site in the Czech Lands. (But the possibility that some of the stone-masons remained in the cathedral cannot be entirely ruled out.) In the meantime the masonic lodge began to teem with fresh labour, not only from Peter Parler's birthplace in Swabia and his father's native town of Cologne, but from almost the whole of Germany and Austria. Under Parler's leadership there worked some twenty-eight Czechs, three or four Poles, one 'Brabantian', one Hungarian and one stone-mason from Spiš in Slovakia. The total number of masons in the Parler lodge in those years surpassed 150. Many of them were only passing through Prague on their compulsory 'journeying' whereby they spread further afield the experiences they had gained.   :

: For supervising the work on the cathedral Peter Parler received a weekly pay of 56 groschen and a special emolument for the completion of each individual stage of construction and for sculptural work. On 30 August 1377 fifteen threescores of groschen were paid out to him from the counting-house for the stone tomb of Přemysl Otakar I. The bill for the choir stalls which he carved in wood in 1386 have not survived and the work itself was lost during the fire in 1541.   :

: To this should be added income from other construction work of which Parler was in charge or which he designed in Prague, Kolín on the Elbe and Kutná Hora. His popularity in the Czech Lands, which became his second home, is best proved by him being elected First Councillor at Hradčany in 1360, when he was not yet thirty years old.   :

: Though he owned a number of houses and parcels of land there, he himself rented a house for years and used his own estate for speculation. In 1380 he borrowed 30 threescores of groschen from the counting-house of the lodge and gave two of his houses in pawn. An entry in the court proceedings of the archbishop's consistory, so far overlooked, reveals that Peter announced on 23 May 1383 during what was clearly some usurious transaction that he would devote thirteen gold florins to the construction of the cathedral. At about that same time he gave to the St. Vitus's treasure a gilded silver monstrance with his coat of arms, which still survives. The situation in his family was so complicated that the dispute involving his third or fourth marriages had to be solved by the Holy See.   :

: This handful of biographical details does not detract from the obvious fact that Peter Parler entered history as a young man of genius. We know that in later years he showed certain signs of excitability or even of oddness. That is entirely in conformity with his work, which is full of innovation, even revolt. The many new and surprising architectonic solutions which sprang out of Parler's fantasy would

suffice for the life work of several builders. And in view of the slow speed of construction work at the time far from all his designs were executed in the end: only a fraction of his plans have come down to us.   :

: In the whole of Europe at the time there was probably no other person than Peter Parler who more poignantly realized the academic character and dullness of the torso of Prague cathedral built by Matthias of Arras. All the five pentagonal chapels covering seven sides of the twelve-angled chevet have the same vaulting scheme. And such chapels were intended to continue monotonously along both sides of the ambulatory. But Peter terminated the third of the half-built chapels on the southern side (known as the Martinic chapel) with a ground-plan in the form of a square and spanned it with a pentagonal vault that is keeping with its abnormal ground-plan. On the opposite side of the chancel and to cover the two square compartments in the sacristy, finished in 1362, he used two different patterns — star vaulting and net vaulting with suspended keystones.   :

: Parler overcame his predecessor's post-classical linearism in various ways. One way was a return to the mighty plastic forms of architectonic elements of the thirteenth century. In the solid columns with chalice capitals, used in the triforium and elsewhere, he returned to the Burgundian-Cistercian beginnings of the central European architecture of the Gothic period. He also drew inspiration from French classical Gothic. Parler's development was channelled by an important task that he was set in the immediate vicinity of the cathedral: the reconstruction of the palace chapel of All Saints. Outwardly the chapel, consecrated in 1387 and rebuilt in 1580, was based on Sainte-Chapelle, to which Charles had taken such a liking in his childhood in Paris. His architect must therefore have been acquainted with this culminating work of French classical Gothic.   :

/142/
Matthias of Arras and Peter Parler: St. Vitus's cathedral. View of the end of the choir and the ambulatory chapels. 1344—1420.

/143/
Peter Parler: The Golden Gate on the southern side of the cathedral, consecrated in 1367. The mosaic of the Last Judgment was made in 1370—1.

/144/
Nicoletto Semitecolo
and Venetian
mosaic-makers: The
Last Judgment.
1370—1.

: At the end of the choir in St. Bartholomew's church at Kolín on the Elbe (1360—78) Peter Parler had to deal with a ground-plan problem which arose first in the construction of Notre-Dame in Paris. The Old Town bridge tower, which he built at a later stage, shows certain relations to the western façade of Rheims cathedral. The assumption that the master undertook a journey around western Europe is further supported by certain surprisingly advanced architectonic elements (for example, ribs not attached to the vaulting, suspended keystones) and his highly skilful way of building vaulting. That has sometimes been explained by the influence of English architecture, which, as the first in Europe, advanced to late Gothic, e.g. at York Minster and the cathedrals at Wells and elsewhere. In relation to French and English architecture Parler's work is not eclectic in character but represents a creative application of the underlying principles. :

: Peter Parler himself gave impetus to the development of central European architecture in his work. In it the continuous full wall was again assuming its role as a solid cover for the unified space. The layout and elevation that rose to the fore at the time is of older origin, as ancient even as the Prague octagon of Karlov abbey. :

: Parler's St. Wenceslas chapel in the cathedral, consecrated on 30 November 1367, is built on a square ground-plan and spanned by net vaulting derived from the compositional scheme of a quadrangle. What was decisive here was again Charles's wish that the chapel should represent the heavenly Jerusalem, which in chapter 21 of the Revelation of St. John is described as a town of square plan. The

/145/
*Matthias of Arras and Peter
Parler: the choir of St. Vitus's
cathedral. 1344—1420.*

solidity of the chapel walls, only sparsely lit by narrow windows gives it the character of a pre-Gothic room. This is equally true of its northern portal ending in a semi-circle arch with an arched frieze. These forms were deliberately chosen to create a fitting setting for the Romanesque bronze door knocker in the shape of a lion's head with a ring in its mouth affixed to the metal-sheathed door of the portal. (It was believed that this was the door knocker which St. Wenceslas was holding when he was murdered.) The St. Wenceslas chapel is another example of the programmed historicism of art of Charles IV's era, i.e the deliberate use of pre-Gothic types and forms.

: Peter Parler and his imperial master showed great predilection for surprising contrasts. This can be seen in the southern porch of the cathedral, known as the Golden Gate. Its construction was finished by 1367 and then, in the years 1370 to 1371, its façade was decorated with a large mosaic picture. The mosaic decorations cover also the two-sided buttresses of the pillars of the restrainedly profiled tripartite arcades of the porch. These buttresses are a transposition to monumental scale of the principle of the carved and painted frame on Tomasso da Modena's Karlstein diptych. From a distance the Golden Gate in its perfect balance of the horizontal and the vertical and the smooth area of the façade below the heavily profiled cornice of the balcony brings to mind the Italian proto-Renaissance architecture. But as soon as the spectator approaches the shaded area of the porch, his eyes unexpectedly come to rest on a waterfall of unattached ribs. They merge into the vaulting on the central pillar set in front of the level of the door.

: From 1371 Parler was busy on the upper part of the choir. He built a triforium gallery above the dark zone of the arcaded pillars and higher still a broad strip of windows that admit light in plenty. Their ribs are bound by the same rhythm as the smaller pillars upholding the roof of the triforium. As this triforium is enclosed by glass windows, as in the abbey church of Saint-Denis, the whole upper part of the choir forms one single source of light. It is to be regretted that the chapel of All Saints has not survived in its original form. This was Peter Parler's version of Sainte-Chapelle and we un-

fortunately are not able to compare the two.

: In both cases Charles will have participated in the spiritual conception since it is known that he was greatly interested in the neo-Platonic Augustinian metaphysics of light.

: Parler altered the heritage of the thirteenth century to fit in with late Gothic. The canopies on the inter-window pillars in the triforium incline in the direction of the choir and merge with it. Small windows are set above the inclined sections and parallel with them and at an angle to the large windows, rising to an ogee arch with a finial. They have no other function than to intensify the wavy movement that fills the entire upper part of the choir in a horizontal direction and together with the pierced balustrade of the triforium forms a balance to the vertical upward movement. By the time the choir was consecrated on 12 July 1385 Parler had finished the vaulting over the chancel in net vaults, a pioneering feat at that time. He used a continuous network of vaulting to overcome the squares of each vaulting compartment and also to achieve an impression of unified space.

: To assess the broad scope of Parler as an artist it has to be realized that at the same time when he was building the cathedral he also projected Charles Bridge: a structure that is non-Gothic in substance, genetically linked to antique patterns and yet boldly anticipates further development by the rational functionalism of its curved, hydro-dynamic axis. By his open-minded approach to the various tasks that Charles entrusted to him, Peter Parler can be compared to some of the Renaissance architects. Boniface Wohlmut might well serve as an example (died 1579). It was he who made the Gothic vaults in the Old Diet at Prague castle and the abbey church at Karlov and at the same time built the Ball House in the Royal Gardens and other Renaissance works in the Palladian spirit. Peter Parler also conceived style as 'selective style'. He worked with thirteenth century architectonic principles, even with the pre-Gothic forms and at the same time laid the foundations for late Gothic in central Europe. His inventiveness and the ease, naturally only apparently so, with which he did so is remarkable. The creative individuality of the man can be seen in his buildings, some of which bear the mark of pure art.

/146/
*Peter Parler: St. Wenceslas chapel
in the cathedral. 1356—67.*

/147/
The Devil Wrenching the Soul
out of Judas's Mouth. Right-hand
console on the portal of the St.
Wenceslas chapel. Sandstone.
1367.

/148/
The figure of Socrates (?) in the
parable of the Salvation of the
Human Soul. Left-hand console
on the portal of the St. Wenceslas
chapel. Sandstone. 1367.

/149/
Master Oswald: Semi-figures of angels on the right half of the eastern wall of the St. Wenceslas chapel. 1372—3.

: While in the spirit of post-classical linearism Matthias of Arras suppressed the function of foliated decorations to a minimum, the work of Peter Parler's masonic lodge meant a return to the thirteenth century in this regard. Floral motifs on the architectonic elements carved under Parler's supervision have the truthfulness of perfectly observed form in no way inferior to classical Gothic. As time passed Parler's lodge reached an understanding of painting so that his stone-masons created parallels in sculpture to the ancient acanthus with which Bohemian manuscripts were decorated, beginning with the Liber Viaticus of John of Středa. Throughout the Parlerian part of the cathedral a large number of fantastic and grotesque masks, symbolic and animal figures can be found. There are even figural morality scenes, such as the console with a girl undressing in front of a lecherous old man on the upper (i.e. outside) triforium of the transept.   :

: The oldest sculptural decorations in the cathedral, reliefs on the St. Anne altar table of 1358 (today in the St. Wenceslas chapel) belong to a pre-Parlerian stage of development. The first sculpture that can be connected with the work of Parler's masonic lodge is a wooden Virgin and Child at Karlstein castle, dating from around 1360.   :

: Beneš Krabice informs us of the completion in the year 1367 of 'a beautiful work, that is, a large portal and columns by the St. Wenceslas chapel in the Prague church, a work of carving and exceedingly expensive'. It can be deduced from this that statues were set on the cornices in the porch of the Golden Gate which, unfortunately, have not survived.   :

: From the same time date the masks of two fauns on the corners of the St. Wenceslas chapel. The discovery that their maker had previously worked on the decorations of the minster at Colmar conforms with the known fact that the Parlerian lodge included stone-carvers from Alsace, one of whom is given twice in the St. Vitus's accounts as 'Strasbourger'.   :

: The mask of a drunk and singing Silenus below the statue of Wenceslas IV on his throne on the Old Town bridge tower and other Prague sculptures can in all likelihood be ascribed to the same sculptor, in whose work light and shadow are clearly divided. In the cathedral the left console of the portal to the St. Wenceslas chapel is closest to his art. It represents a bald-headed and bearded old man in the garments of a medieval magister leaning over a woman, of whose figure only traces remain. The console is reminiscent of the work of another stone-carver in Parler's lodge, who, after 1380, worked in the church in Silesian Głogówek near Oleśnica. Here he carved two anecdotes that were popular in the Middle Ages. One related how Phillis travelled on Aristotle's back and drove him with a whip and the other how Xanthippe placed a bucket with slops on the head of Socrates. The subject of the Prague console, where the old man has clear Socratean features, is different. It is a no less popular medieval anecdote relating how Socrates cured his wife, the daughter of the Emperor Claudius (!), with her father's blood. A widely read work of the time, Gesta Romanorum, explains this anecdote by stating that 'wife' here stood for the human soul, 'Emperor Claudius'

/150/
Henry IV Parler: St. Wenceslas. Marlstone. Polychromy by Master Oswald. 1373.

for Jesus Christ and his 'blood' referred to the Redemption on Calvary.

: It is hard to imagine a more effective contrast to this allegory of the salvation of the human soul than the opposite right-hand console of the portal, on which the Devil is fiercely wrenching the soul out of Judas's mouth. In its dramatic conception this console recalls the figures of the condemned on the relief of the Last Judgment on the southern portal of the Holy Rood church at Schwäbisch Gmünd. But it differs from it by a greater mobility of the figures and a softer, more picturesque feeling for form. In that respect it is closer to the story of the souls of the good and the evil thief on the Calvary on the upper strip of the tympanum on the church of Our Lady before Týn in Prague (1384—8). In this the conception of the decorations of the portal to the St. Wenceslas chapel have their parallel in meaning.

: The statue of St. Wenceslas standing today on the cornice of the altar wall in the saint's chapel is entirely different in its conception. Its pedestal bears Parler's mark with the T-square. It differs from older local depictions of the saint in a Byzantine coat of mail. Here we have the new type of an elegant Gothic knight and courtier leaning with his left arm

/151/
Peter Parler: Tomb of Přemysl Otakar I. Marlstone. Detail. 1377.

/152/
Peter Parler: Tomb of Přemysl Otakar II. Marlstone. Probably 1377.

on his shield. We find such a depiction for the first time on Tommaso da Modena's triptych at Karlstein castle. The Czech pattern that Tommaso used in his work was close to that applied by a Nuremberg stone-mason on the statue of St. Wenceslas in the local Frauenkirche, except that he omitted the lance. On the Prague statue the aristocratic and courtly character of the saint is still further enhanced. At the same time a tone of melancholy appeared, for the first time in art of Charles IV's era, in the expression of his bent head. Formal aspects link the St. Wenceslas statue to certain works in Cologne (the bust of Daphne with Parler's mark).   :
: According to the St. Vitus's accounts stone-mason Henry received 30 groschen on 3 April 1373 for five days' work on a statue of St. Wenceslas. This stone-mason has been rightly identified as Henricus Parlerius, often given in the accounts as Parler's as-

sistant in running the masonic lodge, with a weekly pay of 16 or 20 groschen. Recent research marks him as Henry IV Parler, son of builder John of Gmünd, and Peter Parler's nephew.   :
: The statue of St. Wenceslas is the only one in the whole cathedral that is not linked to any architecture or tomb. It is a free-standing, portable statue like the later 'beautiful Madonnas', which it anticipates in its idealization of the subject matter, its noble form and its technical brilliance of execution.   :
: The main sculptural ornamentation in the chancel is an extensive set of tombs and busts. Six sarcophagi are placed at regular intervals along the walls of the three eastern chapels on the ground floor. Sculptures of the Přemyslide monarchs are affixed to the lids and coats of arms to the sides.   :
: Twenty-one busts are carved into the pillars of the triforium; they represent Charles IV, members of his family and his courtiers, leading church dignitaries and the two builders of the cathedral. The outside triforium is decorated with a total of ten busts: Christ, the Virgin Mary and the patrons of Bohemia, to whom the Slavonic apostles St. Cyril and St. Methodius have been added.   :
: Although these sculptures vary in subject matter, genre and quality of execution, they are linked by a common theme. The tombs of the Přemyslides were to represent the historical past of the Czech state; the portraits on the triforium its contemporary state and finally the busts of the heavenly beings in the outside triforium to represent eternity. There is a mutual link in that below the bust of Christ is to be found that of Charles IV, whom the Archbishop of Prague, in his funeral speech, called 'The Lord Christ of this Age'. The busts in the outside triforium were renewed in the nineteenth century.
: The tombs in the chapels, on which work began no later than in 1376, were to make St. Vitus's cathedral a royal burial place. This purpose had formerly been served by the monastery church at Zbraslav, where no tomb has survived. The programme of the tombs in St. Vitus's was influenced by the burial place of the kings of France in the church at Saint-Denis, which Charles had seen in his youth and which he visited again at the beginning of 1378.

/154/
Bust of King John of
Luxemburg on the
triforium. Sandstone.
1375 — 8.

/155/
Bust of Elizabeth
Přemyslide on the
triforium. Sandstone.
1375 — 8.

182

/156/
Bust of Emperor Charles IV on
the triforium. Sandstone.
1375—8.

/157/
*Bust of Queen Blanche of Valois
on the triforium. Sandstone.
1375—8.*

/158/
*Bust of Queen Anne of the
Palatinate on the triforium.
Sandstone. 1375—8.*

184

/159/
*Bust of Empress Anne of
Świdnica on the triforium.
Sandstone. 1375—8.*

/160/
*Bust of Empress Elizabeth of
Pomerania on the triforium.
Sandstone. 1375—8.*

185

/161/
Bust of the director of the St. Vitus's masonic lodge and chronicler Beneš Krabice of Veitmile on the triforium. Sandstone. 1378—9.

/162/
Bust of architect Matthias of Arras on the triforium. Sandstone. 1378—9.

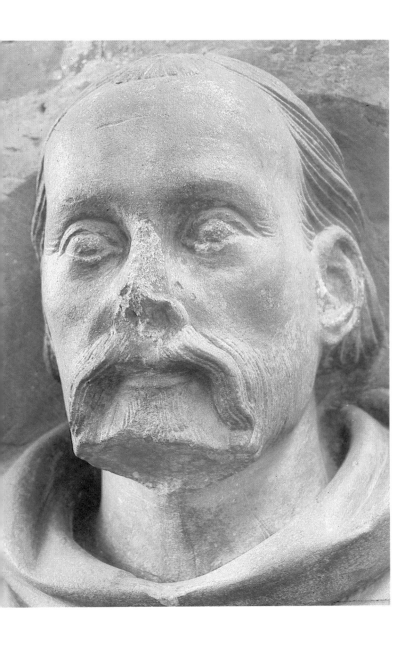

/163/
Bust of architect Peter Parler on
the triforium. Sandstone.
1378—9.

/164/
Engraved tombstone of Peter
Parler in St. Vitus's cathedral.
Sandstone. (The architect died in
Prague on 13 July 1399 at the
age of about 66 years.)

: The sarcophagus of Bořivoj II shows some similarities to the tomb of Philippe III at Saint-Denis, which Pierre de Chelles carved in the years 1298—1307. The sculptor of the Bořivoj sarcophagus must have learnt his craft in France in his youth and at the time when he was working at Prague cathedral he must have been an older man. He may also have made the tomb of Břetislav II. :

: The relatively high sum of fifteen threescores of groschen, which Peter Parler received on 30 August 1377 for the sarcophagus of Přemysl Otakar I, shows that he worked on it for a long time and without assistants. Characteristic of Parler's art is the contrast between the smooth parts on the broad collar, which covers the king's bust almost to the waist and the deeply articulated folds of the cloak below the waist. The mighty figure of short proportions rests heavily on the lid of the tomb. The king's spiritual life is reflected only in the expression of the face with protruding eyebrows, broad cheekbones and a heavy jaw.

: The robustly straddling figure of the militant Přemysl Otakar II, which is also attributed to Peter Parler, makes a vigorous and determined impression. The difference between the two kings results from the need for differentiation in type, which outwardly shows by the former being dressed as a monarch of peace while the latter is presented as a warrior. These two types of monarch appear alternately on all the tombs. The Přemyslide figures on the sarcophagi show some relationship to the figures of the prophets on the portal of older churches built by Parler in Schwäbisch Gmünd, Augsburg and Nuremberg. But they surpass them in the fullness of physical volume, which can perhaps be explained as an influence of Master Theodoric's pictures. :

: The tomb of Soběslav II shows a freer design of the draperies, whose dish-shaped folds anticipate the style of the 'beautiful Madonnas'. The formal purity of the tomb of Soběslav II and its carefully chased surface make it possible to accept the attribution to Henry IV Parler. Similarly the last sarcophagus, that of Břetislav I, is closer to Henry's art than to Peter's. All these tombs are titanic and monumental in scale and show the same architectural style, which has fittingly been characterized as 'anti-Gothic and pre-Gothic'. :

: A serious problem of attribution is presented by the set of twenty-one busts in the triforium. The busts of eleven members of the Emperor's family in the polygon of the chevet were carved in the years 1374—8, the rest in the years 1378—9. The only exception is the marl bust of Canon Wenceslas of Radeč, which was added shortly before the consecration of the choir in 1385. Though it is impossible to ascertain whether Peter Parler personally participated in the work, there can be no doubt that he was consulted in the overall conception of their artistic properties. All the busts bear signs of the typically Parlerian contrast between the natural organic parts of the faces and the abstract geometrical forms of the shoulders, collars, mitres, coats of arms and rims of the crowns (to which gilded metal parts were probably affixed to the one-time polychromy, which was partly renewed in the early seventeenth century).

: The twelve busts represent persons who were no longer alive at the time so that the sculptor could hardly know them personally. The head of the Emperor's father, John of Luxemburg, is very similar to that of St. Henry in the Frauenkirche in Nuremberg. But not even that is a true portrait—which means that in both cases a prototype was used that was known to the masters in the masonic lodge and had proved its worth. :

: The same is true of the bust of the then still living Empress Elizabeth of Pomerania, Charles's fourth wife, where a relationship to the bust of Daphne at Cologne has been ascertained. Certain deviations from reality are also due to consideration for the monarchs. Charles is not depicted as an old man suffering from diseases but as a person of middle age. The style and technical execution of his bust correspond most closely to that of the damaged tomb of Bořivoj II. :

: Recent restoration work removed from the bust of Charles's mother Elizabeth Přemyslide later additions, which gave her the appearance of a kind-hearted, fat matron. It brought her closer to the Emperor's third wife, Anne of Świdnica, who was famous for her beauty. :

: Anne's bust corresponds most closely to the outstanding mask of Daphne, almost hidden under the naturalistically conceived foliage below the cordoned cornice of the southern façade of the Old Town bridge tower. But similarities can also be traced to the heads of the 'beautiful Madonnas'. :

: One might express a hypothesis as to the personality of the sculptor who made these works. According to the medieval inventories of Prague cathedral the picture with its richly carved frame of the St. Vitus's Madonna was made by the 'Junkers of Prague'. :

: In the register of the Prague Guild of Painters the 'Junkers' are named Wenceslas, Janek and Peter, which is identical to the names and the order of Peter Parler's successors in the supervision of work on the cathedral. The first of the three, Peter's eldest son Wenceslas Parler, appears on the weekly accounts of the St. Vitus's masonic lodge from 1375. In 1397, when Peter Parler laid down the function of 'magister fabricae', Wenceslas became his successor. In the winter of 1397—8 he went to Vienna to gain experience. Later, as 'maestro Venceslao di Praga', he appears in written contracts with the masonic lodge of the cathedral at Milan. But before he could move there he died in Vienna in 1404 at about the age of forty-five. :

: This explanation does not contradict the endeavour to limit the share of Henry IV Parler in the work on the busts of the Emperor's family. It is natural enough that Peter should show preference for his closest relatives in his lodge. His son and his nephew might have worked on the sculptures with some older stone-carver. The work of the younger Parler generation includes the charming bust of the youthfully curious Wenceslas IV and his wife, Jane of Bavaria, then still a child. :

: The ten busts along the longitudinal sides of the triforium have quite a different character. They represent the three Prague metropolitans, five canons, directors of building work, and the two builders of the cathedral. The full face of Archbishop Ernest of Pardubice and Archbishop John Očko, together

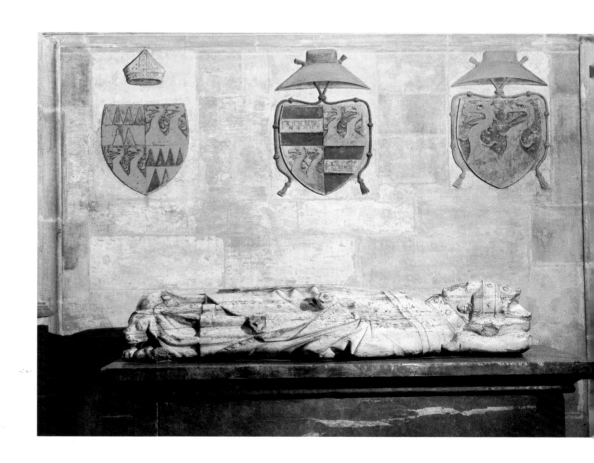

/165/
Tomb of Cardinal John Očko of Vlašim in the chapel of Sts. Erhard and Otylia. Slivenec and Vlašim marble. C. 1378.

/166/
Master Oswald: The Martyrdom of St. Catherine. Mural painting on the western wall of the Vlašim chapel. 1378—9.

with the bust of the corpulent Beneš Krabice form one group. Archbishop John of Jenstein, by contrast, is closer to Canons Kotlík, Bušek and Holubec. These busts are more suggestive of paintings and take the rough structure of the sandstone into account. They may well be the work of the master who made the console with Judas. But in the design of the heads they are a return to the thirteenth century. This can be shown by a comparison with the well-known statues of the founders of the cathedral in Naumburg: Kotlík with Ekkehard and Bušek with Wilhelm. There is great stress on the grimaces on the faces of the canons as is the case on some of the console masks, which are a hundred years older.   :

: Amazement has often been expressed that in the Prague triforium the depiction of the two builders of the cathedral is given in the same row as the Emperor's family and the prelates. What is known as 'builders' portraits' appeared in the Middle Ages often in the form of humorous genre figures on the consoles.   :

: In Prague the matter is different. Here representative busts were made to honour the two builders accompanied by their coats of arms and memorial inscriptions proclaiming their immortal achievement. In fact the inscriptions under their busts are greater in length than under those of some of the less important monarchs.   :

: This fact, at first sight puzzling, can be explained by the exceptional conditions at the court of Charles IV, where creative personalities were given outstandingly high appreciation. By way of example one might cite Charles's reply to Francesco Petrarch's first letter of 1350, which to his orders was composed jointly by the Roman Tribune of the People Cola di Rienzo and Chancellor John of Středa. In the letter the Prince of Poets is called 'imperial friend and husband of the Muses of Helicon'.

: John of Středa recalls in his letter to Charles in 1374 that in the twenty-six years of his service he had carried out 'not matters general, granted to many, but unparagoned, given to few'.   :

: From the men of literature this high assessment of personal merit was then transferred to the fine arts. In expressing his satisfaction at the manner in which Master Theodoric had carried out the decora-

/167/
*Master Oswald: The Baptism of
St. Otylia. Mural painting on the
eastern wall of the Vlašim
chapel. 1378.*

/168/
The Madonna with Sts. Mary
Magdalene, Bartholomew, James
and two kneeling canons. Detail
of mural painting in the Canons'
(Mary Magdalene) chapel.
Seventies of the 14th century.

tions in the imperial chapel at Karlstein castle Charles used the quite modern term 'ingenioso'.   :
: The name of Peter Parler is carved into the memorial tablet on the Golden Gate: otherwise its text includes only the names of the Emperor, the Prague cardinal and several outstanding personalities of contemporary political and Church life.   :
: The busts of the two builders are among the best in the whole triforium. The first, representing Matthias of Arras, is not a true portrait. It is of a type of the prophet Zechariah in the Nuremberg Frauenkirche, except that the dense wrinkles are simplified and the modelling is softer. But Parler's bust corresponds in costume and type to the figure engraved on his tomb. There can be no doubt that this sensitively modelled meditative head with sparse hair of a man in his fifties is a true likeness of that great architect.   :
: It has been suggested that Peter Parler derived the idea for the triforium gallery and its layout from England, in particular Bristol cathedral. There, as in Prague, portrait sculptures are placed on the triforium. Busts were placed above doors already in antiquity and consequently later in the Renaissance. There is, for instance, a painted portrait of Charles IV and his wife above the lintel of the imperial oratory at Karlstein castle. By contrast to Bristol and other Gothic buildings here in Prague we are not concerned with heads or consoles, but with a whole gallery of portrait busts set in the architecture. Along the sides of the triforium a number of recesses are carved into the pillars and these create grooves for the busts done in high relief. This again is a pre-Gothic principle of art. One of its antecedents can be found in the basilica of San Giusto at Trieste (12th century), where a number of Roman sepulchral figures with relief busts are placed around its portal. The sculptor who made the bust of Wenceslas IV and his wife at Głogówek near Oleśnica took the type of queen and the antiquated system of folds on both figures from Roman sculpture in the Emperor's collections.   :
: In the St. Vitus's triforium the connection with Roman antiquity is less obvious than at Głogówek

but it can be ascertained on a number of motifs. The hair style of Wenceslas's wife Jane with small transverse waves corresponds to the hair style customary among noble Roman ladies (e.g. the bust of Julia Domna on the Capitol). The ear lobe of Canon Holubec is bent forward by the edge of his hood as in the case of the statues of Romans at sacrifice. A precedent for the type of narrow ascetic face of John of Jenstein exists on certain Roman portraits. This contrasts with the face of well-being of Beneš Krabice, which has been described as 'absolutely realistic, non-Gothic'. We can find similar corpulent types on the busts of the ancient Romans, e.g. Pompey at Copenhagen.   :

: The bust of Wenceslas of Radeč is not a portrait of that canon, who had a beard, but it interprets very successfully the widely used type of Roman surviving to this day on several busts, e.g. in Frankfurt and elsewhere. Works of antiquity were not only a source of type and motifs for the sculptor of the triforium, but were primarily examples of what could be done in the field of portraiture.   :

: The attitude of the court of Prague to antiquity was different in the thirteenth century. In the famous Rheims Annunciation set forms from antiquity were used to express Christian subject matter. The Prague triforium is indifferent to religious views, for sculpture here served to honour personality. And again it is different from the example of the antiquated (and only fragmentarily surviving) triumphal arch of Frederick II at Capua, where the statue of the Emperor on the throne towers above the marble busts of the two ministers. In Prague the hierarchy of status is respected in the layout of the portrait gallery but all busts are presented in one row. Some of them, those of Parler and Radeč, actually surpass the Emperor's portrait in artistic quality.   :

: Towards the end of his life Cardinal John Očko set up in his chapel in the cathedral, known as the Vlašim chapel, a tomb, the magnificence of which is increased by the colour contrast of the red-grained granite of the sarcophagus and the white marble from which the statue on its lid is carved. This costly work has a direct antecedent in the limestone tomb of Ernest of Pardubice in the parish church at Kłodzko (Glatz).   :

: Even closer to Očko's tomb is another work by the same master, the marble tomb of Bishop Przeslaw of Pogorzela in Wrocław cathedral. Przeslaw died in 1376. At that time work was beginning in Prague cathedral on the Přemyslide tombs, to which Očko's is close in overall conception and in certain details. The fact that the sarcophagi of the two metropolitans are carved in marble, i.e. material with which there was little experience in central Europe, as well as the shape of the narrow folds rising out of the rounded mass, enables one to make the assumption that their makers must have been in contact with Tuscan sculpture. There is a possibility that the master who fashioned them was a Tilman, to whom, on 30 August 1377, three threescores of groschen were paid out of the lodge's funds for the marble stone of a lost tomb of Queen Guta.   :

: Apart from marble, another precious material, used for the decorations of the cathedral and its immediate vicinity, was bronze. The Romanesque door knocker has already been mentioned. It was transferred into the new building together with a bronze pedestal of a large candlestick with rich figural decorations, which had been in Spytihněv's basilica. Originally it had been brought as loot from Milan by King Vladislav II in 1158 or 1162.   :

: There can be little doubt that at the time of the reign of Charles IV a monumental bronze statue of St. George Fighting the Dragon already stood in the vicinity of the cathedral. According to the inscription on the saint's shield, which was still extant in 1757, this work was cast in 1373 by Martin and George of Cluj in Transylvania. They are known to have cast four statues which until the wars with the Turks used to stand in front of the cathedral in the Transylvanian Oradea. The protracted dispute as to whether today's statue in Prague dates from the fourteenth century or whether it is the result of a new cast in the sixteenth century was definitely settled by the discovery of an important archive document. It reveals that repair to the work was carried out in the years 1563—4 by the royal gunmaker Thomas Jaroš, but that the repair was insignificant in scope and did not in any way affect the substance of the masterpiece. Otherwise, it is not surprising that it has been considered a work of the Renaissance. That is the impression made by the mature spatial design of the statue, especially the rotating movement of the horse twisting its head.

: This same motif of movement can be seen on one of the horses on the legend of St. Wenceslas at Karlstein castle. The relationship is an indirect one, provided by both works following a formula in art with its origin in antiquity. From there it came to be applied to certain sculptures, such as the Byzantine ivory relief of the Emperor's Triumph called Barberini (early sixth century) or reliefs by Nicolo and Giovanni Pisano.   :

: The pictorial character of the terrain on the Prague statue with cleft rocks and mushroom-shaped trees recalls the terrain on the panels of the Vyšší Brod altarpiece, which was derived from a Venetian mosaic. One can therefore express the belief that the makers of the statue must have been acquainted with Venice and the famous statue of the bronze horses by the Greek sculptor Lysippus, which was brought from the Hippodrome in Byzantium in 1204 and placed on the balcony of St. Mark's in Venice.   :

: By contrast to the custom in western countries large areas of wall space appeared in Prague cathedral and they required painted ornamentation. The entire façade of the Golden Gate, with an area of about 85 square metres, was covered with an enormous mosaic picture on Charles's orders in the years 1370—1. Chronicler Beneš Krabice calls it 'a picture of glass in the Greek manner'. While the glass lids for the ornamentation of the vaulting in the Holy Rood chapel at Karlstein castle were imported from Venice, the glass material on the mosaic was combined with quartz and came from Bohemian glasshouses. That does not alter the **fact** that the mosaic itself was made by Venetian artists, whose skill Charles had admired during his adventurous stay on the Adriatic in 1337.   :

: In composition the mosaic depicts the Last Judgment. Its left-hand part shows the figures of those risen from their graves. The central part shows Christ as judge in a mandorla. On the right is the archangel Michael, devils and the condemned. The usual number of interceders is enlarged by the presence of the patron saints of Bohemia. At the bottom the kneeling figures of Charles IV and Empress Elizabeth of Pomerania have been added.   :

: In the central field the mosaic is composed on strictly geometrical principles, but along the two sides the composition is looser. In particular, the naked athletic figures rising from the graves on the left of the picture—some with their backs to the spectator—show lively movement. It is usually assumed that the cartoon of the mosaic was made by local artists, but they gave the maker of that cartoon only hasty sketches of the patron saints of Bohemia and of the imperial couple. The heads on the mosaic with full faces, thick noses and full lips, are faintly reminiscent of the types used by the Master of the Emmaus Cycle. But all these are features likewise to be found in the art of Guariento di Arpo. Similarly the angels holding the mandorla have a pattern in the angels that Guariento painted in the Dominican church at Bolzano. From 1365 Guariento worked on the decorations of the Doge's Palace in Venice, where he died before 22 September 1370. The cartoon of the mosaic was then finished (or made) by his closest collaborator Nicoletto Semitecolo, recorded in Venice on 7 March 1353 as 'painter of Saint Luke's' (pictor sancti Luce). The drawing on the St. Vitus's mosaic is closest to the frescoes which Semitecolo painted in about 1370 in the Volto Santo chapel on the Venetian Canal ai Servi. Through the collaboration of Venetian artists with Bohemian painters and glass-makers a grandiose mosaic picture came into existence, which is not only the largest but also one of the most valuable works outside the territory of Byzantium.   :

: Mural painting was to be the only decoration on the large patch of wall space in the St. Wenceslas chapel—as in Italian churches. The extensive cycle with the legend of the patron of the chapel dates from the early sixteenth century though it was planned from the very beginning.   :

: In the lower part of the chapel, scenes from Christ's Passion were painted some time before 1372. In the earliest old Slavonic legend from the period around 940 this is given as a typological parallel to the martyrdom of St. Wenceslas. Portraits of Charles IV, Elizabeth of Pomerania, Wenceslas IV and Jane of Bavaria were added to these Passion scenes on the eastern wall.   :

: The paintings were altered for the first time in the summer of 1373 when polished semi-precious stones were inlaid in the walls. They were given a more important function than at Karlstein castle, for they are a substitute for whole sections of paintings (arcades with semi-circular arches, a throne, a column, a tomb, a cross on a banner, the footprints of Christ's feet, etc.). The technique used here in simplified manner was known as 'opus sectile' and was already applied in late antiquity (e.g. the basilica of the Consul Junius Bassus in Rome).   :

: In the period between the sixteenth and the nineteenth century new pictures were added to the paintings and some were covered by layers of overpainting. It has been possible to remove some of this from several semi-figures of angels on the eastern wall. In this manner it became possible to show an identity in technique between those paintings and the original fragments on the Karlstein staircase cycle and a small part of the typological cycle in the cloisters of the Slavonic abbey.   :

: At the time when the painted decorations in the St. Wenceslas chapel were being made only one master-painter was working in the cathedral. For

/169/
The Adoration of the Magi.
Mural painting in the Saxon
chapel. Seventies of the 14th
century.

/170/
Martin and George of Cluj: St. George and the Dragon. Bronze statue at Prague castle. 1373.

that reason the weekly accounts of St. Vitus's limit themselves on 29 August 1372 to calling his journeymen by the term 'famuli pictoris'. For their share in colouring the coats of arms on the 'spiral' they were given 6 groschen pocket-money. The master himself was called Oswald and for completing the polychromy of the coats of arms on 3 October 1372 he received 80 groschen. A year later, on 18 September, he was paid 90 groschen out of the lodge's funds for 'de pictura ymaginis s. Wenceslai', which, in all probability, can be related to the polychromy on the saint's statue by Henry IV Parler in the St. Wenceslas chapel.   :

: Oswald's relations with the St. Vitus's lodge date back to an earlier period, to judge by the Parlerian motifs on the staircase cycle at Karlstein or the sketch of the stone fireplace on the Stockholm drawing attributed to him. In the meantime, Oswald had become a citizen of Prague and a prosperous financier, who loaned large sums at usurious rates. (On 7 February 1383 he managed to have excommunicated by the consistory an insolvent debtor, an unnamed parish priest, living at Tuchlovice in the Kladno district. This was the area where the St. Vitus's chapter was trying every method to extend its land holdings.)   :

: A damaged inscription on a fragment of the master's tombstone found in the cathedral can probably be reconstructed as follows: 'Anno Domini *(1383 + x)* died the careful man Osvaldus, painter of Charles, the Emperor *(of Rome and Wenceslas, the King of Bohemia)*.'   :

: Oswald enjoyed the protection of the Prague primate John Očko, for whom he painted the Vlašim chapel in the cathedral. On its eastern side the founder is depicted still as archbishop, on the western side as cardinal, to which office he was appointed on 17 September 1378. It can therefore be assumed that the ornamentation of the chapel was finished before his death on 14 January 1380.   :

: On the scene of the Baptism of St. Otylia on the eastern wall the primate is kneeling below the figure of St. Erhard to express their equal status in the Church. On the opposite side Očko's predecessor, St. Adalbert, is given to the left of Christ embracing his cross. On the right, there is the scene of the Martyrdom of St. Catherine, the patron saint of

Charles University, where the metropolitans of Prague held the chancellorship. The three polychromed coats of arms above Očko's marble tomb, which show all the church offices held by him in turn, serve a representative function. The scene of St. Otylia miraculously regaining her sight during the baptism was clearly selected with a view to the founder of the chapel being blind of one eye (hence his nickname 'Očko'—the 'One-Eyed'). This scene enlarges and enriches the spatial composition of the picture of the Baptism of St. Ludmilla, which Oswald had painted almost twenty years previously on the Karlstein staircase. The master seems to have lived longest of the old group of Charles's painters. He also underwent a remarkable personal development: on his later paintings in the cathedral the 'cult of the beautiful form' can be detected, typical of the artistic endeavours in the Czech Lands towards the end of the fourteenth century.   :

: It was not until recent restoration work that it became possible to distinguish reliably the painted decorations in two other chapels in St. Vitus's in the period around 1378 from Oswald's work.   :

: In the first place there is the chapel of St. Adalbert and Dorothy, called the Saxon chapel, founded by the Elector of Saxony Rudolph I, who selected it as his burial place. In this chapel there is a relatively well preserved part of a monumental Adoration of the Magi on the western wall. Related to it in style is the picture of the standing Madonna with Sts. Mary Magdalene, Bartholomew, James, saints and two kneeling canons on the eastern wall of the Mary Magdalene chapel. The painter of these two pictures is close to Oswald in the technique of soft, outline-free painting with an endeavour to achieve purity of form. But he differs from him by a more lively rhythm of outlines, a richer colour scale using chiaroscuro and more energetic modelling. The possibility exists that he once worked as assistant at Karlstein castle. He must have been acquainted with the work of Master Theodoric. He adopted from him the physical fullness of the figures, alternating gently flattened parts of the draperies with distended, superficially articulated volume as well as using richly embossed gilded hallmarks on the crowns and the gifts of the Three Kings.   :

: The picture in the Saxon chapel has a grandiose

composition. Almost one half of it is taken up by a broadly spread figure of the Virgin, a type of the Italian Madonna dell' Umiltà. The somewhat more intimately conceived picture in the Canon's chapel was to serve as an altar retable so that it is closer to panel painting.   :

: All other paintings in the cathedral are either the result of later overpainting or did not come into being until later. Only a watercolour copy of an overpainted picture of the Holy Family in St. Anne's chapel enables us to express the belief that this chapel must have been decorated during the Emperor's lifetime.   :

/171/
Peter Parler: Choir of the Dean's church of St. Bartholomew at Kolín on the Elbe. View of the vaulting in the ambulatory. 1360—78.

Chapter XI

The Spread
of Court Art

172

*Peter Parler — masonic lodge:
Mask of a 'wild man'—a faun,
on the console of the northern
double nave in the church of St.
Castullus in Prague. Seventies of
the 14th century.*

Charles changed Prague into one immense building site. He built simultaneously many castles and other structures in the Kingdom of Bohemia, in the countries bordering upon the Crown of Bohemia and in Germany. The speed of construction of some of these works was remarkable. Karlstein castle and the Slavonic abbey were built and richly decorated in roughly two decades after the laying of the foundation stones and likewise the building of Prague cathedral went rapidly ahead during the Emperor's lifetime. This was not true everywhere. In the case of the monastery church of Our Lady of the Snows in the New Town of Prague the speed of construction slowed down to a critical point and in the end the building programme had to be reduced substantially. Nor did the building of another New Town abbey church, the octagon at Karlov, proceed as fast as its founder would have wished. The same can be said of certain buldings in Germany where many were obviously close to his heart, such as the new choir at Aachen cathedral.   :

: The Emperor's personal supervision was needed if the building work was to go ahead successfully. This can be gathered from a report by Beneš Krabice: in Silesian Fürstenberg Charles built in the years 1370—1 'a strong castle, fortified the town and then built a bridge across the river Oder there. To make sure that the work should go ahead successfully, His Majesty stayed for almost the entire spring season'. :

: From time to time Charles's foundations encountered unforeseeable problems. The hermits of the Order of the Celestines, whom Charles invited to Prague from Avignon, did not wish to settle in the busy town. He therefore established them at Oybin near Zittau where the masonic lodge of Matthias of Arras built a monastery and church for them on a steep rocky cliff in the years 1366—84. On an enlarged scale the church has the same ground-plan as the single naved church of St. Apollinaris in the New Town of Prague (founded 1362). The exceptionally high Oybin church is today a ruin.   :

: The riches of healing springs near Charles's hunting lodge in western Bohemia led to the foundation of the world renowned spa town of Karlsbad (Karlovy Vary) in 1370. At the same time, however, such chance events prevented the concentration of means and manpower.   :

: In his passion for foundations Charles went beyond his limits. He himself came to realize this and withdrew some of his decisions. For instance he ordered the work on Kašperk castle in south-western Bohemia to be stopped soon after its foundation in 1356. For Charles did not have unlimited resources at his disposal. He was not able to carry through some of his foundations on the planned scale or speed although he was greatly aided by the circle of his counsellors, who understood his aims and helped to carry them through by their own initiative and their own funds. But even this cooperation did not suffice to finance the construction of the cathedral; this was ensured among other factors by the tithe from the Kutná Hora silver mines. In the end it became necessary to resort to a public collection.   :

: Charles's search for investors can be demonstrated by an order he issued in 1369 that part of the income of the provostry at Prague Vyšehrad be turned over for the reconstruction of the church of Sts. Peter and Paul. In this way Charles found the investors he had been looking for and encouraged. :

: The main reason for this must be ascribed to the remarkable fact that for decades, beginning with the reign of King John of Luxemburg, not a single foreign soldier dared set foot in the Kingdom of Bohemia. Charles punished all who did harm to the country with an iron hand and rooted them out completely. In the first few years of the reign of Wenceslas IV such peace reigned in the kingdom that it was possible — in the words of the chronicler — to carry a bar of gold across it on the head and no one would touch it. The fruit of this peace was relatively great economic prosperity.   :

: During the reign of Charles IV about one thousand monasteries and churches were reconstructed or newly built. Later development was to show that this number was too great, for the sudden upswing in the power of the Church became the main cause of the Hussite revolution. But not even then did the entire artistic wealth of the preceding decades vanish, for it was still greatly admired by Aeneas Sylvius in the middle of the fifteenth century.   :

: Side by side with the Church prelates in Charles's entourage and with the leading aristocratic families, artistic development was supported to a much

/173/
Peter Parler — masonic lodge:
Head of a Moor on the repository
for the pyx in the northern wall
of the apse of St. Bartholomew's
church at Kolín.

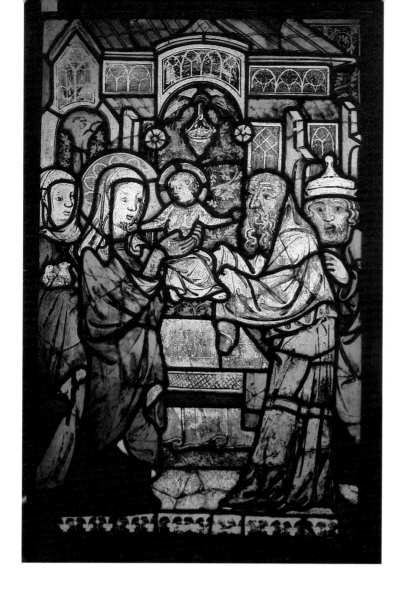

greater degree than in the preceding century by a novel factor—the towns.   :

: It would be interesting to trace in greater detail how the Czech towns tried to adapt themselves to the humanist atmosphere at the imperial court. Here we can only illustrate this briefly by the report that the Old Town of Prague presented a magnificently illuminated manuscript of Pliny to the newly founded Charles University.   :

: The growing economic power of the towns showed itself in the first place in the building of parish churches and their ever more demanding artistic decorations. Details in the erection books show that the burghers participated to a large extent in the setting up of new altars.   :

: In the New Town of Prague two new parish churches, those of St. Henry and St. Stephen, were founded by the town, even though the consecration

/174—175/
The Sacrifice in the Temple. The Death of the Virgin. Stained glass in the church of St. Bartholomew at Kolín. Before 1378.

/176/
Sázava, former Benedictine monastery. Chapter hall. Vaulting from the forties, mural paintings from the seventies of the 14th century.

of the former to the saintly Emperor suggests that Charles contributed his share to it. :

: In 1348—60 the church of the Holy Ghost was built in the Old Town of Prague out of funds bequeathed by the burgher Nicholas of Rokycany. This church was adapted in the 17th century. Another Old Town church, St. Castullus, was erected before 1375 by a builder who was a member of Peter Parler's lodge. In the double nave four times two vaulting compartments are upheld by circular piers similar to those in the church of the Jacobins in Toulouse (1230—40). :

: There is a remarkable console with a faun in the church. Branches and leaves grow out of his mouth and form a canopy above it. The effective contrast of illuminated and shaded parts is reminiscent of the mask of two fauns in the St. Wenceslas chapel in the St. Vitus's cathedral and also of the sculptural decorations in the church of Our Lady before Týn in the Old Town of Prague. :

: The construction of the main church in the Old Town began in the last few years of Charles's life and employed the stone-masons of Parler's lodge long after the Emperor's death, as did the bay window in the Carolinum and the alcoves and older parts of the astronomical clock on the Old Town Hall. The close cooperation of the stone-masons with the town can also be demonstrated by the house signs which they made. :

: Peter Parler remained true to the burgher's environment from which he came, although he became famous as the Emperor's successful Master of Works. Soon after his arrival in Bohemia he was offered the job of building a new choir for the church of St. Bartholomew at Kolín on the Elbe. The old choir, finished before 1300, had been destroyed by fire in the middle of the fourteenth century. The offer was attractive to Parler, the more so as he could start the building from its foundations and did not have to take account of the ground-plans of his predecessors as in Prague cathedral. :

: For that reason the choir of St. Bartholomew's, which Peter erected in the years 1360—78, is perhaps his most characteristic piece of architecture. It has a cathedral ambulatory and yet it involved a radical reform of the cathedral structure. This can be

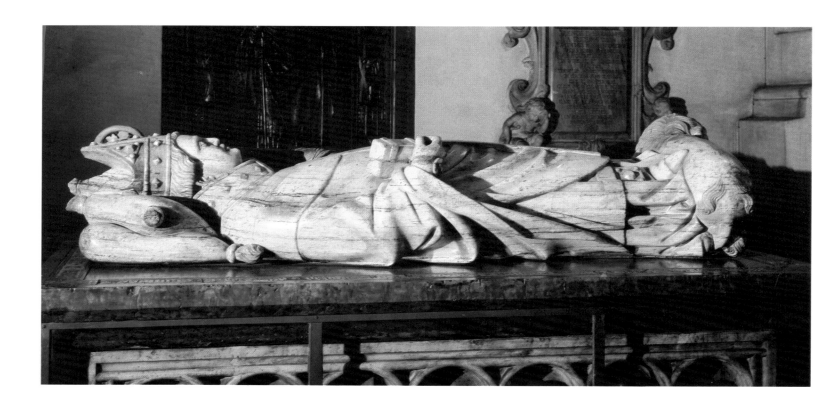

/177/
Wrocław, cathedral. Tomb of
Bishop Przeslaw of Pogorzela.
Marble. C. 1376.

seen in its non-gigantic, truly human scale, and the abolition of the traditional dividing line between ambulatory and chapels, which broaden funnel-like and merge into its space. It can also be seen on the chapels which form an exterior ring. The most complex constructional problem arose at the termination of the choir. Peter solved this in magnificent manner by building a pier in its axis to support the vaulting. This enabled him to unify the inner ground-plan of the choir, which forms four sides of an octagon, with its outer ground-plan of the five sides of a decagon. :

: Another example of Peter Parler's inexhaustible creative imagination is the unheard-of division of the supporting pillars in the axis of the choir. He removed all non-essentials from the body of the structure: the ribs merge directly into the round piers; the walls and the pillars are bare, void of any linear drawing with the aid of panels. :

: The building was intended to leave its mark by the inventiveness of architectural treatment, not its wealth of stone decorations. The gargoyles of the choir were carved anew in the 19th century. Inside, the original, noble shaped repository for the pyx in the northern wall of the apse has survived. The sections below the repository hold remnants of curly cabbage leaves and three heads: those of Christ, the Virgin Mary and a Moor. The first two heads are of ideal type while the third shows exceptional realism and plasticity of form. It is difficult to know why the head of a Moor was placed on the repository. This subject must have corresponded to the predilection in court art for exotic matters; this can be seen also on the negroes on the paintings by the Master of the Emmaus Cycle, Master Theodoric and John of Opava. :

: Work began on the stained glass windows even before the choir of the Kolín church was consecrated on 12 October 1378. Four windows have survived: the Sacrifice in the Temple, the Crucifixion, the Death and the Coronation of the Virgin. They do not have the sovereign craftsmanship of the stained glass at Osek nor the dramatic pathos of the Karlstein stained glass with the Crucifixion. They do, however, show a certain similarity to older works in glass done in the manner of a drawing. :

: The Kolín Death of the Virgin relates with some simplification to the composition on the same subject on the little panel in the Morgan collection, while the Sacrifice in the Temple is a different version of a miniature in the manuscript of the Laus Mariae. The maker of this glass window adopted the Italianized architectural setting from court art of this type. Particularly striking is the relationship of his puppet-like figures of naive expression to a group in the manuscript of the Breviary of Grand Master Leo and the work of the Master of the Karlstein Apocalypse. :

: It was in all probability Peter Parler who designed the church of St. Barbara in the rich mining town of Kutná Hora, where his second son John was in charge of construction work from 1388. The chancel of the church in many ways resembles that in Kolín. But it differs from it by having the outer circumference of its ambulatory chapels forming fifteen sides of a twenty-eight-angled form so that it is not far removed from a semicircle. It seems that even at the later stage of building (interrupted by the Hussite wars) some regard at least was paid to the original plans. :

: Apart from town churches Parler's masonic lodge also built monastic churches. In the porch of the church of Our Lady below the Chain in Prague's Little Quarter, belonging to the Order of St. John (1370—80), the architectonic principles of the St. Vitus's Golden Gate appear in a different version. :

: Another member of the Parler family who worked in the Czech Lands was Peter's brother Michael. In 1359 there is a record of him at the Golden Crown abbey (Zlatá Koruna) where work was continuing on the construction of the Cistercian abbey founded by King Přemysl Otakar II in 1263. Michael's contribution includes certain highly skilful architectural features, for example a rose window in the wall of the right arm of the four-sided monastic church. :

: Other monastic buildings include the Benedictine monastery on the Sázava river, where St. Procopius lived and died in 1053. Although this saint followed the Church Slavonic liturgy of the Eastern rites he was canonized by the Pope and became one of the patron saints of the Kingdom of Bohemia. :

: The complex building history of the monastery can be reconstructed on the basis of historical reports and the results of archeological research. The church, originally Romanesque, was first altered in the Gothic period and later underwent baroque adaptations. The Sázava monastery was supported by the squires of Lipá who held the office of High Marshal of the Kingdom of Bohemia from generation to generation. At some time before the middle of the fourteenth century the Roudnice masonic lodge of John IV of Dražice worked on constructing the basilican nave and aisles with an elongated chancel. Their work includes two remarkable bosses. One has a sculptured head of a king with a noble face, stylized in the spirit of post-classical Gothic. The head on the second keystone is quite different. It represents a grimacing man with a flat nose, perhaps a jester, composed into a foliated wreath. His uncouth expression anticipates the naturalistic consoles of the second half of the fourteenth century. Around 1360 changes were made in the building plans. The Roudnice lodge was replaced by that of Matthias of Arras, who was to build a hall church instead of the planned basilica. But building work was interrupted even before the Hussite wars broke out.   :

: Roughly half of the Sázava chapter hall escaped baroque reconstruction. Here rich decorations survive which provide proof of the original colourfulness of the Gothic interior and the perfect attunement of architecture and painting. Painted decorations covered not only the entire vaulting and the walls but all architectural members and the window jambs. Epic scenes from the life of Christ and the Virgin are painted here together with devotional pictures relating to the Benedictine cult of the Virgin. On the vaulting her Triumph is celebrated by jubilant angels surrounded by clouds. The painting must date from the end of the 1370s. It shows close relations to the older strata of art under Charles IV, especially the typological cycle in the Slavonic abbey. Certain parts, especially the heads of the angels, show the influence of northern Italy (Guariento di Arpo). The Sázava painters could have adopted many features of Italian origin from the stock accumulated by the preceding development of court art, such as fluted pilasters, illusively painted recesses, profiled landings, and a console cornice.   :

: The annexation of Silesia to the Czech state is reflected even in the arts. Charles did not manage to have the Wrocław bishopric subordinated direct to the Archbishop of Prague, but he found a faithful ally for his policies in the Wrocław Bishop Przeslaw of Pogorzela. This art-loving metropolitan did a great deal to improve the appearance of his cathedral, where the name of the Czech stone-mason Pešek is mentioned in connection with its construction. It is likely that he worked on the bishop's funeral chapel, which was painted in the years 1369—71. Although it is a rectangle in ground-plan, it is spanned by intricate net vaulting. From it vaulting of this type was adapted for Krakow, where it can be found in the small lady choir and in the presbytery of the church in the Wawel.   :

: The bishop's marble tomb was made by a master who also carved the older tombstone of Ernest of Pardubice at Kłodzko and roughly at the same time worked on the marble tomb of Cardinal John Očko in Prague cathedral. There exist many common features in the overall conception of the figures, their stoutish faces and the solid bodies. Przeslaw's tomb is richer and even has figural decorations along its sides. In this it follows the older Silesian tombstones, which have survived in much better condition than the works of stone sculpture in the Czech Lands prior to Peter Parler.   :

/178/
Peter Parler—masonic lodge: Statue of Charles IV Enthroned on the Old Town bridge tower in Prague. 1376—80.

Chapter XII

The Emperor as Portrayed
in the Works
of his Artists

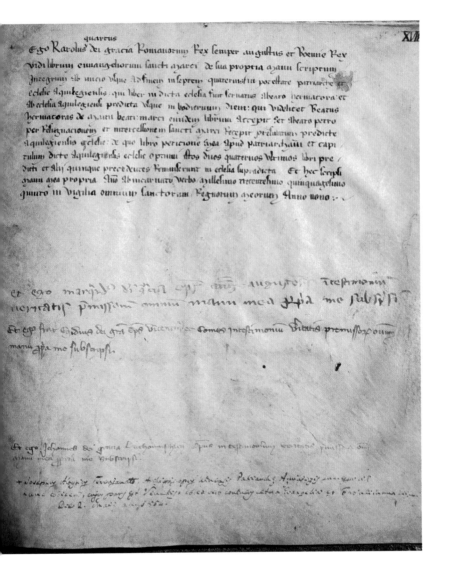

Charles had an average figure and was not very tall. He stooped slightly and his head and neck leaned forwards. He had a broad face with protruding cheekbones and large eyes, a bald patch on his forehead and his chin was hidden under a thick black beard.

: These characteristic features, given by chronicler Matteo Villani around 1364, were confirmed when the Emperor's skeleton was examined in 1928 and 1977. Charles was about 173 to 177 cm in height. His large and strong skull is far greater in length and circumference than the other ten skulls in the royal tombs. It is egg-shaped in profile with a strickingly projecting face and rather high. The arches above the eye cavity are well marked. The cheekbones are very strong. The slightly receding forehead moves in an arch across the short crown to the full nape. The chin, the spina nasalis and the nose bones protrude noticeably. The nose itself appears broad. The spine is bent forward. The exostosis of the bones show that Charles suffered from gout. During recent investigations it was discovered that Charles had an incurable haematoma on his back as a result of an injury during battle or a tournament. This explains the slight forward bend of the spine so that Villani saw him as stooping, 'gobeto'. Other war injuries were to be found on his skull and nose.

: Charles's physical appearance must be judged in relation to his life story. This reveals that he showed signs of unrestrainable impetuosity in his youth. The risky operations that he led as Condottiere of the Venetian League in 1337 and later on Italian soil exceed normal courage and border on hazard. He did not manage even later to tame his explosive nature: in 1356, when he defeated the perfidious knight of the road John Pancíř of Žampach he choked him with his own hands.

: On the other hand, he showed true magnanimity where other monarchs might have felt riled in their majesty. When Tribune Cola di Rienzo, the son of an inn-keeper, made out in front of him that he was the illegitimate son of Emperor Henry VII (in other words, Charles's uncle), he replied that he did not wish to interfere in things that were known to the Lord alone. He ignored without comment an accusation on the part of Milíč of Kroměříž who point-

208

/180/
Vienna, St. Stephen's cathedral.
Statue of Charles IV on the Tall
Tower. Sandstone. C. 1370.

ed a finger at him at a public meeting and called him the great Antichrist. He gladly forgave his second wife, the kind but somewhat dull-witted Anne of the Palatinate, who nearly caused his death by poisoning him with an aphrodisiac.   :

: A most valuable source that reveals Charles to us as a person is the report that Francesco Petrarch gave to his friend about his encounter with Charles in Mantua in 1355. The two men were greatly attracted to each other by mutual interests and, at the same time, kept apart by the strength of their individuality. At a banquet in Avignon Charles paid too much attention to Laura. Francesco reacted in his famous Sonnet 201, in which he shows his anger and jealousy. In Mantua Charles asked Francesco to relate his whole life to him with every detail. He listened with great attention and when the poet omitted anything he immediately filled in the gap, astounding him by knowing so much about him.   :

: The main qualities of Charles's character as Petrarch saw them were ambition, courtesy, joviality, curiosity, a trace of suspiciousness, obstinacy, loquaciousness, and immense quarrelsomeness. In the latter respect the temperamental Francesco was his match, and so their 'quarrels went on in long and witty speeches'. Once they argued 'from the first light of dawn into the depth of the night'. 'A new quarrel broke out and went on for many days and took no end' over Charles's request that his friend should stay by his side. One of Petrarch's valuable comments shows that Charles would smile from time to time as he spoke.   :

: Other facts are added by the even more detailed report on Charles's last visit to France at the end of 1377 and the beginning of 1378, included in the Grandes Chroniques de France.   :

: When after forty-eight years he again met in Paris the Duchess of Bourbon, his sister-in-law and the former close friend of his long deceased sister, he began in front of all the courtiers 'to weep so loudly and equally the said Duchess that it was a very grievous sight'. They followed this with a long conversation over dinner.   :

: Charles's talks with his nephew the King of France and his family were equally long and sincere. The Emperor was not only pleased with precious and artistically valuable gifts but also with small presents, such as two dogs which he was given by his grand-nephew. :

: Tormented by gout, he could hardly walk but he had himself taken in a sedan-chair to the abbey of Saint-Denis. There by the tombs of Charles le Bel, Philippe of Valois and their wives he remembered with gratitude how they had entertained him in their houses and the many kind deeds done to him. He showed 'a passionate longing to see the relics' and spent a long time looking at them, 'deriving great pleasure from so doing, as could be seen on his face'. :

: According to Villani, Charles had a great predilection for carving. Whenever he gave audience he would sit and carve soft wood with a sharp knife and his eyes roamed over those present as if he were not listening to any supplicant kneeling before him. But he never missed a single word and always gave short and convincing answers. The view has been expressed that he did not look a supplicant in

the eye as perhaps, like the Emperor Henry VII, King John and other Luxemburgs, he was afflicted by an inherited eye disease or possibly an inflammation of the iris. This illness is frequently found in those suffering badly from gout. Petrarch, however, relates that during one of his debates with Charles he underlined his reply 'with a bright look in his eyes'. In 1377 the Emperor sent Charles V a hand-written letter to Paris, which means that he could see well at the age of sixty-one. :

: Charles's handwriting is known from the notes he personally added to the Gospel according to St. Mark. It has a better quality than the following signatures of three bishops, including Chancellor John of Středa. The lettering reveals a trend towards calligraphic swings with a certain artistic quality. In that connection Villani's remark about Charles's hobby is interesting. This must be regarded as an inherited disposition. It is known that his mother, Elizabeth

/181/
The Royal Seal of Charles IV.
Wax. Prague, Chapter Library.
1354.

/182/
The seal of Charles University.
Prague. Archives of Charles
University. 1348.

Přemyslide was outstanding at needlework. She was greatly admired in 1310 when she appeared at the imperial court as a bride in valuable embroideries which were her own work. She would often adorn these embroideries with pearls and gemstones. :
: Villani related of Charles that he dressed in simple cloth without any adornments and that his garments, reaching below the knee, were always buttoned up. This refers, however, only to one aspect. For other sources we find tell us that in the course of his life Charles wore an almost unbelievable quantity of clothes. He inherited from his father King John a liking for incognito and changes of clothes and he passed this on to his son Wenceslas IV. This may be connected with the remarkable

/184/
Gold ducat with a picture of Charles IV as King of Bohemia. 1346 — 78.

/183/
The seal called the Golden Bull of Charles IV. Prague, Chapter Library. After 1348.

/185/
Gold ducat with a picture of Charles IV as Emperor of Rome. 1355 — 78.

acting ability that these three monarchs possessed, especially Wenceslas who used to entertain his entire court by parodying Archbishop John of Jenstein. :

: Charles was naturally surrounded by musicians and jesters. He gave entertainments, held tournaments and found his place in the history of the theatre by laying the foundations for the subsequent development of the well-known carnival plays in Nuremberg. :

: After the defeat at the battle of Crécy in 1346 he took a big risk and, dressed as a groom, travelled through the whole of Germany, then under the control of his sworn enemy, King Ludwig of Bavaria. :

: There were many occasions when he donned the garments of a merchant or poor pilgrim or when he fought at a tournament unknown under a strange coat of arms. In the Imperial Diet in Mainz in 1349 he borrowed luxurious robes from one prelate and having put them on, questioned the gathering whether he looked like a servant of God or like a prince. :

: On Christmas Day 1347, during solemn mass at Basle cathedral, he himself, wearing the chasuble and holding a sword, read the pericope of the gospel: 'These are the Orders of Emperor Augustus'. Immediately after this liturgical act to which he was entitled by his consecration as king, he paid court to the beautiful ladies of Basle at a dance. Reports of this quickly spread across Europe and angered his former Parisian teacher Pope Clement VI. He chastized Charles in a special epistle, in which he also reproved him for his habit of dressing like a dandy in short, tight coats. He recommended that he should wear 'garments that are long and loose, which are a mark of maturity'. Such garments might be of advantage to Charles on certain occasions, but certainly not when on horseback which until to his death he greatly preferred to using a carriage. :

: Naturally there were occasions when Charles had to resort to armour. At the age of fifty-seven, although ill, he personally led his army into the field. :

: On his frequent diplomatic trips he needed comfortable travelling clothes. He wore a beret during any frost and a large hat over the top. He often changed his overcoats. One of them, which he left on the tomb of St. Victor and St. Corona at Feltre, has survived to this day. :

: During festive occasions he wore a cloak and slippers of valuable Byzantine brocade with a cloak that had a Greek collar of golden scales. The Chinese material found in the royal tomb is perhaps a remnant of his attire. Each of the rings that Charles wore was worth a fortune. :

: He had himself crowned six times. He was also six times present at the coronations of his wives and of his son Wenceslas. :

: He was last seen in imperial robes in Prague. He lay on his bier on a gold cloth and a gold pillar. Around him were placed the crowns of Lombardy, Bohemia and the crown of the Holy Roman Empire, the orb, the sceptre and a bared sword. He had white gloves and many rings on his fingers. He was dressed in gold and purple trousers and a purple cloak, and on his head he wore the crown of his majesty. Twelve knights carried a golden canopy above him and the bier. :

: Charles set his court sculptors, painters and craftsmen an important, if not their main task: to depict him with his wives and his family. He was convinced that everything that referred to his person and his family was to be documented and so kept for all time in the minds of his descendants. For this reason he wrote his own biography and gave his chroniclers various items of information and orders as to what they were to write. :

: Charles was greatly interested in the Roman emperors and there can be no doubt that he knew their life stories from Suetonius. (It is highly probable that the miniatures in the Vatican manuscript of Suetonius from the period around 1380 are based on some manuscript, now lost, in the Emperor's library.) Suetonius, as is known, made interesting reading, for he dealt with everything in which the rulers of ancient Rome deviated from the normal. And as Charles was interested in natural rarities and curiosities, certain places in the Czech chronicles have an almost Suetonian character. We can read in the chronicle of Beneš Krabice, for instance, that Charles organized highly original tournaments, in which his fourth wife, Empress Elizabeth of Pomerania, competed in the presence of many princes,

squires and knights with the strongest men. 'She broke with her own hands...' a new horseshoe made for a large horse, which no one could even bend, '...likewise thick and very strong soldiers' knives and those of the cooks did she break with her hands like carrots. Further, she rent apart from top to bottom the armour or coat of mail of the knights and courtiers of His Majesty the King'. :

: The bust of that Empress in the triforium of Prague cathedral stands out in size from the entire row, for it is the largest of them. What might appear as a crude formal mistake on the part of the stone-carver in Parler's lodge, finds its full justification in the report quoted. :

/187/
Master Oswald: The figure of
Charles IV on the eastern wall of
the St. Wenceslas chapel in St.
Vitus's cathedral. 1372—3.
Overpainting from the early 18th
century.

213

/188/
Charles IV at a banquet at the French royal court in the year 1378. (On the right actors are performing the conquest of Jerusalem by the Crusaders.) Illustration in Grandes Chroniques de France. Paris, Bibliothèque Nationale. 1378—80.

: In another place in his chronicle Beneš Krabice writes that during his travels about the Rhineland 'Charles lost a tooth in his sleep, without any pain, a molar it was. And in its place there grew another tooth, although His Majesty, the Emperor was fifty-seven years old . . . I am writing the truth because I saw it with my own eyes'. This must mean that Charles had shown to Beneš, and undoubtedly to other courtiers, the new tooth in his mouth, for he wished the report about his strange tooth to be recorded as an attested fact.   :

: Charles's physical appearance as a man with a stooping backbone, strikingly projecting cheekbones and a broad, slightly deformed nose corresponds as little to the Gothic canon as to our present ideal of beauty. Nevertheless, the Emperor's great interest in his own person made him insist that he be depicted in that form, which distinguished him so markedly from all others.   :

: In 1842 the father of modern Czech history, František Palacký, stated that there was a complete identity between Villani's description of Charles's appearance and the Emperor's portraits. He mentioned the bust on the triforium of St. Vitus's, the statue on the Old Town bridge tower, mural paintings at Karlstein castle, the votive panel of John Očko of Vlašim and other miniatures.   :

: There are many other examples. But Palacký did not know the results of anthropological research, which not only confirmed the identity but explained the injuries. They are entirely comprehensible in view of the fact that Charles was a very militant fighter and a dashing captain. He was not ashamed of his appearance: it included wounds he had suffered in battle waged in knightly manner according to the rules of the time.   :

: There is yet another way of explaining the relationship of these descriptions of Charles to their model. A total of sixty such documents have been recorded. Some of them are 'crypto-portraits'. According to a principle already known in antiquity and popular in the Middle Ages, the Emperor is shown on these in the figure of one of the three Magi. The number of such portraits is likely to grow as research continues.   :

: In Hoepli collection in Milan, for instance, a miniature has been discovered representing Charles IV on a charter of knighthood, which the Emperor granted to the Paduan burgher Jacopo di Santa Croce in 1355. That same year Charles knighted about fifteen hundred young men in Rome. The elongated face of the monarch in imperial robes on that miniature does not correspond to Charles's appearance.   :

: There exist a number of works which set out to represent Charles IV but which are not true portraits. They are a continuation of the art of the preceding period when it was sufficient in representing a monarch to give him the attributes of sovereignty. Most of them came into being outside the Czech Lands. Among them are works of considerable artistic value, e.g. the statue of Charles IV on the tower of St. Stephen's cathedral in Vienna, built in 1358—65. The figure of the Emperor, elongated in Gothic manner, stands on a lion here in an ingenious, almost Mannerist posture. His head resembles that of Rudolph IV on the same tower. The Vienna statue has little in common with Charles's skeleton nor with Villani's description. It is not related to the art of the Prague court even in style. Otherwise, it is artistically proof of the political and dynastic relations between the two courts.   :

: Small glyptic works, seals and coins, are very valuable for the iconography of Charles IV. Some of them did not set out to portray Charles. They continued the tradition of the older Bohemian royal seals which had already reached a high standard under Přemysl II, Wenceslas II and King John.   :

: An example of this kind is Charles's Royal Seal on two documents of the year 1354. On the seal of the University of Prague of 1348 and then on the Royal Seal of Charles IV of 1355 some of the characteristic features of the monarch's face, as known from later portraits, begin to appear.   :

: The artist who made the design of the gold florin on which Charles is depicted as King of Bohemia and Emperor of Rome did a remarkable thing. Although the semi-figure of the monarch is of miniature size, it is important as a breakthrough in the development of Charles's portraits. The florin clearly shows the brow arches and the protruding cheekbones, which gave the Emperor's face a slightly 'Mongolian' appearance. (His great-grandmother was Kunigunde of Hungary.) The broad nose is flattened as if from a blunt stroke; the moustache merges with the pointed beard.   :

: These small works of glyptics presume the existence of a monumental portrait in sculpture, which must have served as example. Unfortunately the head of Margrave Charles, like that of King John, is missing on the relief of the church of Our Lady of the Snows and no other sculptured portrait has survived in the Czech Lands from that period. But it should not be overlooked that Charles spent his youth in Paris. A major development in funeral

sculpture was taking place there; as in antiquity it began to be based on the wax masks of the deceased. The culmination of these efforts is represented in the statue of Philippe III in the abbey church at Saint-Denis. :
: This was later followed by the sculptor who made the tomb of Bořivoj in Prague cathedral; he also comes into consideration as the artist who made the bust of Charles IV in the triforium. The physiognomic features of Charles's face, which are depicted without any embellishment on the gold florin, are somewhat suppressed in the triforium. Here

/189/
Master Wilhelm(?): Charles IV as King of Rome. Mural painting in the town hall at Cologne (Hanseatic Hall). 1346—55.

the face is a little younger than it actually was at the time when the bust was made. The mouth is half open in a faint smile, and seen en face he appears satisfied and kind. In profile Charles's image corresponds to that of one of the most clever diplomats of all times. The statue of the Emperor on the throne on the Old Town bridge tower does not in any way hide his physical defects: Charles is stooping and his body is slightly twisted.
: The relationships between Charles's portraits in his oratory at Karlstein castle and the relic scenes in the church of the Virgin Mary there and the development of Parisian portrait realism have now been clarified. The importance of a report of a lost quadriptych should not be underestimated. It depicted the French King Jean le Bon, his son the Dauphin and later King Charles V, Edward III of England and the Emperor Charles IV. The well-known bust of Jean le Bon in the Louvre is perhaps a remnant of a similar quadriptych. According to later reports such a work existed also in Bohemia, one part of which was formed by a bust of Charles IV. Such portraits served as diplomatic gifts. This would explain how the depiction of the Dauphin Charles at Karlstein castle tallies fully with his portraits in France. Moreover, we can deduce from this that the Karlstein portraits of Charles IV did not in any way lag behind those in Paris in their realistic depiction. This is, in fact, confirmed by the rich pictorial accompaniment to the said report of his travels in France in the years 1377 and 1378. :
: The miniatures show how the Emperor's appearance changed in the course of time. His originally black beard began to show grey hairs on the votive panel of John Očko. In Paris it was already white and gave Charles a patriarchal appearance. Most of the miniatures do not reach the realism of the fifties. Nonetheless, that representing a banquet with a theatrical performance in the royal palace shows by the Emperor's painful expression on his face how much suffering his disease brought him. :
: On the façade of the southern transept of the church of Our Lady in Thuringian Mühlhausen the well-known 'balcony scene' was carved some time after 1362 showing Charles IV, his wife, a courtier and a court lady. The boldly conceived figure of the

Emperor bending down from the balcony recalls late antiquity or baroque illusionism. Does this scene represent a man who is stooping or not? The answer could be either—which suggests the idea that one of the motifs leading to the quite unusual conception of the Mühlhausen scene was an attempt to hide Charles's physical defects.   :

: The same is true in different manner of the engraver who made the reliquary cross of Pope Urban V in the St. Vitus's treasure. Here it can be seen that Charles's stooping had progressed considerably by 1370. This is not surprising in view of the fact that the Emperor did not look after his health. Right up to the last years of his life he undertook long and strenuous journeys, which must have given him great pain. To our surprise, however, even the Pope himself is depicted in a forward stoop so that the outlines of the two figures facing each other create an arch. We do not possess any report that indicates that the Pope was afflicted by the same bodily defect as Charles. For that reason the explanation would seem more natural that the Pope's figure was intentionally adopted to that of the Emperor. That opens up a new question, one that stands apart from the iconography of Charles IV. The figures of the saints painted in the Holy Rood chapel at Karlstein castle have often been characterized as figures without necks and in a stooping posture. This is a physical canon that is entirely non-Gothic. To what extent is this canon related to what is revealed by Charles's skeleton and Villani's characterization of his appearance?   :

: Several miniatures were made after the Emperor's death but follow older works now lost. They are equally important for the iconography of Charles IV. One of these is a miniature made in 1442. It represents Charles IV on the throne (Frauenkirche in Nuremberg). It must have been based on stained glass in that church dating back to c. 1360. The glass painting showed the Emperor, his wife and his coat of arms.   :

: There must have been many more works of this kind in many different places. They can be looked upon as taking the Emperor's place in his absence, a promise of his return and a threat to those who dared thwart his commands.   :

/191/
*The Holy Rood chapel at
Karlstein castle. Detail of the
original lighting. Before 1367.*

The catalogue comprises works of medieval art made in Bohemia and Moravia and shown in the illustrations

Architecture

ZVÍKOV Founded before 1230
/6/
Castle on a rocky cliff above the confluence of the rivers Vltava and Otava. The royal palace with a chapel in the shape of an irregular pentagon and an arcaded gallery on the first floor opening over the courtyard dates from the period of Přemysl II. It was restored in the second half of the 19th century.
D. Menclová, České hrady I (Czech Castles), Prague 1972, 213 ff; J. Kuthan, Gotická architektura v jižních Čechách (Gothic Architecture in Southern Bohemia), Prague 1972, 79 ff, 95 ff.

SEDLEC near KUTNÁ HORA, former Cistercian church 1280—1320
/5/
The church was built on a cathedral ground-plan as a basilica with nave and double aisles and a transept with nave and side aisles, an ambulatory and a ring of nine chapels off the ambulatory. The builder was under the influence of Swabian architecture (Mencl).
The reconstruction of the interior, carried out in the years 1701—6 by Jan B. Santini Aichl in the spirit of Gothic baroque, is of outstanding artistic value.
V. Mencl, U 1969, 324 ff; E. Bachmann, GiB, 76 ff.

Prague, CHURCH OF OUR LADY OF THE SNOWS 1347—97
/117/
The former monastery church of the Carmelites is the choir of an originally planned nave with side aisles. The architectonic details show a relation to the court masonic lodge of Matthias of Arras. During the Hussite wars the church was badly damaged. Renovated after 1606.
V. Kotrba, ČUG, No. 81

Prague, CHURCH OF OUR LADY AND CHARLEMAGNE (KARLOV)
After 1350 /115, 116/

The church belonged to the canonry of the Lateran Augustinians. The architectonic style of the short choir (consecrated in 1377) shows relations, in its details, to the masonic lodge of Matthias of Arras. A big eight-sided nave adjoins the choir. Bachmann's theory that it had vaulting upheld by one pier has not been confirmed by research; it is more likely that there were four piers (Mencl). The present vaulting was made by Boniface Wohlmut in 1575 with 18th century alterations. (In 1376 Charles had the 'royal throne' at Rhens built on an octagonal ground-plan.)
V. Kotrba, ČUG, 96 ff; E. Bachmann, GiB, 96 ff.

KARLSTEIN 1348—1367
/78—81, 83—95, 98—100, 102—110, 191/
Castle founded on 10 June 1348. By 1355 Charles IV already lived in it. Repairs to the castle were carried out after 1487 and 1508. Partial reconstruction was undertaken by O. Aostalis de Sala in 1588—96. In the years 1887—1904 the castle ruin was reconstructed to plans by F. Schmidt and J. Mocker. This affected the external appearance, in particular the Great Tower. The best surviving interior is that of the Emperor's oratory (known as St. Catherine's chapel) in the church tower. The double portrait of the Emperor and the Empress on the lintel was overpainted in the early 17th century, the other paintings are damaged but without overpainting. The paintings in the church of the Virgin Mary were already partly repaired after 1508. The relic scenes were painted again in the early 17th century. The cycle of the Apocalypse was overpainted in the 19th century but this has been removed. The wooden statue of the Virgin Enthroned has its original polychromy. The cycle of the Legend of St. Ludmila and St. Wenceslas in the Great Tower was crudely overpainted during Mocker's reconstruction (original fragments and copies have survived). Mocker successfully repaired the Holy Rood chapel, adding certain features on the basis of

Abbreviations:

ČNM — Časopis Národního Muzea ('Journal of the National Museum')
ČUG — České umění gotické ('Czech Gothic Art'), Prague 1970
GiB — Gotik in Böhmen (ed. K. M. Svoboda), Munich 1969
U — Umění ('Art'), Journal of the Czechoslovak Academy of Sciences

Catalogue

219

originals. The paintings in the chapel remain untouched. The medieval origin of five brush drawings on the walls of the chapel was recognized by Friedl and Krofta. The set of 130 panel paintings by master Theodoric and his workshop have largely remained in situ (with the exception of five pictures, which were transfered to the National Gallery — inv. No. Do 1880—83, 6852). They are painted directly on wood. The largest is the Crucifixion (220 × 176 cm); the pictures of the saints are all larger than 100 cm.
V. Dvořáková, D. Menclová, Karlštejn, Prague 1965; V Kotrba, ČUG, 88 ff; K. Stejskal, ČUG, No. 256—67; J. Pešina, ČUG, No. 303.

Prague, SLAVONIC ABBEY
(EMMAUS)   1348—72
/118, 121—129/
The abbey was built for the Croatian Benedictines, using Church Slavonic. The abbey hall church of Our Lady and the Slavonic Patrons is the work of two builders, the first of whom also probably built the imperial chapel and the chapter hall. The monastery building with cloisters and a cloister garth in the centre was ready by 1367. The painted right-angled sedile with the coat of arms in the abbey church has its analogy in the church of Our Lady of the Snows. The console of the church portal and the stone work in the cloisters are examples of pre-Parlerian sculpture. The typological cycle in the cloisters, amounting originally to 85 scenes, was overpainted in the 16th and the 19th centuries. The overpainting has largely been removed. In 1640—1769 the abbey was partly rebuilt in baroque style and in neo-Gothic after 1880. It was badly damaged in an air-raid on 14 February 1945.
E. Bachmann, GiB, 29; V. Kotrba, ČUG, 95 ff; K. Stejskal, ČUG, No. 268; H. Ječný, V. Píša, Slovanský benediktinský klášter v Praze (The Slavonic Benedictine Abbey in Prague), Monumentorum tutela 4, 1972, 127 ff; K. Stejskal, The Slavonic Abbey, Prague 1974.

MATTHIAS OF ARRAS, PETER PARLER:
ST. VITUS'S CATHEDRAL, Prague
                        1347—1420
/135, 139—169, 187/
It is easy to distinguish the contribution of each of the two builders of the nave and aisle of the choir with ambulatory and ambulatory chapels as well as keeping apart the pseudo-Gothic transept, the nave and aisles of the basilica and the western façade, which were built on to the old choir by

J. Mocker and K. Hilbert in the years 1873—1929. In recent decades St. Wenceslas chapel has been restored, its northern portal with figural consoles in sandstone and the statue of St. Wenceslas dating from the year 1373 in marlstone; it is 210 cm in height with original polychromy by Master Oswald. In three of the chapels at the end six tombs of Přemyslide princes and kings have been restored in marlstone (176—196 × 71—82 cm); the heads were damaged during the devastation of the cathedral in 1620. The tomb of John Očko of Vlašim is slightly damaged; it measures 204 × 90 cm and is made of white Vlašim marble. Restoration has favourably influenced the appearance of the twenty busts carved into the sandstone and the one of Canon Wenceslas of Radeč, carved into marlstone, on the triforium; their height and width is approximately 50 cm. Constant care has been given to the mosaic picture of the Last Judgment, 85 square metres in size, on the façade of the Golden Gate. Restoration has at last made it possible to distinguish the painting of Master Oswald in the St. Wenceslas and the Vlašim chapels from that done by an outstanding anonymous painter in the Saxon and the Canon's chapels.
E. Bachmann, GiB, 99 ff; V. Kotrba, ČUG, 77 ff; K. Stejskal, ČUG, No. 274—9; G. Schmidt, Wiener Jahrbuch für Kunstgeschichte 1970, 108 ff; V. Mencl, U 1971, 217 ff; K. Stejskal, U 1972, 234 ff; J. Vítovský, U 1976, 473 ff.

PETER PARLER—MASONIC
LODGE:
NORTHERN DOUBLE NAVE IN THE PARISH CHURCH OF ST. CASTULLUS in the Old Town of Prague   Before 1375
/172/
In the double nave of the northern transept of the church a console of a 'wild man' of Parlerian type has survived, which Master Klaret, Charles's lexicographer, called a faun. A similar subject is depicted in the medieval Prague house 'At the Faun'.

V. Mencl, Česká architektura doby lucemburské (Czech Architecture of the Luxemburg Period). Prague 1948, 103; K. Stejskal, U 1972, 234 ff.

PETER PARLER: CHURCH OF ST. BARTHOLOMEW at Kolín on the Elbe—CHOIR   1360—1378
/171, 173—175/
Two epitaphs confirm that Parler built the cathedral choir, attached to the early Gothic hall church from the second half of the 13th century: the inscription above his bust in the St. Vitus's triforium and an inscription carved into a stone in the sacristy of the Kolín church. The stone repository for the pyx with its sculptural decorations, including the head of a Moor, was affected by restoration in the 19th century.
V. Mencl, U 1969, 301 ff; V. Kotrba, ČUG, 83 ff.

PETER PARLER: CHARLES
BRIDGE   1357—78
/111, 178/
The inscription above his bust in the St. Vitus's triforium confirms that Peter Parler made the plans for Charles Bridge. Master John Otlín, whom other sources cite in connection with the bridge, was probably only the builder in charge of construction work. With its span of 516 m and its technical perfection, it is one of the boldest building feats of the Middle Ages. The Old Town bridge tower was also built to a design by Peter Parler, and the Emperor must have approved this personally. Its southern façade is dominated by monumental statues of Charles IV and Wenceslas IV on the throne. The tower was not completed until the end of the 14th century.
R. Chadraba, Staroměstská mostecká věž, triumfální symbolika v umění Karla IV. (The Old Town Bridge Tower, Triumphal Symbol of the Art of Charles IV), Prague 1971; V. Kotrba, ČUG, 85 ff; J. Homolka, Studie k počátkům umění krásného slohu v Čechách (Study on the Beginnings of the 'Beautiful Style' in the Czech Lands), Prague 1971, 11 ff.

TOMBSTONE OF GUTA, DAUGHTER OF WENCESLAS II
1294—7
/9/

Prague, National Museum. Marlstone, 85 × 41.2 cm. An inscription in Gothic majuscules around the edge: *Obiit Guta filia domini Wenceslai sexti regis Bohemie.* The figure is engraved with remains of resinous infill in the groove. Guta died at an early age in 1294 or 1297. She was buried in the convent of the Blessed Agnes in Prague At the Franciscans, where her tomb was discovered in 1960.
E. Pochitonov, V. Radoměrský, ČNM 1961, 1 ff; K. Stejskal, ČNM 1976, 10 ff.

THE MADONNA OF STRAKONICE
Early 14th century
/7/

Prague, National Gallery, inv. No. P 677. Pine wood, height 183 cm. The left hand of the Virgin is missing. Remnants of the original polychromy. Comes from the chapter hall of the commandery of the Knights Hospitallers of St. John at Strakonice. Kramář pointed out the French roots of this type. Probably mediated through Freiburg or Strasbourg. There is, however, no reason to assume that the statue is thirty years younger than its western patterns.
V. Kramář, Strakonická gotická madona (The Gothic Madonna of Strakonice), Volné směry 1935; J. Homolka, V. Kesner, ČUG, Catalogue of the National Gallery, Prague 1964, No. 2.

TYMPANUM WITH THE RELIEF OF THE TRINITY, THE CORONATION OF THE VIRGIN, KING JOHN AND MARGRAVE CHARLES
Before 1346
/26/

Prague, National Gallery. Sandstone. All heads and parts of the figures are damaged. The tympanum comes from the portal of the church of Our Lady of the Snows in the New Town of Prague, where it was probably taken from an older building. The figure of the donor in the right-hand corner is marked with a Moravian eagle and the monogram K on the belt (the Moravian Margrave Charles). The kneeling figure opposite represents King John of Luxemburg.
A. Kutal, U 1973, 480 ff; J. Mayer, U 1974, 426 ff.

THE CRUCIFIXION
Before 1350
/27/

Prague, National Gallery, inv. No. P 2831. Linden wood, height 123 cm. Back worked in detail. Movable arms probably from the 15th century. Well preserved original polychromy. Comes from the former convent of the Carmelite nuns in Prague-Hradčany. The Crucifixion is loosely connected with the group of the Madonna of Michle. Kutal showed that its maker was influenced by the circle of Giovanni Pisano.
A. Kutal, České gotické sochařství 1350—1450 (Czech Gothic Sculpture, 1350—1450), Prague 1962, 12; A. Kutal, J. Homolka, ČUG, No. 145.

PETER PARLER—MASONIC LODGE

Stone sculpture: see catalogue entries on: St. Vitus's cathedral, church of St. Castullus, Charles Bridge, church of St. Bartholomew at Kolín on the Elbe. Wooden sculpture: see catalogue entries on: Karlstein, Madonna.

MARTIN AND GEORGE OF CLUJ: BRONZE STATUE OF ST. GEORGE at Prague castle
1373
/170/

Prague, National Gallery. Original. Bronze with considerable addition of lead. Height of the rider 135 cm. Rests are of original gilding. B. Balbín in 1677 printed the text of an inscription on the shield of the rider (lost today): *A. D. MCCCLXXIII* (1373) *hoc opus imaginis S. Georgii per Martinum et Georgium de Clussenberch conflatum est.* Kutal showed that in the 15th century the statue stood in front of St. George's convent at Prague castle. But the author's references to the Parlerian character of the work are not convincing.
A. Kutal, Bemerkungen zum Reiterstandbild des hl. Georg auf der Prager Burg, Yearbook of the Faculty of Arts of Brno University F. 16, 1972, 35 ff; A. Kutal, J. Homolka, ČUG, No. 166.

TOMB OF PRZESLAW OF POGORZELA
c. 1376
/177/

Wrocław, cathedral. Bishop's funeral chapel (known as the Little Choir). Marble. The tomb was probably imported from Prague. It was made by the sculptor of the marble tomb of John Očko of Vlašim in Prague cathedral (Opitz considers Przeslaw's tomb of older date).
J. Opitz, Sochařství v Čechách za doby Lucemburků (Sculpture in the Czech Lands at the Time of the Luxemburgs), Prague 1935, 60.

FIGURE OF JOHN THE BAPTIST AND FIVE APOSTLES Before 1330
/23/
Strakonice, former commandery of the Knights Hospitallers of St. John, church of St. Procopius (now Adalbert), west wall of the choir loft. The central part of the large fragment has survived in a relatively good condition. The same master painted the second part of the extensive typological cycle in the cloisters.
V. Dvořáková, J. Krása, A. Merhautová and K. Stejskal, Gothic Mural Painting in Bohemia and Moravia, 28 ff, 146 ff.

COURT PAINTERS OF CHARLES IV
See catalogue entries on: Karlstein, Slavonic abbey, St. Vitus's cathedral.

SCENES FROM THE LIFE OF THE VIRGIN, FIGURES OF THE MADONNA and ANGELS After 1370
/176/
Sázava, former Benedictine monastery of St. Procopius. Paintings survive in the chapter hall built in the years 1315—40 by commission of the squires of Lipá and partly rebuilt in the 17th century. They are the work of two painters and follow the older phase of court painting closely.
V. Dvořáková, J. Krása, A. Merhautová and K. Stejskal, Gothic Mural Painting in Bohemia and Moravia, 128 ff, 145; K. Stejskal, ČUG, No. 280.

THE MADONNA OF MOST
After 1340
/33/
Prague, National Gallery. Linden wood covered with canvas, 53 × 40 cm. Comes from the Capuchin parish church at Most. One of the oldest surviving types of the *Madonna di Consolazione,* which probably arose as the result of the merger of two separate types, one Byzantine, the other Italian. Venice played a role as mediator.
J. Pešina, ČUG, No. 291; G. Schmidt, GiB, 179.

THE DEATH OF THE VIRGIN FROM KOŠÁTKY After 1340
/28/
Boston, Museum of Fine Arts. Oakwood covered with canvas, 100 × 71 cm trimmed along the sides and along the lower edge of the panel. Comes from the chapel in the chateau at Košátky. During the second world war it was taken to Boston from the State Collections of Old Art in Prague. Schmidt discovered that the painter followed a picture on the same subject by Paolo Veneziano at Vicenza of the year 1333.
A. Matějček, J. Pešina, Czech Gothic Painting, Prague 1950, No. 17; G. Schmidt, GiB, 174; R. Salvini, Arte Veneta 1976, 105 ff.

THE WROCŁAW TRINITY
Before 1353
/29/
Wrocław, Muzeum śląskie, inv. No. D 423/1. Oak-wood covered with canvas, 56 × 39 cm. Karlowska-Kamzova showed that the picture is a remnant of a diptych belonging to Ludwig, Prince of Legnica and Brzeg, closely connected with the court of Emperor Charles IV. It was made in the same workshop as the Death of the Virgin from Košátky (Boston). In 1353 an unknown illustrator of the Legend of Hedwig followed his strict composition. Similar relationships can be found in the Vyšehrad antiphonary.
J. Pešina, ČUG, No. 297; A. Karlowska-Kamzova, Roczniki sztuki śląskiej, 1970, 143 ff.

THE VYŠŠÍ BROD ALTARPIECE
c. 1347
/35/
Prague, National Gallery, inv. No. 06786—6794. Nine panels represent the Annunciation, the Nativity, the Adoration of the Magi, Christ on the Mount of Olives, the Crucifixion, the Lamentation, the Resurrection, the Ascension, and the Descent of the Holy Ghost. Maple-wood covered with canvas, 99—99.5 × 90—93 cm. The altarpiece was made for the Cistercian monastery at Vyšší Brod. The donor depicted on the Nativity is clearly Peter I of Rožmberk (d. 1347). The leading master of the workshop derived his main source of knowledge from the Adriatic school (Pešina). This is confirmed by an analysis of technique. The almost three metre high wall of pictures covered by the panels has no analogy in the west. Schmidt pointed out similar Byzantine patterns in Sinai. Similar sets of pictures can, of course, be found also among the work of the Master of the Triptych of St. Clare at Trieste.
J. Pešina, ČUG, No. 292; J. Pešina, Česká gotická desková malba (Czech Gothic Panel Painting), 14 ff; G. Schmidt, GiB, 177.

THE MADONNA OF VYŠEHRAD
After 1355
/50/
Prague-Vyšehrad, collegiate church of Sts. Peter and Paul. Pine-wood covered with canvas, 68.5 × 54 cm (painting 57.5 × 43.5 cm). It is highly likely that the work came from the one-time church of S. Maria de humilitate at Vyšehrad, founded by the Prague Archbishop John Očko of Vlašim. It is close to the picture of the Madonna dell' Umiltà by the Genoa painter Bartolomeo da Camogli of the year 1346 at Palermo.
J. Pešina, ČUG, No. 296; J. Pešina, Česká gotická desková malba (Czech Gothic Panel Painting), 22 ff.

THE MADONNA OF KŁODZKO
After 1350
/42/
Berlin, Stiftung Preussischer Kulturbesitz, Gemäldegalerie. Wood covered with canvas, 186 × 95 cm, trimmed along the lower edge of the panel. The picture was commissioned by the Archbishop of Prague Ernest of Pardubice. He is depicted on it kneeling

in front of the throne of the Madonna of Sienese-Florentine type.

A. Matějček, J. Pešina, op. cit. 14; J. Pešina, Česká gotická desková malba (Czech Gothic Panel Painting), 25.

DIPTYCH WITH THE MADONNA AND THE MAN OF SORROWS
Before 1360
/32/
Karlsruhe, Staatliche Kunsthalle, inv. No. 2431 A/B. Wood covered with canvas, 18.5 × 12.3 cm without frame. The pattern of the two semi-figures are Byzantine in origin; they reached Czech painting through Venice. They have their analogy in the miniatures of the group of the Liber Viaticus. This suggests that the diptych was made for a prelate at the imperial court.
J. Pešina, ČUG, No. 298.

THE ADORATION OF THE MAGI and THE DEATH OF THE VIRGIN
c. 1355
/38/
New York, M. Pierpont Morgan Library. Wood covered with canvas, 29 × 18.5 cm. The little pictures are damaged in places. They are perhaps the remains of a polyptych, or an altar wing, whose probable reconstruction can be based on the miniature of the Annunciation and the Presentation in the Temple in the manuscript of the Laus Mariae, both of which are closely similar in style. The picture of the Death of the Virgin loosely follows a panel on the same subject from Košátky (Boston). On the Adoration of the Magi motifs from the Adoration and the Nativity on the Vienna polyptych of Count Černín by Guariento di Arpo are merged. The design on the robes of the king in the centre, a crypto-portrait of Charles IV, is identical with that of a cushion on the Wrocław Trinity. With its loose drawing the panels are very similar to stained glass at Osek. Oettinger pointed out their close relationship to the heads of the patrons of Bohemia in the Emperor's oratory at Karlstein castle.
A. Matějček, J. Pešina, op. cit. No. 16; K. Oettinger, Zeitschrift für Kunstge-

schichte, 1937, 402; K. Stejskal, Umění a řemesla (Art and Crafts), 1974, No. 4, 43 ff.

MASTER THEODORIC called ZELO
Before 1367
/108—110/
Panel pictures in the Holy Rood chapel: see catalogue entry on Karlstein

THE EMMAUS CRUCIFIXION
c. 1370
/131/
Prague, National Gallery, inv. No. 1252. Fir-wood covered with canvas on both sides, 132 × 99 cm. Comes from the abbot's chapel in the Slavonic abbey. Similarities to the votive panel of John Očko of Vlašim suggest a return to the original dating to the period around 1370.
J. Pešina, ČUG, No. 302.

VOTIVE PANEL OF JOHN OČKO OF VLAŠIM
1371
/52, 186/
Prague, National Gallery, inv. No. 084. Pine wood, 181 × 96 cm. Comes from the archbishop's chapel at Roudnice castle, consecrated in 1371. The figures of the kneeling Charles IV, Wenceslas IV and Archbishop John Očko are depicted on it on the same scale as the figures of the Madonna and the six patrons of Bohemia. The novel stress on the autonomy of the calligraphic line can be explained by western (French) influences.
J. Pešina, ČUG, No. 304.

Stained Glass

STAINED GLASS WITH THE FIGURE OF JOHN THE BAPTIST
c. 1350
/36/
Prague, Museum of Applied Arts, inv. No. 0648. Composition in coloured glass held together by lead strips and additional painting in 'Schwarzlot', 64.5 × 39.5 cm. Comes from the chapter hall at Osek, where the reconstruction of the cloisters was finished around the year 1350. That date also corresponds with the form of the Italianized terrain and the architectonic setting on the stained glass. Matouš and Stejskal have shown relations to the typological cycle in the cloisters of the Slavonic abbey.
F. Matouš, Mittelalterliche Glasmalerei in der Tschechoslowakei, Prague 1975, 80 ff; K. Stejskal, Umění a řemesla (Art and Crafts), 1974, No. 4, 43 ff.

THE KARLSTEIN CRUCIFIXION
Before 1370
/88/
Karlstein castle, imperial palace (originally imperial oratory in the church tower). Glazed and painted glass, 64 × 60 cm. Almost the entire lower third of the scene is missing. In technical respects the glass is close to that of Osek.
A. Friedl, Theodorikův epigon (Theodoric's Epigon), Kniha o Praze (Book on Prague), Prague 1958; E. Poche, ČUG, No. 448; F. Matouš, op. cit., 40 ff; K. Stejskal, Umění a řemesla (Art and Crafts), 1974, No. 4, 43 ff.

STAINED GLASS FROM THE ARCHDEACON'S CHURCH OF ST. BARTHOLOMEW at Kolín on the Elbe
Before 1378
/174, 175/
Stained glass representing a cycle of the life of Christ was made for the new Parlerian choir before its consecration in 1378. Four scenes have survived from the Presentation in the Temple and the Death of the Virgin. Glazed and painted glass, 89.5 × 55.6 cm and 69.5 × 54 cm. In compositional layout the glass follows an older stage of court painting (the Morgan panels, Laus Mariae). The details show relations to the manuscript of the group of the Breviary of Grand Master Leo and the Karlstein Apocalypse.
E. Poche, ČUG, No. 450; F. Matouš, op. cit., 44 ff; K. Stejskal, Umění a řemesla (Art and Crafts), 1974, No. 4, 43 ff.

THE OXFORD ARCHER After 1350
/37/

Oxford, Christ Church. Brush drawing on parchment, 26.7 × 16 cm, cut out of a larger sheet or a workshop pattern-book. Some scholars (Bell, Dusler) take it to be of Sienese origin. Pächt attributed it to the Master of the Parament of Narbonne (c. 1380), while Meiss and Stejskal, independently, to the court circle of Charles IV. Its position in the development of drawing can be clarified by comparison with the Death of the Virgin from Košátky (Boston), the Wrocław Trinity and the Vyšehrad Madonna. There is an especially close relationship to the Morgan panels. A similar type appears on the Emmaus typological cycle (the Stoning of Christ) and in the Zagreb Bible of Purkart of Janovice.

Catalogue: Painting and Drawings from Christ Church, Oxford, London 1960, No. 21; O. Pächt, Burlington Magazine 1956, 150; M. Meis, French Painting in the Time of Jean de Berry, Phaidon 1967, 190 ff; K. Stejskal, U 1967, 53.

MASTER OSWALD: DRAWING OF THE MADONNA WITH ST. WENCESLAS   1360 – 70
/101/

Stockholm, Royal Library. Pen drawing, partly washed, included in a missal of Bohemian origin. The pattern of St. Wenceslas has a close analogy in the figure of Prince Boleslav on the scene of Washing Away the Blood on the staircase cycle at Karlstein castle. The fine modelling of the shapes on the drawing is identical to the semifigures of angels on the right half of the eastern wall of the St. Wenceslas chapel in Prague cathedral, which are the authentic work of Master Oswald.

Z. Drobná, Gotische Zeichnung in Böhmen, Prague, 1956, 41; K. Stejskal, U 1961, 1355 ff.

THREE SHEETS CUT OUT OF A WORKSHOP PATTERN-BOOK
c. 1370
/133/

Erlangen, Universitätsbibliothek, sign. I A 1, I A 2; Dessau, Staatliche Galerie. Parchment. Pen, brush, reddish-brown ink. On the first sheet in Erlangen, 13.8 × 13.5 cm, there is a philosopher and an astronomer with a sextant; on the second, 12.7 × 17.2 cm, a sitting prophet, a figure of a youth and an old man with a stick. The drawing at Dessau, 15 × 7.8 cm, represents John the Evangelist. The inscriptions *Juncker von Brag* (Prague) *gemacht* date from the 16th or 17th century. The drawings show a relationship to the votive panel of John Očko of Vlašim and particularly to the Emmaus Crucifixion. Their dating is based on similarities to the miniatures of John of Opava of the year 1368.

Z. Drobná, ČUG, No. 406; K. Stejskal, U 1976, 35 ff.

LECTIONARY OF ARNOLD OF MEISSEN CALLED OF OSEK
c. 1290
/8/

Prague, State Library of the Czech Socialist Republic, Ms 76, depositary Osek. Parchment, 246 ff., 42.5 × 32.3 cm, binding from the year 1306. Two-volume lectionary written by Arnold of Meissen, Wenceslas II's Chancellor, for the Cistercian convent of Mariae Stella in Lusatia. It contains Franciscan motifs, for it was made in the same workshop as a slightly older Franciscan Bible (Prague, Library of the National Museum, XII B 13). Its ornamentation comprises a total of 125 large initials with figural scenes and ornamental designs and a number of drolleries.

A. Friedl, Lekcionář Arnolda Míšeňského (The Lectionary of Arnold of Meissen) Prague 1928; K. Stejskal, ČNM 1976, No. 1, 13 ff.

THE LIFE OF ST. FRANCIS   c. 1300
/10/

Prague, Nostitz Library (today Library of the National Museum), Ms 13. Parchment, 116 folios, 20.2 × 14.5 cm. Original binding. The Bohemian origin of the manuscript is given by the description of miracles that happened to squire Wenceslas of Němčice in Prague (fol. 60 v) and squire John of Vinařice (fol. 77 r). The first illuminator, who painted 33 small figural scenes and all ornamental initials, was trained in Paris. The remaining 15 miniatures are the work of the second illuminator, trained in Bologna.

J. V. Šimák: Rukopisy majorátní knihovny hrabat z Nostic a Rienecka v Praze (Manuscripts of the Family Library of the Squires of Nostitz and Rieneck in Prague), Prague 1910, 102. (I am indebted to Dr. J. Krása for the reference to this manuscript.)

THE PASSIONAL OF ABBESS KUNIGUNDE 1313—21
/12/
Prague, State Library of the Czech Socialist Republic, Ms XIV A 17. Parchment, 37 folios, 30 × 25 cm, old binding. The manuscript comprises mystical tractates, two of which were composed by the Dominican Kolda of Koldice. He is depicted on folio 1 b, handing his work to Kunigunde, the daughter of King Přemysl Otakar II, the Abbess of the convent of the Benedictine nuns of St. George's at Prague castle. By his side there is a picture of the St. George's Canon Beneš, the scribe and editor of the Passional, whose text he accompanied by his own verses and by outstanding illustrations on 26 pages.
K. Stejskal, Le chanoine Beneš, scribe et enlumineur du Passionnaire de l'abbesse Cunégonde, Scriptorium XXIII (Gand 1969), 52 ff; E. Urbánková, K. Stejskal, Pasionál Přemyslovny Kunhuty (The Passional of Kunigunde Přemyslide), Prague 1975.

ASTRONOMICAL CODEX OF THE KINGS OF BOHEMIA 1301—34
/25/
Bernkastel-Cues, Library of the Hospital of St. Nicholas, cod. Cus. 207. Parchment, 155 folios, 33 × 24 cm, new binding. The first part of the codex (folios 1—92) was written for King Wenceslas II in 1301. The second part (folios 93—155) was finished in 1334 for his grandson, then Margrave and later Emperor Charles IV. Folios 115v and 116r have drawings of seven planetary gods based partly on antique, partly on Babylonian-Arab patterns. Another astronomer drew 48 figures of the constellations on folios 124 v to 135 r, based on Sicilian-Arab patterns.
A. Krchňák, Mitteilungen und Forschungsbeiträge der Cusanusgesellschaft 3, Mainz 1963, 117 ff; E. Urbánková, K. Stejskal, op. cit. 47, 89 ff, 117 ff.

POSTIL OF NICHOLAS OF LYRA
Before 1350
/34/
Krakow, Biblioteka Jagiellońska, cod.

1472. Parchment, 190 folios, 35.2 × 26 cm, old binding. The manuscript comprises eight figural initials, a proof of Venetian influences.
Z. Ameisenowa, Rekopisy i pierwodruki iluminowane Biblioteki Jagiellońskiej, Wrocław—Kraków, 1958, No. 108; J. Krása, U 1971, 395.

THE VELISLAV BIBLE Before 1350
/41/
Prague, State Library of the Czech Socialist Republic, XIII C 124. Parchment, 188 folios, 30.7 × 24.5 cm, new binding. The book contains a total of 747 drawn illustrations divided into two strips. Subject matter is drawn from the Old Testament, the Apocrypha, writings on the Antichrist and legends, among others about St. Ludmilla and St. Wenceslas. On folio 188 r there is a picture of the person who commissioned the work, Velislav; he can be identified with a canon of the same name who was a high court dignitary of Charles IV. The illustrators used patterns in Romanesque manuscripts for many of the illustrations.
K. Stejskal, Velislai biblia picta, Pragae MCMLXX; G. Schmidt, GiB, 170.

THE PSALTER OF THE KARLSTEIN CHAPTER Before 1350
/97/
Prague, Library of the National Museum, XVI BA 18. Parchment, 79 folios, 41 × 28 cm., Renaissance binding. The manuscript was made for the convent of the Benedictine nuns of St. George's in Prague. In the years 1357—9 it was transferred to the Karlstein chapter. It contains entries on the death of Charles IV and some of the canons. Its ten biblical scenes in the initials are matched by small scenes along the lower margin of the pages selected according to the method of typological parallelism. The ornamentation of the manuscript, partly damaged by damp, belongs to the older works of the workshop of the Breviary of Grand Master Leo.
J. Krása, ČUG, No. 343.

THE OLOMOUC MISSAL c. 1360
/96/
Olomouc, State Archives (Chapter Library), No. 134. Parchment, 257 folios, 37.7 × 27.5 cm, original binding. Calendar of the Prague diocese. The codex with several ornamental and 10 figural initials was made in the workshop of the Breviary of Grand Master Leo. The type of faces reveals a close relation to the Karlstein Apocalypse.
J. Krása, ČUG, No. 345; K. Stejskal, U 1971, 381 ff.

GRADUAL OF ERNEST OF PARDUBICE 1363
/45/
Prague, Chapter Library, P 7. Parchment, 310 folios, 52 × 35.5 cm, original binding. This is one of a set of nine choral books which Archbishop Ernest of Pardubice presented to the St. Vitus's chapter before the year 1364. Six of these have survived. All were made in the workshop of the Breviary of Grand Master Leo, partly by one of the weaker masters. In the ornaments of these manuscripts Romanesque shapes alternate with massive acanthus adopted from the illuminator of the Latin Emmaus Bible. It can be assumed that the figural ornamentation is largely an echo of the mature works of panel painting, stained glass and so on.
J. Krása, ČUG, No. 346.

MISSAL OF PROVOST NICHOLAS
c. 1355
/47/
Brno, City Archives. St. Jacob's Library, 10/1. Parchment, 406 folios, 38 × 27 cm, original binding. On the cross bar of initial A on folio 1 r there is the inscription: *Dominus Nicolaus praepositus Brunensis.* The oldest surviving element of the group of Liber Viaticus. Apart from several ornamental initials it contains three figural miniatures. On the canon's sheet with the Crucifixion (fol. 181 v) there can be detected a trend towards looser drawing and softer shapes, which was then to continue in book and panel painting (Laus Mariae, the Morgan panels). Dostál proved, contrary to Dvořák, that the ornamentation of the manuscript and the entire group of Liber Viaticus derived directly from Italy, not through the intermediary of Avignon.
E. Dostál, Čechy a Avignon (Bohemia and Avignon), abstract in the journal of the Matice Moravská 46, Brno 1922; J. Krása, ČUG, No. 347.

MINIATURE OF THE RESURRECTION Before 1360
/49/
Olomouc, Archbishop's Library. Parchment, initial in a frame, 8.4 × 8.9 cm. The miniature was cut out of an unknown manuscript; it comes from the workshop of the Master of the Liber Viaticus.
J. Krása, ČUG, No. 348.

LIBER VIATICUS OF JOHN OF STŘEDA Before 1360
/48/
Prague, Library of the National Museum, XIII A 12. Parchment, 319 folios,

42.5 × 31 cm. Original binding altered in the 16th century. The luxurious breviary was made for the Bishop of Litomyšl, John of Středa, Charles's chancellor. Folios 307 to 319 contain, among others, the offices of St. Wenceslas, composed by the Emperor himself. Apart from figural initials, semi-figures of the prophets and genre scenes along the margin of the sheets there is an exceptional wealth of filigree and calligraphic initials with motifs of astragal, masks, etc. A large part of the ornamentation was made by the Master of the Viaticus, the most outstanding personality among the chancellor's illuminators. The adligatum to the manuscript was made in the workshop of the Breviary of Grand Master Leo.

J. Krása, ČUG, No. 349; ditto, U 1971, 396 ff.

LAUS MARIAE or MARIALE ARNESTI c. 1360

/43, 44/

Prague, Library of the National Museum, XVI D 13. Parchment, 170 folios, 30 × 20 cm, 15th century binding. Apart from filigree initials the manuscript contains two outstanding full-page pictures of the Presentation in the Temple (folio 34 v) and the Annunciation (folio 55 v). They are closely related to the Missal of Provost Nicholas and to some works of panel paintings (the Boston Madonna and especially the Morgan panels). In the conception of the painted architecture they follow up the Death of the Virgin from Košátky (Boston).

J. Krása, ČUG, No. 350.

ORATIONALE ARNESTI Before 1364

/46/

Prague, Library of the National Museum, XIII C 12. Parchment, 153 folios, 30.5 × 21 cm, 16th century binding. Collection of prayers, meditations and period mystical writings. The final prayer was composed by Archbishop Ernest of Pardubice, who had commissioned the manuscript. The formal purity of the ornamentations is made up of four figural initials, with short acanthus decorations and small initials with filigree made by the scribe. The author of the miniatures is the illuminator of the Missal of John of Středa.

J. Krása, ČUG, No. 351.

MISSAL OF JOHN OF STŘEDA After 1364

/51/

Prague, Chapter Library, Cim 6. Parchment, 235 folios, 44.5 × 32 cm. Added to the text of the psalter are Marian hymns and verses in honour of

St. Jerome, some of which were composed by the bishop's friend Francesco Petrarch. The ornamentation includes 16 figural and 48 ornamental initials. The scene of the Annunciation, in which the angel comes to the Virgin with a letter, is not inspired by the Gospel but by Dante's verse: *L'angel che venne in terra col decreto.* The illuminator was a disciple of the Master of the Viaticus.

J. Krása, ČUG, No. 352.

THE EVANGELIARIUM OF JOHN OF OPAVA 1368

/53, 54/

Vienna, Österreichische Nationalbibliothek, cod. 1182. Parchment, 191 (189) folios, 37.5 × 25.6 cm. The original gilded binding was enhanced in 1446 with an engraved symbol of Frederick III. It contains the complete texts of the four Gospels. It was made for Duke Albrecht III of Austria (1350—95), Charles's son-in-law. The explicit on folio 190 v runs: *Et ego Johannes de Oppavia presbiter canonicus Brunensis plebanus in Lantskrona hunc librum cum auro purissimo de pena scripsi iluminavi et deo cooperante complevi in anno domini millesimo trecentesimó sexagesimo octavo.* The splendid written execution of this gold codex is in keeping with the exceptional wealth of its painted ornaments. The acanthus ornament and heraldic motifs merge into a perfect unit with figural subjects. Full-page initials are placed on the opposite side to scenes from the life of the four Evangelists, set out in the manner of a polyptych of twelve pictures. The individual chapters of the Gospels comprise a total of 85 small initials with epic scenes. The painter who made the Missal of John of Středa cooperated with John of Opava on the ornamentation of the manuscript. Both of them used ancient patterns, of Carolingian and Byzantine origin.

J. Krása, ČUG, No. 353.

THE EMMAUS BIBLE c. 1360

/130/

Prague, Chapter Library, A 2. Parchment, 165 folios, 47 × 32.7 cm, original binding. The second volume of the Latin Bible, beginning with the Book of Kings as far as the Book of Job. (The first volume has likewise survived and is deposited in the same library under the signature A 3; the Bible was transferred there probably at the beginning of the 18th century.) Its origin is given both in a Czech entry and in the miniature on folio 129 v, representing St. Jerome teaching the bearded Benedictines of his Prague

monastery. The Bible contains figural initials at the beginning of each individual book or prologue. Its author used examples based on mural paintings in the Slavonic abbey and at Karlstein castle. Connections can be traced back to the stained glass at Osek. It is highly probable that the illuminator was trained as a glass painter.

J. Krása, ČUG, No. 354; K. Stejskal, The Slavonic Abbey, Prague 1974, 87 ff.

THE VYŠEHRAD ANTIPHONARY 1360—61

/30, 132/

Vorau, Chorherrenstift, cod. 259. Parchment, 397 folios and 419 folios and 407 folios and 326 folios, 38 × 56 cm. The four-volume antiphonary was presented to the Vyšehrad chapter by its provost Dětřich of Portice, Bishop of Minden. 37 miniatures were made in the same workshop as the ornamentation of the Breviary of Grand Master Leo. The remaining 43 miniatures are the work of the illuminator of the Latin Emmaus Bible. Most of them are details of the monumental paintings at Emmaus, Karlstein castle and elsewhere.

P. Buberl, Die illuminierten Handschriften in Steiermark IV/1, Leipzig 1911, 205 ff; J. Krása, ČUG, No. 354; K. Stejskal, Osobnost mistra emauzského cyklu (The Personality of the Master of the Emmaus Cycle), Gotyckie malarstwo ścienne v Europie środkowo-wschodniej, Poznań 1977, 74 ff.

THE PONTIFICAL OF ALBRECHT OF STERNBERG 1376

/55/

Prague, Library of the Museum of National Literature (Strahov), Dg I. 19. Parchment, 151 folios, 41.5 × 30.5 cm, binding from the year 1581. According to an authentic inscription on folio 1 r this codex was written for Albrecht of Sternberg, Bishop of Litomyšl and Magdeburg by scribe Hodík. It is possible that he was also the illuminator of 45 initials with pictures relating to church ceremonies. They are a simplified version of the principles of Bohemian court paintings of the 1360s. The miniature on folio 34 v, on

which Charles IV worships the Man of Sorrows by the side of the man who commissioned the work, has a parallel in another work by the same illuminator, the unfinished Bible of Albrecht of Sternberg in the Jagiellon Library in Krakow, MS 284.
J. Krása, ČUG, No. 358; Z. Ameisenowa, Rękopisy i pierwodruki iluminowane Biblioteki Jagiełłońskiej, No. 110.

THE CHRONICLE OF PŘIBÍK PULKAVA OF RADENÍN   c. 1374
/72/
Krakow, Muzeum narodowe, Biblioteka Czartoryskich, cod. 1414. Parchment, 139 folios, 32 × 23 cm, new binding. The manuscript contains the Latin text of the Czech chronicle of Přibík Pulkava of Radenín and two works of the Emperor Charles IV (*Ordo ad cornandum regem Bohemorum, Ordo ad benedicendum reginam*). The painted ornamentation is limited to the title page. The young Wenceslas IV is depicted on the throne in the initial C. The ornamentation is based on the group of manuscripts of John of Středa; the motif of the herons appears here, which is known from later manuscripts of Wenceslas IV. The ornamentation in the Czech manuscript of the Six Books of Thomas of Štítný in the State Library of the Czech Socialist Republic in Prague is attributed to the same illuminator (XVII A 6).
J. Krása, ČUG, No. 355; K. Stejskal, U 1974, 554.

THE LEGEND AND OFFICE OF ST. ELIGIUS   1378
/77/
Paris, Bibliothèque historique de la ville de Paris. Parchment. The codex was written and magnificently illuminated in the Czech Lands. From there it was sent to Paris in return for the mitre of St. Eligius, which Charles brought back from his journey through France in early 1378. It is decorated with figural scenes on rectangular fields which reveal a relationship to the group of the Liber Viaticus and also anticipate the work of the illuminators of Wenceslas IV.
La bibliothèque historique de la ville de Paris, 1969, 30, 57.

THE ZBRASLAV CHRONICLE   1393
/1/
Jihlava, City Archives, cod. Ms 118. Parchment, 185 folios, 46 × 32.3 cm. The manuscript includes pen drawings of standing figures of the Přemyslides, Luxemburgs and their wives and on folio 6 v a picture of Charles IV.
Z. Drobná, ČUG, No. 409.

MATTHEW PTÁČEK-ORNYS: CODEX OF EMPEROR MAXMILIAN II, called CODEX HEIDELBERGENSIS   1574—5
/134/
Prague, depository of the Czechoslovak Academy of Sciences in the National Gallery, sign. AA 2015. Paper, 65 folios, 38.5 × 25.5 cm. Miniatures on paper were cut out at the beginning of the 18th century, partly re-arranged and glued on to paper sheets. The second, larger example of the codex is kept in the Österreichische Nationalbibliothek in Vienna, cod. Ms 8330. Both codices are the work of the imperial surveyor and illuminator Matthew Ptáček-Ornys of Lindperk (1526—1600). Its most important part is the genealogical series which was probably designed to serve as pattern for the renovation of the destroyed Karlstein family tree. The names and titles of the monarchs were copied by Ornys from an older document *Linea Caroli IV.* Apart from the figures of the cycle of Kings of Bohemia, painted in the early 16th century at Prague castle and other Renaissance patterns, he used a Gothic pattern book from the years 1370—90. Part of this pattern book corresponds in style to the drawings at Erlangen and Dessau.
K. Stejskal, Matouš Ornys a jeho „Rod císaře Karla IV." (Matthew Ornys and his 'Genealogy of Emperor Charles IV'), U 1976, 13 ff.

Applied Arts

PLENARY FROM ST. GEORGE'S CONVENT called STRAHOV PLENARY   c. 1307
/11/
Prague, Church of Our Lady at Strahov, St. Norbert's altar in the chapel consecrated to that saint. Plenary No. 1. Wood covered with silver foil, crystal, gemstones, enamel, 65 × 45 cm. Medallions with impressed reliefs of the Evangelists are affixed to the corners of the plenary. Plenary No. 2 has richer ornamentation, and is of the same provenance and deposition. A quatrefoil with a relief of the Annunciation is, among others, attached to it, identical with that which adorns the crossing of arches on the funeral crown of the Czech King Rudolf Kaše († 1307).
E. Poche, Plenáře svatojiřské (The St. George's Plenaries), U 1972, 226 ff; E. Urbánková, K. Stejskal, op. cit. 91 ff.

THE MAJESTIC AND RIDER'S SEAL OF JOHN OF LUXEMBURG   1310—19
/24/
Prague, State Archives. Circular wax seal, 11.5 cm. In typological respects it follows up an older seal of the Kings of Bohemia. Its outstanding execution makes it one of the leading works of French oriented post-classical Gothic.
F. Beneš, České panovnické pečeti z let 1310—1526 (Seals of the Bohemian Monarchs from the years 1310—1526). Muzejní zprávy pražského kraje IV (Museum Records of Prague Region IV), 1959, 1 ff; J. Krása, U 1976, 456.

ANTEPENDIUM OF PIRNA   After 1340
/31/
Meissen, Staatliche Kunstsammlungen (Albrechtsburg). Canvas, brightly coloured silk, gold braid, 125 × 370 cm. The figures of nine saints are set around the central scene of the Coronation of the Virgin, including the patron saints of Bohemia, Sts. Wenceslas, Adalbert, Procopius and Vitus.
E. Poche, ČUG, No. 453.

THE ST. WENCESLAS CROWN   1346
/59/
Prague, treasure of St. Vitus's cathedral. Gold, pearls, sapphires, spinels, emeralds, rubies—a total of 20 pearls and 91 gemstones. Height 21 cm. The four parts of the headband are linked together with hinges. A lily rises from each part. On the crossing of the

arches there is a Byzantine cameo from the 13th century (sapphire) with a cross and a Greek inscription. The crown was first used during the coronation of Charles IV in 1347; it was altered after 1354 but before the year 1387.
E. Poche, ČUG, No. 417.

CASE FOR THE ST. WENCESLAS CROWN   1347
/58/
Prague, treasure of St. Vitus's cathedral. Cut and hammered leather, coloured, height 25.3 cm, width 32 cm. Petal-shaped coats of arms of the empire, Bohemia, the Prague archbishopric and that of Ernest of Pardubice. Inscription of dedication with the date 1347.
E. Poche, ČUG, No. 160.

RELIQUARY CROSS WITH CAMEOS   c. 1349
/60/
Prague, treasure of St. Vitus's cathedral, inv. No. 25 (97). Gold, cameos, sapphires, height 62.5 cm. Cross of Greek shape corresponding by the lilies at the end of its smooth arms to the crown of the kings of Rome in the treasure of the cathedral at Aachen; this was made on Charles's orders in 1349. It is adorned with three antique cameos, five Byzantine and one from the 13th century representing the Emperor Frederick II of Hohenstaufen on the throne.
E. Poche, ČUG No. 427.

CRYSTAL DISH IN A SILVER MOUNT   After 1353
/62/
Prague, treasure of St. Vitus's cathedral, inv. No. L 16 (112). Crystal, gilded silver, height 9.5 cm. The crystal dish from Venice (13th century) was adapted on Charles's orders in 1353 to hold the alleged veil of the Virgin.
E. Poche, ČUG, No. 424.

CRYSTAL JUG IN A GILDED SILVER MOUNT   1348
/63/
Prague, treasure of St. Vitus's cathedral, inv. No K 33 (103). Crystal, gilded silver, pearls, malachites, sapphires, emeralds, height 47 cm. Charles had a magnificent mounting made for the drilled and polished crystal jug of Egyptian or Italian provenance and its lid. Altered in the 16th century.
E. Poche, ČUG, No. 419.

ONYX GOBLET   1350
/61/
Prague, treasure of St. Vitus's cathedral, inv. No. K 32 (222). Onyx, gilded silver, partly enamel, height 15.4 cm.

Charles had a stem made for the semi-egg-shaped onyx bowl of Venetian origin; it bears an enamel coat of arms with an inscription of dedication and the date 1350.
E. Poche, ČUG, No. 420.

BINDING OF THE CAROLINGIAN NEW TESTAMENT WITH A CONSUL'S DIPTYCH
c. middle of 14th century
/64/
Prague, Chapter Library, Cim 2. Ivory, gilded copper, carved, crystals, gemstones, 35 × 27 cm. The relief of a late Roman consul's diptych from the 5th century is set in a broad metal frame divided by twisted gold wire into eight fields. The semi-figures of the patron saints of Bohemia are engraved around gemstones set in oval rectangular mounts. Semi-figures of saints are set in the centre of the lateral fields under crystal lenses.
E. Poche, ČUG, No. 462.

RELIQUARY CROSS, said to belong to POPE URBAN V   1368—76
/65/
Prague, treasure of St. Vitus's cathedral, inv. No. K 36 (94). Gold, black enamel, crystal, gemstones, height 31.3 cm. Cross of Greek type, smooth. In the centre on the front, below an oval crystal lens, is a particle of the alleged garment of Christ, which Charles received from Pope Urban V in Rome in 1368. The Pope is depicted on the cross together with the Emperor, Wenceslas IV and Cardinal Pietro de Bellifortis. The upper field on the horizontal bar of the cross bears a scene of the Crucifixion. The figures are engraved into the gold and filled with black enamel. Cibulka showed the important developments of this technique.
J. Cibulka, Zlatnická rytina jako předchůdce grafické rytiny (Gold Engraving as Predecessor to Graphic Engraving), Umění (Štencovo), 1932, 107 ff; E. Poche, ČUG, No. 430.

CASE FOR THE TUNIC OF ST. JOHN THE EVANGELIST
1368—76
/66/
Vienna, Weltliche Schatzkammer. Gold, black enamel, crystal, height 15 × 24.8 cm. The flat lid is covered with eight scenes from the life of John the Evangelist, engraved by the artist who decorated the cross of Pope Urban V. The mature style of his composition shows that he had received his training in Italy. The same artist made the case for the bonds of the apostles kept since 1423 also in Vienna.

J. Cibulka, op. cit.; E. Poche, ČUG, No. 430.

THREE RELIQUARIES OF CHARLES IV
Third quarter of 14th century
/70/
Aachen, cathedral treasure. Reliquary for the rope from the scourging of Christ: gilded silver, crystal, pearls, gemstones, cameos, height 54 cm. Reliquary for Christ's belt: gilded silver, crystal, gemstones, cameos, height 69.5 cm. Reliquary for the belt of the Virgin Mary: gilded silver, crystal, gemstones, enamel, height 62.5 cm. Reliquaries of outstanding wealth with remarkable refinement of architectonic and figural motifs.
E. G. Grimme, Der Aachener Domschatz, Düsseldorf 1973, No. 73 — 75.

RELIQUARY BUST OF CHARLEMAGNE   Probably 1376
/71/
Aachen, cathedral treasure. Beaten silver, partly gilded, cameos, gemstones, height 86.3 × 57.2 × 33 cm. The mature modelling of the facial muscles and the stylization of the hair and beard of the bust correspond to the head of Christ on the Pietà in St. Thomas's in Brno. The same radical proto-Renaissance trend can be found on the bust of Wenceslas of Radeč in the St. Vitus's triforium. The gilded silver crown, 21 cm in diameter, was probably made for the coronation of Charles IV in Aachen in 1349. It is set with gemstones, three large pearls and seven cameos.
E. Poche, Einige Erwägungen über die Kameen Karls IV., Collection in Honour of J. Květ's Seventieth Birthday, Prague 1965, 88 ff; E. G. Grimme, op. cit, No. 69.

RELIQUARY FOR THE MITRE OF ST. ELIGIUS   1378
/76/
Prague, National Museum, inv. No. 60701. Gilded silver, crystal, height 32.5 cm. The metal framework of the reliquary surrounding the rock crystal infill has the shape of the mitre. The inscription on the elliptical base

of the reliquary indicates that the Emperor Charles IV gave the mitre of St. Eligius to the Brotherhood of Prague Goldsmiths in 1378, having received it from the King of France (Charles V).
E. Poche, ČUG, No. 432.

THE SEAL OF CHARLES UNIVERSITY   1348
/182/
Prague archives of Charles University. Silver, circular, diameter 6.05 cm. The work is memorable for Charles being depicted on it in the same robes as St. Wenceslas, before whom he is kneeling in a Byzantine coat of mail.
K. Chytil, Typ sv. Václava na pečeti Karlovy university a ve viatiku Jana ze Středy a jeho deriváty (The Type of St. Wenceslas on the Seal of Charles University and in the Liber Viaticus of John of Středa and its Derivations), Památky archeologické (Archeological Monuments) 1928—30, 201 ff.

THE ROYAL SEAL OF CHARLES IV   1354
/181/
Prague, Chapter Library, sign. XI, 2. Circular wax seal, diameter 10 cm. Charles is sitting on the throne in majesty and on the inscription is given as King of Rome and Bohemia. As regards typology, the seal follows up an older seal of the Kings of Bohemia.
E. Poche, ČUG, No. 418.

THE SEAL CALLED THE GOLDEN BULL OF CHARLES IV   After 1348
/183/
Prague, Chapter Library. Gold foil, wax, diameter 6.1 cm. The monarch, sitting in majesty on the imperial throne, is marked as King of Rome and Bohemia in the inscription.
E. Posse, Die Siegel der deutschen Kaiser und Könige II. Dresden 1910, Table 3, pict. 6—7.

GOLD DUCAT WITH A PICTURE OF CHARLES IV AS KING OF BOHEMIA   1346—78
/184/
Prague, National Museum. Gold, diameter 21 mm, weight 3.25 g. The picture represents the semi-figure of the young Charles with the royal crown of Bohemia. Inscription: *KAROLUS DEI GRACIA.*
E. Nohejlová-Prátová, Krása české mince (The Beauty of the Czech Coin), Prague 1955, 122 ff.

GOLD DUCAT WITH A PICTURE OF CHARLES IV AS HOLY ROMAN EMPEROR   1355—1378
/185/
Prague, National Museum. Gold, diameter 22 mm, weight 3.482 g. The picture of faithful portrayal shows Charles with the imperial crown. Inscription: *KAROLUS DEI GRACIA.*
E. Nohejlová-Prátová, op. cit. 124 ff.

PILGRIM'S BADGE WITH CHARLES IV AND THE POPE   1350—78
/57/
Prague, Museum of the City of Prague. Cast metal, height 6 cm. The pilgrim's badge with one surviving attachment for a chain, on the right. It represents the Pope with the key of St. Peter and the Emperor Charles with the Longinus's lance, standing on each side of the Cross. Coats of arms at the foot: to the left, that of the Pope, in the middle the imperial, and on the right that of Bohemia.
D. Stará, Cín — z dějin českého kovářství (Pewter, Chapters from the History of Bohemian Metal-Casting), catalogue of an exhibition in the National Museum, Prague 1972, 12, pict. 1.

Some Political Events

1316 (14 May)
Charles IV born in Prague

1322
John of Luxemburg helps Ludwig IV of Bavaria to win the battle of Mühldorf and gets the Cheb (Eger) region in reward

1323—1329
Charles educated at the Royal Court of France (1323 confirmed in Avignon)

1328
Ludwig IV of Bavaria crowned Emperor in Rome

1331—1333
Charles helps his father to assert his right to the Luxemburg signoria in Italy

1333—1335
Charles Regent of the Kingdom of Bohemia—participates in the meeting of monarchs at Trenčín

1336—1337
Charles accompanies King John to Lithuania—enters the Venetian League—travels from Buda to Venice via Croatia and Dalmatia—made Captain of Belluno and Feltre for life

1339
Charles takes part in the campaign against Edward III, King of England

1340
Charles prepares the campaign against the Saracens at Montauban—extends his signoria in northern Italy

Chronological Table

Economic and Cultural History	The Most Important Foundations by Czech Monarchs and Prelates	Other Data of Art and Historical Interest
		1315—1323 Nine liturgical codices of Queen Elizabeth Rycheza
		1316 The Seal of King John of Luxemburg
1318 John IV of Dražice, Bishop of Prague, leaves for Avignon	**1319** John of Luxemburg founds the church of St. James in Prague	**1318** John of Luxemburg remunerates goldsmith John of Greece
		1321 Canon Beneš finishes the illuminations of the Passional of Abbess Kunigunde
1323 Poet Guillaume de Machaut enters the services of John of Luxemburg		**1324** The Brotherhood of Goldsmiths established in Prague
		1325 Gold florins of John of Luxemburg
1329 John IV of Dražice, Bishop of Prague, returns from Avignon—has his Prague palace reconstructed	**1329** Queen Elizabeth Přemyslide founds nine chapels and altars in the monastery church at Zbraslav	**before 1330(?)** Sculptural decorations of the House at the Bell in Prague
	1332 Bishop John IV of Dražice lays the foundations of the Augustinian monastery at Roudnice	**1333** Arrival of builder William of Avignon in the Czech Lands
	1333 Charles founds the castle and town of Monte Carlo near Lucca—the beginning of the reconstruction of Prague castle	**1334** The Atlas of the Constellations of the Czech Kings completed (Cod. Cus 207)
		1335 Queen Elizabeth Rycheza remunerates painters Oldřich and Pešek
		1336 Paintings in the Dominican church at Opava (painter Nicholas)
1338 The Prague burghers given the right to set up a town hall in the Old Town		**before 1338** John of Brabant casts the (now lost) tomb of Wenceslas II
	1339 Bishop John IV of Dražice has the church of St. Giles in Prague rebuilt (consecrated in 1371)	
	after 1340 Charles founds Karlsburg-Tepenec castle in Moravia	

Political Events

1342
Charles's teacher Cardinal Pierre Roger de Rosiers made Pope Clement VI

1344—1345
Charles accompanies King John to Lithuania for the second time

1346
Charles elected King of the Holy Roman Empire at Rhens — crowned that same year in Bonn — John of Luxemburg killed at the battle of Crécy

1347
Charles crowned King of Bohemia — death of Emperor Ludwig IV of Bavaria

1348
The plague spreads in Europe with the exception of Bohemia

1349
Charles crowned King of the Holy Roman Empire at Aachen for the second time

1351
Francesco Petrarch appeals to Charles to revive the old Roman Empire

1354
Death of Charles's great-uncle, the Archbishop and Elector of Trier Balduin — Charles enters the Venetian League against the Viscontis and undertakes his first Roman progress — meeting with Francesco Petrarch in Mantua

1355
Charles crowned King of Lombardy in Milan and Emperor of the Holy Roman Empire — death of the 'Czar of the Serbs and Greeks', Stephen Dushan — beginning of the Turkish occupation of the Balkan peninsula

1356
Charles issues the Golden Bull (set of rules for the election of the kings of the Romans) — King Jean II le Bon of France taken prisoner by the English in the battle of Poitiers

1356—1357
Charles accepts the homage of the Dauphin of France (Charles V) at the Imperial Diet at Metz and part of the Crown of Thorns of Christ

Economic and Cultural History

1341
John of Luxemburg sets aside a tithe of the profits of the silver mines for the construction of Prague cathedral

1344
The bishopric of Prague raised to archbishopric (Ernest of Pardubice made its first archbishop)

1346
Charles composes the 'Coronation Order of the Kings of Bohemia'

1347
Charles holds theatre performances in Prague — partial renewal of the Church Slavonic liturgy in Prague

1348
Charles lays the foundation to the New Town of Prague, the University of Prague and establishes vineyards, gardens and fishponds in Bohemia

1350
The Crown Jewels of the Holy Roman Empire brought from Germany to Prague — mass pilgrimage of Prague craftsmen in Rome — the Roman Tribune Cola di Rienzo in Prague — Charles requests the King of Poland Kazimir to grant the Bohemian and Silesian merchants free transit to Prussia and Russia

1353
Traveller and chronicler Giovanni Marignolli in Prague — John of Středa appointed Imperial Chancellor

1354
Charles sends relics acquired in Germany to Prague — Introduction of the Milan (Ambrosian) liturgy to Prague

1356
Charles grants John, the scribe of the Slavonic abbey, an emolument for copying Slavonic books — Francesco Petrarch in Prague

1358
Charles concludes trade agreements with the Venetian Doge John Delphin — Reformer Conrad Waldhauser begins to preach in Prague — the plague and poor harvests in the Czech Lands (until 1362)

Foundations

1341
John of Luxemburg founds the Carthusian monastery in Prague

1344
John of Luxemburg and Charles found Prague cathedral (choir consecrated in 1385)

1347
Building work begins on the monastery church of Our Lady of the Snows in Prague

1348
Building work begins on the Slavonic abbey — foundation of Karlstein castle

1348—1350
The walls of the New Town of Prague built — renovation of the royal palace at Vyšehrad

1349
Archbishop Ernest of Pardubice established the Augustinian monastery at Kłodzko (Glatz)

1350
Foundation of the monastery of St. Charlemagne in the New Town of Prague (Karlov)

1351
Charles fortifies Stará Boleslav and founds the Augustinian church of St. Dorothy in Wrocław

1354
Charles founds the monastery of St. Ambrosius in Prague and the St. Wenceslas chapel in Lower Ingelheim on the Rhine

1355
Charles founds the St. Catherine's convent in the New Town of Prague, the Augustinian monastery at Tarenzo and the Gothic choir of Aachen cathedral

1356
John Henry, Margrave of Moravia, founds the Augustinian monastery of St. Thomas in Brno — Bishop John of Středa establishes an Augustinian monastery at Litomyšl

1357
Laying of the foundation stone of Charles Bridge — foundation of Karlsfried castle near Zittau

1358
Consecration of the Frauenkirche in Nuremberg

Other Data

before 1343
Bishop John IV of Dražice builds the (now lost)
tomb of St. Adalbert in Prague cathedral

1344
Matthias of Arras arrives in Prague

1346
The Crown of the Czech Kings, known as the
'St. Wenceslas Crown'

1347
The Vyšší Brod Altarpiece

1348
Foundation of the Brotherhood of Painters in
Prague

1352
Death of Matthias of Arras

1355
The Imperial Seal of Charles IV

1356(?)
Tommaso da Modena sends his pictures as
decorations for Karlstein castle

1356
Arrival of Peter Parler in Prague (died here in
1399)—Breviary of Grand Master Leo

1357
Charles has a (now lost) tomb of St. Wenceslas
set up in Prague cathedral—Nicholas Wurmser
given as Imperial Painter living in the Czech
Lands

/191/
*The Lands of the Czech Crown
before the death of Charles IV.
Before 1377.*

1361 (26 February)
Wenceslas IV born at Nuremberg

1363
The two-year-old Wenceslas IV crowned King of Bohemia in Prague

1365
Charles crowned King of Arles at Arles

1368 (15 February)
Birth of Sigismund of Luxemburg

1368–1369
Charles undertakes his second Roman progress—Elizabeth of Pomerania crowned Empress in Rome

1371
Birth of Master John Hus

before 1372
Emperor John V Palaeologus of Constantinople sends Charles relics

1373
Charles joins Brandenburg to the Kingdom of Bohemia

1374
Death of Francesco Petrarch

1376
Wenceslas IV crowned King of Rome at Aachen

1377
Pope Gregory XI settles permanently in Rome

1377–1378
Charles journeys to France

1378
Archbishop John Očko of Vlašim raised to Cardinal

1378 (29 November)
Death of Emperor Charles IV in Prague

1359–1361
The biggest medieval textile store, 'The Booths', built in Prague

after 1360
Charles contributed personally to the Latin-Czech-Slavonic Glossary of Master Bartholomew of Chlumec, said Klaret—Bible of Leskovice (Dresden), the oldest Bible written in Czech

1364
Ernest of Pardubice gives a thousand talents of silver for the building of Prague cathedral—the Emperor's Secretary John Očko of Vlašim made Archbishop of Prague—John Milíč of Kroměříž begins to preach in Prague and builds the 'House of Men of Literature'

1366
The Doge Marco Cornaro assures the Prague merchants that they may again safely enter Venice—Charles sets rules for trade on the Vltava—the foundation of Charles College and the library of Prague University

1367
The Old Town and the New Town of Prague protected by the united system of walls

1369
100,000 pilgrims come to see the Imperial Coronation Jewels exhibited in Prague

1370
The oldest document written in Czech

1372
The solemn consecration of the Slavonic abbey

1374
Preacher John Milíč of Kroměříž chastised in the Bull of Pope Gregory XI

1376
The Czech writings of Thomas of Štítný copied and illuminated in the Clementinum Codex

1359
Charles builds Wrocław castle and fortifies the outlying districts

1360
The Little Quarter, Hradčany and Pohořelec surrounded with a wall—foundation of the Servite monastery in the New Town of Prague—beginning of building work on the cathedral choir of St. Bartholomew's at Kolín on the Elbe (consecrated in 1378)

1364
Charles establishes Wenzelsburg castle at Lauf near Nuremberg

1366
Charles founds the monastery of the Celestines at Oybin near Zittau

1368
Charles sets up a hospice for pilgrims from the Czech Lands in Rome

c. 1370
Beginning of the building of All Saints' chapel at Prague castle (consecrated in 1387)—foundation of Karlsbad (Karlovy Vary)—Charles establishes Fürstenberg castle and a bridge across the Oder

1371
Archbishop John Očko of Vlašim consecrates the chapel of the Patrons Saints of Bohemia in his castle at Roudnice

1372
Bishop Albrecht of Sternberg founds the Augustinian monastery at Moravian Sternberg

1374
Charles builds Tangermünde castle in Brandenburg

1375
John Henry, Margrave of Moravia, founds the Carthusian monastery at Brno-Královo pole

1376
Charles founds the 'Königsstuhl' at Rhens on the Rhine

c. 1378
Beginning of the construction of the Old Town bridge tower

1359
Michael Parler works on the construction of the
Golden Crown monastery (founded in
1263) — Master Theodoric named Imperial
Painter

1360
Nicholas Wurmser of Strasbourg remunerated
by Charles IV

1360 — 1361
The Cycle with the Legends of St. Ludmilla and
St. Wenceslas at Karlstein castle — the
Vyšehrad Antiphonary

after 1361
The St. Moritz chapel in the church of St.
Sebald at Nuremberg decorated with scenes
from the life of Charles IV and Wenceslas IV

1363 — 1364
A set of choir books of Ernest of
Pardubice — stone tomb of Ernest of Pardubice
at Kłodzko (Glatz)

1367
Master Theodoric remunerated for the
ornamentation of the Holy Rood chapel at
Karlstein castle

1368
Canon John of Opava finishes the decorations
of the Vienna evangeliarium

1370 — 1371
Mosaic picture of the Last Judgment on the
Golden Gate of Prague cathedral

1371
Votive panel of John Očko of Vlašim

1372 — 1373
Records of Imperial Painter Oswald at Prague
cathedral (died after 1383)

1373
Henry IV Parler remunerated for work on
a statue of St. Wenceslas in Prague
cathedral — Martin and George of Cluj cast the
statue of St. George and the Dragon at Prague
castle

1374(?)
The Krakow manuscript of Pulkava's Chronicle

1375
Beginning of work on the busts in the triforium
of Prague cathedral

1376
The Pontifical of Bishop Albrecht of Sternberg

1377
Peter Parler paid for the tomb of Přemysl
Otakar I in Prague cathedral

1378
Vlašim chapel in Prague cathedral
decorated — the mitre of St. Eligius — the Offices
of St. Eligius

Genealogical Tree of Charles IV

HENRY VII OF
LUXEMBURG, Emperor
of Rome
* c. 1274
† 20 Aug. 1313
× 9 June 1292

MARGUERITE OF
BRABANT
* 4 Oct. 1276
† 14 Dec. 1311

JOHN OF
LUXEMBURG,
King of Bohemia
* 10 Aug. 1296
⚔ 28 Aug. 1346
× 31 Aug. 1310

I. ELIZABETH
PŘEMYSLIDE
* 1292
† 28 Sept. 1330

CHARLES IV,
Emperor of Rome
and King of
Bohemia
* 14 May 1316
† 29 November 1378

WENCESLAS II, King of
Bohemia
* 27 Sept. 1271
† 21 June 1305
× 24 Jan. 1285

I. GUTA OF HAPSBURG
* 13 March 1271
† 18 June 1297

Key to the Genealogy
· born
† died
⚔ died in battle
× married

HENRY III, Count of
Luxemburg
* c. 1240
† 3 June 1288
× 1260/1

BEATRICE OF AVESNES
† 1320

HENRY II, Count of Luxemburg
* 1217
† 24 Dec. 1281
× c. 1240

MARGARET OF BAR
† 23 Nov. 1275

WALRAM III, Prince of Limburg
† 1226
× 1214
II. ERMESINDE OF LUXEMBURG
* 1186 † 9 May 1246

HENRY II, Count of Bar
† 1239/40
× 1219
PHILIPPA OF DREUX
* 17 March after 1240

BALDUIN OF AVESNES, Squire of
Beaumont
* Sept. 1219
† 1289
× . . .

FELICITAS OF COUCY
† 1307

BURKARD OF AVESNES
* 1243
× July 1212, divorced 1221
MARGARET OF FLANDERS
* 1202 † 10 Feb. 1282

THOMAS I OF COUCY
† 1252
× 1212
MATILDA OF RETHEL

JOHN I, Duke of Lorraine,
Brabant and Limburg
* 1252/3
† 3 May 1294
× 1273

II. MARGUERITE OF
DAMPIERRE AND
FLANDERS
† 3 July 1285

HENRY III, Duke of Lorraine and
Brabant
† 28 Feb. 1261
× . . .

ADELHEID OF BURGUNDY
† 23 Oct. 1273

QUIDO, Count of Dampierre and
Flanders
† 7 March 1305
× c. 1246

MATHILDE OF BÉTHUNE
† 8 Nov. 1264

HENRY II, Duke of Lorraine and Brabant
† 1 Feb. 1248
× bef. 22 Aug. 1215
I. MARIA OF HOHENSTAUFEN
† 1235

HUGO IV, Duke of Burgundy
* 9 March 1212 † Feb. 1273
× 1229
I. YOLANDE OF DREUX
† 1255

WILLIAM II, Count of Dampierre
† 1231
× 1223
MARGARET OF FLANDERS
* 2 June 1202 † 10 Nov. 1280

ROBERT VII OF BÉTHUNE
† 1248
× ELIZABETH OF MAURIALMÉ

PŘEMYSL OTAKAR II, King
of Bohemia
* c. 1230
× 26 Aug. 1278
× 25 Oct. 1261

II. KUNIGUNDE OF
HUNGARY (Galicia)
† 9 Sept. 1285

WENCESLAS I, King of Bohemia
* 1205
† 22 Nov. 1253
× 1224

KUNIGUNDE OF
HOHENSTAUFEN
† 13 Sept. 1248

ROSTISLAV, Prince of Novgorod and
Galicia, Viceroy in Serbian Mačva,
King of Bulgaria
† 1294
× c. 1244

ANNE OF HUNGARY

PŘEMYSL OTAKAR I, King of Bohemia
† 15 Nov. 1230
× c. 1198
CONSTANCE OF HUNGARY
† 4 Dec. 1240

PHILIP OF SWABIA, King of Germany
* c. 1176 † 21 Aug. 1208
× 25 May 1197
IRENE ANGELOS
* 1172 † 27. Aug. 1208

MICHAEL, Prince of Chernigov
* 1179 † 20. Sept. 1246
× N(oncognita), daughter of Prince
Daniel of Galicia

BELA IV, King of Hungary
* 1206 † 3 May 1270
× 12
MARIA LASKARIS

RUDOLPH I, King of
Germany
* 1 May 1218
† 15 July 1291
× 1245

I. GERTRUD OF
HOHENBERG
* 1225
† 16 Feb. 1281

ALBRECHT IV, Count of Hapsburg
† 13 Dec. 1239/40 (?)
× 1217

HEDWIG OF KYBURG
† 30 April 1260

BURKARD III, Count of Hohenburg
† 14 July 1253
× . . .
? MECHTILD OF TÜBINGEN

RUDOLPH II OF HAPSBURG, Landgrave of
Alsace
† bef. 10 April 1232
× AGNES OF STAUFEN

ULRICH III OF KYBURG
† 1227
× c. 1180
ANNA OF ZÄHRINGEN
† c. 1230

BURKARD II, Count of Hohenburg
† bef. 1225
× N(oncognita) of Aichelberg

RUDOLPH II, Count-Palatine of Tübingen
† 1224/47
× MECHTILD (Beatrice) of Eberstein

Works of art in the index are registered according to their place of deposition. For the place see catalogue.

Page numbers within brackets refer to illustrations.

Index